Quality in Business Process Modeling

John Krogstie

Quality in
Business Process Modeling

 Springer

John Krogstie
Norwegian University of Science
 and Technology (NTNU)
Trondheim
Norway

ISBN 978-3-319-82596-0   ISBN 978-3-319-42512-2   (eBook)
DOI 10.1007/978-3-319-42512-2

Printed on acid-free paper

This Springer imprint is published by Springer Nature
The registered company is Springer International Publishing AG Switzerland

Preface

Let no one despise symbols!, Without symbols we could
scarcely lift ourselves to conceptual thinking.
Gottlob Frege, *On the Scientific Justification of a Conceptual Notation*, 1882

Business processes are the core of organizational activities, both in private and in public sectors. A (*business*) *process* is a collection of related, structured tasks that produce a specific service or product to address a certain (organizational) goal for a particular actor or set of actors. Owing to its increasing importance, the management of business processes is receiving increasing interest. Business process management (BPM) generally focuses on how work should be performed in and across organizations to ensure consistent outputs by taking advantage of improvement opportunities—e.g., reducing costs and carbon footprint; ensuring socially responsible actions, execution times, or error rates; or improving the quality or service level.

An important area of BPM is the modeling of processes—business process modeling—which is what this book is about.

So why this focus on modeling?

One can argue that the main reason why humans have excelled as a species is our ability to represent, reuse, and transfer knowledge across time and space. Whereas in most areas of human conduct, one-dimensional natural language is used to express and share knowledge, we see the need for and use of two- and multi-dimensional representational forms to arise. One such representational form is called *conceptual modeling*. A *conceptual model* is historically defined as a description of the phenomena in a domain at some level of abstraction, which is expressed in a semiformal or in a formal diagrammatical language. Business process modeling is a special type of conceptual modeling.

In business process modeling, a mature practice has recently been established around the more formal aspects of the processes necessary for the development of executable models. In many areas, however, although much work has been done, we still have not developed a common agreement relative to central notions—either in research or in practice. In particular, we can mention differing opinions and inputs on, for example:

- Quality of business process models, so they can be used to achieve their purpose,
- Appropriate modeling formalisms and extensions of modeling formalisms and approaches to support achievement and maintenance of model quality,
- Needs for tools and methods to support different approaches to process modeling.

Business process modeling is usually accomplished in some organizational setting but for a myriad of usage areas, including human sense-making, communication, simulation, activation, quality assurance, compliance management, and context for systems development.

Given that modeling techniques are used in such a large variety of tasks with very different goals, it is important to appropriately use the techniques to achieve a proper overview of different uses of modeling and guidelines for what makes a model sufficiently *good* to achieve the decided goals. A main purpose of this book is to discuss how to achieve quality in business process models.

To address issues of the quality of conceptual models in general, we have for many years worked with SEQUAL, a framework for understanding the quality of models and modeling languages, which can subsume all main aspects relative to the quality of models.

SEQUAL has three unique properties compared with other frameworks for model quality:

- It distinguishes between quality characteristics (goals) and means to potentially achieve these goals by separating what you are trying to achieve from how to achieve it.
- It is closely linked to linguistic and semiotic concepts. In particular, the core of the framework—including the discussion of syntax, semantics, and pragmatics—is parallel to the use of these terms in the semiotic theory of Morris. A term such as "quality" is applicable to all semiotic levels. We include physical, empirical, syntactical, semantical, pragmatic, social, and deontic quality in the work on SEQUAL.
- It is based on a constructivist worldview, recognizing that models are usually created as a part of a dialogue between those involved in modeling, whose knowledge of the modeling domain changes as modeling takes place.

A limitation of SEQUAL is that it can be too abstract because it is meant to be able to support the discussion of the quality of all sorts of visual models and modeling languages and thus is difficult to apply in practice.

In this book, we specialize SEQUAL to investigate the quality of business process models. By starting from a generic framework, we can reuse a number of aspects that have general relevance in modeling and thus better ground the proposals—for both the quality of business process models and modeling languages and the accompanying approaches, methods, and tools—to achieve and maintain models of high quality.

A large body of literature has been developed on business process modeling and business process management. The existing works address only a limited set of the usage areas of modeling, whereas this book covers the whole spectrum of modeling goals to find balance in practice by achieving the optimal quality of the process model developed. Some of these usage areas have become popular only recently, thus warranting an update of the coverage of the area with a focus on how to balance quality considerations across all semiotic levels when models are used for different purposes.

Audience

This book has two intended audiences:

- It is primarily for computer science, software engineering, and information systems students at the postgraduate level (master/PhD), after they have been introduced to information systems analysis and design (e.g., based on UML or BPMN), who want to know more about business process modeling and quality of models in their preparation for professional practice.
- Professionals with detailed experience and responsibilities related to the development and evolution of process-oriented information systems and information systems methodology in general who need to formalize and structure their practical experiences or update their knowledge as a way to improve their professional activity. This book include a number of case studies from practice that will make it easier for practitioners to grasp the main theoretical concepts, of this book helping in the application of the approaches described.

At this level, many students have learnt modeling as a predefined tool and have limited training in evaluating the appropriateness of models and modeling languages to achieve a specific goal. They also have limited practical experience with more than a few notations and seldom have real-life experiences with large-scale modeling and systems development. Many of the concepts and principles underlying the concrete modeling notation easily become abstract, and there is a need to exemplify the points and bridge the theoretical parts of the course in terms of how it can address problems in practice, which is also an important takeaway for practitioners as described above.

Outline of This Book

Chapter 1 contains the theoretical foundation by introducing the topic area of business processes and business process modeling and the most important concepts underlying the modeling of business processes. The thinking is grounded in general model theory and highlights the overall philosophy underlying the approach to the quality of models by providing a high-level overview of the most important goals of modeling. We also exemplify this by introducing some of the cases and modeling notations used later in this book.

Chapter 2 describes existing work on the quality of models including SEQUAL and covers in particular work on the quality of business process models.

Chapter 3 describes a specialization of SEQUAL for the quality of business process models including examples of means to achieve model quality at different levels.

In Chap. 4, we provide examples of the use of business process models in practice. We present results from detailed case studies evaluating how to achieve and maintain quality in business process models and how to choose and/or make appropriate business process modeling notations to achieve this goal.

Chapter 5 presents a process modeling value framework: Whereas most modeling approaches (and methodologies) are related to development projects for single information systems, in this chapter, we will discuss how one can achieve a more long-term and improved return on investment of using (business) process and enterprise models. We will then consider how more specific techniques for business process modeling can be applied in this setting (such as tool functionality, use of reference models and modeling techniques, and notations appropriate for the development of high-quality models).

Chapter 6 contains a summary of the main content of this book and discusses the potential for business process modeling in the future through integration with other types of modeling, attacking a new set of challenges particularly across organizational borders to support digital ecosystems based on open big data and systems of systems.

Acknowledgements

A large number of people deserve mention relative to the content of this book as collaborators and cowriters of projects and research work that has brought us to the point at which we are today. Whereas many of our debts in this regard are visible through the references in the text, many people have contributed more subtly, introducing inspiration or roadblocks to be overcome.

When I started working in the field of modeling, including process modeling in the early 1990s, the research group around Arne Sølvberg was very important. Important collaborators at the time were Guttorm Sindre, Odd Ivar Lindland,

Jon Atle Gulla, Anne Helga Seltveit, Gunnar Brattås, Rudolf Andersen, Geir Willumsen, Mingwei Yang, and Harald Rønneberg. In the Tempora project, I worked also with Benkt Wangler, Peter McBrien, and Richard Owens. The international collaboration led me to the IFIP WG 8.1 community and the CAiSE conference, which I have followed over the years, collaborating with Wil van der Aalst, Jan Recker, Michael Rosemann, Andreas Opdahl, Sjaak Brinkkemper, Kalle Lyytinen, Barbara Pernici, Keng Siau, Terry Halpin, Antoni Olive, Oscar Pastor, Erik Proper, Janis Bubenko, Colette Rolland, Peri Loucopoulos, Hajo Reijers, Neil Maiden, Barbara Weber, Janis Stirna, Anne Persson, Peter Fettke, Peter Loos, and Constantin Houy, among others.

When working as a researcher at SINTEF in the early 2000s, another group became important through a number of Norwegian and EU projects in which modeling of information systems was central. In particular, I would like to thank Steinar Carlsen, Håvard Jørgensen, Dag Karlsen, Frank Lillehagen, Snorre Fossland, Oddrun Ohren, Svein Johnsen, Heidi Brovold, Vibeke Dalberg, Siri Moe Jensen, Rolf Kenneth Rolfsen, Arne Jørgen Berre, Asbjørn Følstad, Reidar Gjersvik, Jon Iden, Harald Wesenberg, and Bjørn Skjellaug on the national front and Joerg Haake, Weigang Wang, Jessica Rubart, Michael Petit, Kurt Kosanke, Martin Zelm, Nacer Boudlidja, Herve Panetto, Guy Doumeingts, and Thomas Knothe on the international front.

In the years connected to NTH and NTNU, I also have had the pleasure of collaborating with a number of master and PhD students and post-docs, including Sofie de Flon Arnesen, Maria Rygge, Anna Gunnhild Nysetvold, Yun Lin, Csaba Veres, Shang Gao, Sundar Gopalakrishnan, Gustav Aagesen, Merethe Heggset, Stig Vidar Nordgaard, and Alexander Andersson.

A number of people at NTNU have also been influential through normal scientific discourse, including Hallvard Trætteberg, Reidar Conradi, Monica Divitini, Dag Svanæs, Birgit Rognebakke Krogstie, Eric Monteiro, Agnar Aamodt, Pieter Toussaint, Letizia Jaccheri, Alf Inge Wang, Kjetil Nørvåg, Arild Faxvaag, Rolv Bræk, Sobah Abbas Petersen, Peter Herrmann, Frank Kraemer, Michael Giannakos, and Tor Stålhane.

Finally, I would like to thank my wife, Birgit Rognebakke Krogstie, who also has contributed to parts of the research reported in this book, particularly aspects of the reflection processes in Chap. 4.

Trondheim, Norway   John Krogstie
January 2016

Contents

**1 Introduction to Business Processes and Business
Process Modeling.** 1
  1.1 Quality of Business Processes. 4
  1.2 Process Thinking. 7
       1.2.1 Process Improvement and Innovation Patterns 10
       1.2.2 Process Types and Process Maturity. 10
  1.3 BPM in the Large and in the Wild 14
  1.4 Introduction to Modeling 18
       1.4.1 Abstraction Mechanisms and Levels of Modeling 20
       1.4.2 Perspectives of Modeling 23
  1.5 Business Process Modeling. 27
       1.5.1 Goals of Process Modeling. 27
       1.5.2 Perspectives to Business Process Modeling. 33
       1.5.3 Combined Behavioral and Functional Approaches 38
  1.6 Summary 46
  References 46

2 Quality of Business Process Models 53
  2.1 Quality in Information Systems Development and Evolution. 53
       2.1.1 Data and Information Quality 55
       2.1.2 Quality of Requirements Specifications. 58
       2.1.3 Quality of Data Models 60
       2.1.4 Quality of Enterprise Models 63
  2.2 Comprehensive Frameworks for the Quality of Models 64
       2.2.1 SEQUAL—Semiotic Quality Framework 65
       2.2.2 Quality of Models According to Nelson et al 70
  2.3 Quality of Business Process Models. 75
       2.3.1 Quality of Business Processes 75
       2.3.2 Guidelines of Modeling—GoM. 85
       2.3.3 Seven Process Modeling Guidelines (7PMG) 86
       2.3.4 Pragmatic Guidelines for Business Process Modeling. . . . 88

2.3.5   Quality Through the Use of Reference Models   91
2.3.6   Successful Business Process Modeling Projects   96
2.4   Summary   97
References   97

3   **SEQUAL Specialized for Business Process Models**   103
3.1   Sets in the Quality Framework   104
3.2   The Physical Quality of Business Process Models   109
3.3   The Empirical Quality of Business Process Models   111
3.4   Syntactic Quality of Business Process Models   117
3.5   Semantic and Perceived Semantic Quality of Business Process
        Models   120
3.6   Pragmatic Quality of Business Process Models   125
3.7   Social Quality of Business Process Models   130
3.8   Deontic Quality of Business Process Models   134
3.9   Summary   135
References   136

4   **Business Process Modeling in Practice**   139
4.1   Business Process Modeling in International Projects   139
        4.1.1   Model Use   141
        4.1.2   User Satisfaction   145
        4.1.3   Process Impact   145
        4.1.4   Process Model Quality in the Case   146
        4.1.5   Developing Specialized Process Modeling Language   148
4.2   Business Process Modeling Across the Organization   157
        4.2.1   History of Modeling in the Company   157
        4.2.2   Description of Current Modeling Structure and Tool   158
        4.2.3   Use of Models in the Organization   167
        4.2.4   Guidelines of Modeling Relative to SEQUAL   170
        4.2.5   Influence of Syntactic Quality on Pragmatic Quality   177
        4.2.6   Evaluation of the Quality System Models   182
4.3   Summary   185
References   185

5   **Organizational Value of Business Process Modeling**   187
5.1   A Framework for Increasing the Value of Process Modeling   189
        5.1.1   Identifying Context   190
        5.1.2   Identifying Potential Value   191
        5.1.3   Choosing Practice   191
5.2   Applying the Value Framework   201
        5.2.1   Identifying Potential Value   201
        5.2.2   Addressing Challenges to Modeling   202

5.3 Evaluation of Process Modeling Languages 205
    5.3.1 Quality of BPMN 205
    5.3.2 Ontological Analysis Using the Bunge–Wand–Weber
          Framework 206
    5.3.3 The Workflow Pattern Framework 207
    5.3.4 Evaluating BPMN Using SEQUAL 208
    5.3.5 Evaluation of the BPMN Notation 209
    5.3.6 Combined Semiotic, Ontological,
          and Workflow Pattern Evaluation 212
    5.3.7 Semistructured Interviews of BPMN Users 212
    5.3.8 Case Study of BPMN in Practice................ 213
    5.3.9 Statistical Analysis of BPMN Models 214
    5.3.10 Business Processes Are More Than What Is Possible
          to Represent in BPMN........................ 215
    5.3.11 Evaluation of BPMN Modeling Tools 216
5.4 Achieving Quality in Business Process Models Through
    Modeling Methodology 218
    5.4.1 Socio-Technical WalkThrough (STWT) 220
    5.4.2 The Modeling Conference Technique.............. 221
5.5 Summary 224
References 224

6 Some Future Directions for Business Process Modeling 227
6.1 Business Process Modeling Integrated with other Types
    of Modeling 227
6.2 Beyond the Activity—Business Process Modeling across
    Organizational Levels............................... 229
6.3 Welcome to the Machine—Tools from Interpreters
    to Modelers as Part of Big Data Ecosystems............. 231
6.4 Summary 237
References 238

Appendix: Special BPMN Notation in the Petroleum
          Industry Case 241

Index 249

Abbreviations

4EM	For enterprise modeling
7PMG	7 process modeling guidelines
ADT	Abstract data type
AKM	Active knowledge modeling
ARIS	Architecture of integrated information systems
BPEL	Business process execution language
BPM	Business process management
BPMN	Business process model and notation
BPMS	BPM system
BWW	Bunge–Wand–Weber
CAiSE	Conference for Advanced Information Systems Engineering
CDIF	Common data interchange format
CFP	Call for paper
CIS	Computerized informations system
CMM	Capability maturity model
CRC	Camera-ready copy
DBMS	Database management system
DFD	Dataflow diagram
DSL	Domain-specific language
DSM	Domain-specific modeling
ECA	Event condition action
EEML	Extended enterprise modeling language
EM	Enterprise modeling
EPC	Event process chain
ER	Entity relationship
ERL	External rule language
ERP	Enterprise resource planning
ERT	Entity, relationship, time
FRISCO	Framework for information systems concepts
FSM	Finite state machine

GD	Governing documentation
GEMAL	Generic enterprise modeling and activation language
GoM	Guidelines of modeling
HCI	Human–computer interaction
IBIS	Issue-based informations system
ICOM	Input, control, output, mechanism (in IDEF0)
ICT	Information and communication technology
IDEF	Integration DEFinition
IETF	Internet Engineering Task Force
IS	Information system
ISO	International Standards Organization
ITM	IT Management
KPI	Key performance indicator
LNCS	Lecture Notes in Computer Science
MDA	Model-driven architecture
MDSD	Model-driven software development
MOF	Meta-object facility
OMG	Object management group
OSS	Open source software
PB	Program Board (in conference)
PC Chair	Program Committee Chair
PEP	Process excellence principles
PID	Process interaction diagram
PIM	Platform-independent model
PLM	Product lifecycle management
PML	Process modeling language
PSM	Platform-specific model
RACI	Responsible–accountable–consulted–informed
RAD	Role activity diagram
REA	Resources, events, and agents
RFID	Radio frequency identification
RIN	Role interaction network
SADT	Structured Analysis and Design Technique
SEQUAL	Semiotic Quality Framework
SOA	Service-oriented architecture
SRS	Software requirements specification
STWT	Socio-Technical WalkThrough
TOGAF	The Open Group Architecture Framework
UML	Unified modeling language
VLDB	Very large databases
WfMC	Workflow Management Coalition
XML	Extended Markup Language
YAWL	Yet Another Workflow Language

Chapter 1
Introduction to Business Processes and Business Process Modeling

The term "business process" is defined in various ways in the literature (Dumas et al. 2013). In this book, we will use the following definition:

A *business process* is a collection of related *tasks* that *produce* a specific *service* or *product* to address one or more *goals* for a particular *actor* or set of *actors* with the optimal use of *resources*.

Business processes are the core of organizational activities, both in private and public sectors. All organizational activities contain explicit or implicit processes, and a large body of literature has been developed over the years within both organizational science and information systems/computing. Owing to its increasing importance in business, the management of business processes is receiving increasing interest (Von Brocke and Rosemann 2015). As the definition conveys, however, there are several aspects that must be considered simultaneously:

- A process consists of several coordinated *tasks*; the total result of performing all tasks in concert is the matter of importance.
- There are people (*actors*) involved who receive benefits from the process.
- The process is not there for its own sake; it is meant to help the actors reach one or more *goals*.
- A goal is reached through production of a *service* or *product*.
- Producing the service and/or product takes *resources*. These can be human resources (employees), natural resources, or financial resources. The production mandates the availability of a capability and must occur somewhere in time and space.

All these aspects of a business process as depicted in the upper part of Fig. 1.1 are important to represent, i.e., to model. Business processes are the core of the wider area of business process management (BPM), and central aspects of BPM are discussed in Sects. 1.1–1.3. An important component of BPM is the business process model. Business process models are a type of conceptual model, which we

© Springer International Publishing Switzerland 2016
J. Krogstie, *Quality in Business Process Modeling*,
DOI 10.1007/978-3-319-42512-2_1

describe in more detail in Sect. 1.4. Central aspects and approaches in business process modeling are then described in Sect. 1.5.

Modeling can be viewed according to Fig. 1.2: Based on one or more goals that the modeling is meant to support the achievement of and the existing resources (which might include existing references or bespoke models and

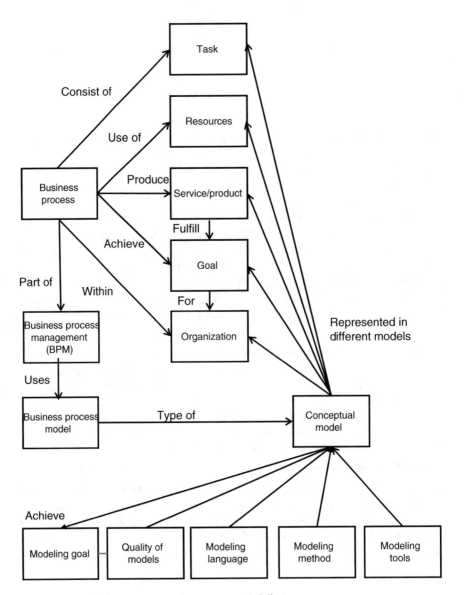

Fig. 1.1 Structure of the area of business process modeling

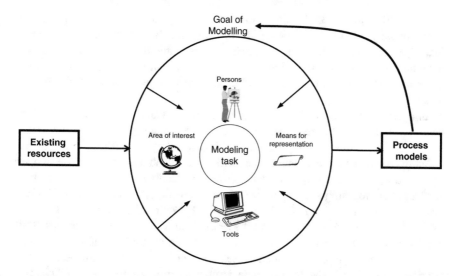

Fig. 1.2 Actors and activities in development of business process models

modeling languages), persons gather (physically or virtually, and synchronously or asynchronously) to represent some area of interest (aka domain) using some means of representation (in which our focus is on the use of modeling languages and accompanying documents). The modeling task is supported by tools—in these days, both supporting human modelers and extracting meaning into models from available data by performing process mining and big data analytics. The modeling activities result in models that help address the goals of modeling.

BPM is focused on how work should be performed in and across organizations to ensure consistent outputs by taking advantage of improvement opportunities. Whereas the results from some business process improvements such as reduced costs can be looked upon by many as trivial, others represent the difference between life and death. In Kolata (2015), we read about the improved process for working with heart attacks in US hospitals. No new medical discoveries or technologies in recent years have reduced the time necessary to clear a blockage in a patient's arteries and resume blood flow to the heart. The changes have been driven by a detailed analysis of the bottlenecks in treating patients and in a nationwide campaign. Hospitals across the country have adopted best practices that include paramedics transmitting electrocardiogram readings directly from the ambulance to the emergency room and summoning medical teams with a single call that sets off all beepers at once.

From 2003 to 2013, the death rate of coronary heart disease decreased by approximately 38 %. The National Heart, Lung and Blood Institute, the primary federal agency that funds heart research, says that this decline has many causes, including better control of cholesterol and blood pressure, reduced smoking rates, and improved medical treatments—and faster care of people when suffering a heart attack.

In a heart attack, a blocked artery prevents blood from reaching an area of the heart. At first, cells are merely stunned, but as the minutes pass, they begin to die. The way to save the heart is to open the blocked artery by pushing in a catheter, inflating a tiny balloon that shoves the blockage aside, and holding the artery open by inserting a stent, a tiny wire cage. However, leading cardiologists were pessimistic about reaching a national goal of accomplishing this for at least half of the heart attack patients within 90 min of arrival at a hospital. Often, it took more than two hours for blood to flow to a patient's heart again. Currently, however, nearly all hospitals treat at least half of their patients in 61 min or less. At Yale–New Haven Hospital, where half of the patients used to wait at least 150 min before their arteries were opened, the median time is now 57 min. At the Mayo Clinic and major academic centers like New York–Presbyterian Hospital, it is 50 min.

In this medical case, time is essential; but even in other settings, significant benefits can be realized through compliance with the proper process. A global oil company with more than 20,000 employees in more than 30 countries has spent significant resources on process modeling over the years. They report to have achieved fair success with enterprise modeling in their corporate management system (Heggset et al. 2014) in which workflow models are used extensively to communicate requirements and best practices throughout the enterprise. The current management system contains more than 2000 business process models with associated requirements and best practices, all available through a corporate Web portal from anywhere in the company. The models are used daily in large parts of the organization and are a significant contributor to reducing operational, environmental, and safety risks. As an example, the important SIF index (serious injury frequency), which counts the number of incidents per million work hours, has been reduced from 6 to approximately 0.8 in the period since the models were introduced. Every week, employees and subcontractors perform approximately 2 million work hours; thus, only 2 rather than 12 people are seriously injured each week.

As indicated by these two examples, there are different aspects of the business process that are important in different settings; what is most important to optimize must be considered when improving business processes.

1.1 Quality of Business Processes

A *good* business process is a process that produces results by optimizing one or more of a set of quality features. The main goal of most enterprises is to achieve economic profit. In addition to this, and as a way to reach this goal, the business wants to gain satisfied customers. Reijers and Mansur (2005) present four dimensions of value that are valid for most customer groups. These dimensions are presented in Table 1.1.

A customer will experience improvement in an enterprise process if he/she receives his/her product faster, cheaper, and/or with better quality or service than before. Improvement in one of these dimensions could result in your enterprise gaining more customers, increasing its market share, etc.

However, looking only at economic profit is too limited. The goal of the organizational activity will vary, but it is normal to aim at some sort of *value*. Based on the use of resources to perform the change, we can briefly highlight types of value as follows (Krogstie 2012a):

- Ensure economic gain (i.e., profit),
- Ensure personal gain,
- Ensure organizational (business) gain,
- Ensure societal gain.

Reaching personal and societal gain might result in economic gain but can also raise a number of additional goals that are not purely economic. For instance, when the systems for reimbursement of health expenses in Norway were automated, the cost incurred by the government rose (because people no longer needed to track this themselves and ask for reimbursement, they were refunded the amount to which they were entitled rather than only what they remembered to reclaim), thus making it possible to provide the actual benefits determined by law. Economic value is highly tangible and can be viewed from different stakeholder perspectives. Business value is somewhat less tangible and includes all forms of value that determine the health and well-being of an organization in the long run. Business value expands the concept of economic value to include other forms of value such as employee value, customer value, supplier value, managerial value, and potentially also societal value (related to areas such as corporate social responsibility). Business value also often embraces intangible assets not necessarily attributable to any stakeholder group such as intellectual capital and a firm's business model and public opinion.

Thus, the underlying set of dimensions of value against which a process can be potentially optimized is larger than what is listed in Table 1.1, as summarized in Table 1.2:

Table 1.1 Four dimensions of value from Reijers and Mansur (2005)

Component of value	What a customer wants
Time	Fast
Quality	Right
Cost	Cheap
Flexibility	High

Table 1.2 Dimensions of value of a business process

Dimension of value	What is wanted
Time	Fast
Quality of product/service	Right
Cost	Low
Flexibility	Sufficient
Resource usage	Sustainable
Unwanted side effects	None
Operations according to regulations	Compliant

- Time: Time from the start to the conclusion of the process.
- Quality of product/service: That the quality of the resulting product or service is as expected (or better). For a given product/service, a large number of potentially competing quality dimensions might be relevant.
- Cost: Direct monetary costs.
- Flexibility: It often relates to how one is able to treat discrepancies with the normal path of the process. As discussed later, the needed flexibility is very different for different types of processes.
- Resource usage: This can relate to several areas. With regard to employees, they would not like to work in a process in which they feel exploited. With regard to natural resources, a recent area called Green BPM (Recker 2011) has appeared in which the overall carbon footprint of the process or any other type of pollution resulting from the process is considered. Another important aspect for many infrastructure resources is increased resource utilization, a driver behind much of the initiatives in the sharing economy such as AirBnB.
- Unwanted side effects: Examples include a process that jeopardizes the security of the customers (e.g., an Internet bank with inadequate security) or the reputation of the company (e.g., using child laborers to produce their products).
- According to regulations: In most areas, in both public and private sectors, you must act according to the regulations in the area (country) in which you operate. You can also consider here the situation in which you are certified to be following a certain process or achieve a specific maturity level that might be necessary to deliver a certain product or service at all or is important to be regarded as a good provider (e.g., as part of the company image). Process maturity levels are further described in Sect. 1.2.2.

As illustrated in Reijers and Mansur (2005), Dumas et al. (2013) even with only the 4 first dimensions, process improvement always involves a trade-off between these dimensions; it is impossible to optimize along all dimensions at the same time. Thus, the goal of the business process should be clear on the dimension and, if possible, metric within this dimension to be measured against.

When considering guidelines for process improvement and process innovation, one can find material on several levels:

1. Overall principles and mind-set (what is often referred to as process thinking) and
2. Concrete improvement strategies (aspects for improving the individual process).

1.2 Process Thinking

As an example of an overall mind-set, we here present PEP—process excellence principles (Andersen Consulting 1997). Five principles are described.

Principle 1: Process outcomes create value

- Process thinking involves focusing on outcomes rather than tasks—on producing "a result of value." As we saw above, this is already entailed in our definition of business processes.
- Value can be defined as what the customer (and other stakeholders of the result) cares about and will pay for. As discussed above, value can include but often goes beyond conventional financial measures.
- Processes, no matter how innovative and finely tuned, must be improved regularly—sometimes changing incrementally and sometimes changing radically.

Principle 2: Target high-value processes
In targeting which processes to change, companies should achieve the following:

- Evaluate processes based on their strategic importance and the size of the improvement opportunity.
- Keep the big picture in mind. Evaluate how a selected process fits with other processes and within the business as a whole. It is easy to end up suboptimizing, especially when too narrowly considering what will be influenced by changing the process.
- Assess the organization's capacity to change. Select a change approach (streamlining, reengineering, etc.) that matches the level of expected benefit and people's tolerance for change.

Principle 3: Innovate, do not duplicate
The design of excellent processes depends heavily on innovation. To help uncover new possibilities and opportunities for process design, one can structure the thinking using the seven Rs:

- **Rethink** (why)—the rationale and assumptions behind processes and their outcomes. In the heart attack case, saving lives is an obvious goal. For an American health institution, there is also the issue that one wants to avoid being sued. An earlier requirement that long consent forms be filled out before the team could get to work was removed. The hospital's lawyers advised that in an emergency, the team could proceed with the patient's name, date of birth, and social security number.

- **Reconfigure** (what)—the activities involved. In the heart attack case, they decided to have paramedics perform an electrocardiogram, which can show the characteristic electrical pattern of the heart that signals a heart attack, as soon as they reached the patient and transmit it directly to the emergency room before arriving at the hospital.
- **Reassign** (who)—the process performers. In the heart attack case, they eliminated the requirement that a cardiologist looks at the electrocardiogram and decide whether an interventional cardiologist, who would open the blocked artery, should see it too. Instead, the emergency room doctor was given the authority to call in the specialist.
- **Resequence** (when)—the timing and sequencing of the work. In connection with treatment of heart attacks, the relatively slow step-by-step preparation of patients in the emergency room was transformed. Now, when a patient arrives, staff members swarm the stretcher, and within five minutes, undress the patient, place defibrillator pads on the chest, insert two intravenous lines, shave the patient's groin where the catheter will be inserted and snaked up to the heart, supply oxygen through a cannula in the nose, and provide medications such as morphine, a blood thinner, and a drug to control heart rhythms.
- **Relocate** (where)—the location and physical infrastructure. In the heart attack case, one room has been designated for heart attack patients and is kept stocked with the necessary supplies to avoid last-minute scrambles for wires or catheters.
- **Reduce** (how much)—the frequency of activities. In the heart attack case, reduction was accomplished through the deletion of many control steps by giving more authority to the emergency room doctor. Earlier, the procedures had been very different, with a long telephone chain of doctors and other staff members called one by one.
- **Retool** (how)—the technologies and competencies that enable work to be accomplished. In the heart attack case, the hospital operator began to summon members of the heart attack team with a single phone call that sounded their beepers simultaneously rather than calling people one by one.

This set of heuristics provides process designers with a systematic approach to view processes in a new light—to see past the obvious, to question the status quo, and to overcome convention and habit. We look in more detail at these and other more detailed patterns of process change in Chap. 2.

Principle 4: Excellent processes need excellent owners

- Process owners are essential in a process-centric organization.
- A process owner is a hands-on, multifaceted role that is different—in style and substance—from the conventional role of functional manager.
- Process owners manage the day-to-day process and are the catalysts for process improvement.

Principle 5: You get what you measure

To evaluate whether a new process is better than the existing one, some means of measurement are necessary. Some characteristics to help develop good measures are as follows:

- Accuracy. Accuracy will be useful in the evaluation, providing the ability to measure how well or to what extent you reached the goal.
- (Perceived) objectivity. Objectivity is important to ensure that you will reach the same conclusion independent of which person or persons perform the evaluation.
- Using more dimensions (e.g., time). The main advantage of using more than one dimension in the goals is that it provides the opportunity to evaluate the results against different criteria of success. If the measures focus on only one dimension, there is a danger of suboptimization, which means that an improvement in one field entails a poorer result for the total process.
- Specific target. A specified target will yield a better evaluation of the result. A general target like "We want the process execution to become faster" is not as good as "We want the process execution to become 75 % faster." This also applies to the need for linking goals and processes.
- Balancing the trade-offs among cost, quality, speed, flexibility, and other measures. Unfortunately, lower costs often will entail decreased quality; higher speed will entail decreased flexibility and vice versa. When developing goals, one must consider the trade-off to find combinations of goals that can be reached at the same time.
- Comprehended by all involved. The goals and measures must be clear to all persons involved. To achieve an effective and productive working process, everyone must pull in the same direction. Understandable and motivating goals and measures are prerequisites for this.
- Supporting the organization's strategies. If some of an organization's goals and measures conflict with its strategies, it will never be able to reach its main goal.

One should always have to stretch to reach a goal. According to psychology and organizational theory, both overly low and overly ambitious goals can be demotivating.

Measures should be designed with the metrics tree in mind. The tree encompasses the following:

- Organizational outcomes: At the top of the tree are the business's overall objectives such as market share and profitability.
- Process outcomes: The next level includes the outcomes needed from each process to deliver on the organizational outcomes.
- Balanced outcomes: For each process, a series of measures is required to ensure a balanced outcome.
- Key performance indicators (KPIs): There may be a need to decompose each balanced measure further into its component parts or tie it back to specific factors within the business that affect the measures.

- After establishing a set of high-level measures, the organization must agree on a small number (5–20) that can be used to measure and monitor the business. These measures must, in aggregate, focus on achieving the organizational outcomes and provide a holistic view of the business. These measures tend to serve as the primary measures of teams and individuals as well. In addition, it is important to:
- Set stretch targets early in the design effort to foster innovation.
- Use future-oriented measures that communicate the organization's strategy clearly.

1.2.1 Process Improvement and Innovation Patterns

In Rosemann and Recker (2015), 4 overall approaches to process innovation and improvement are discussed:

1. Enhance current practices.
2. Derive a better practice by focusing on the practices of other types of organizations.
3. Utilize underutilized assets in new ways. This can involve better use of other people (e.g., in crowdsourcing or for self-servicing), available data (e.g., for feeding recommender engines), or available technology.
4. Design new practices from scratch in collaboration with the customers and other stakeholders.

Based on Andersen Consulting (1997), Dumas et al. (2013), Rosemann and Recker (2015), and Willoch (1994), a number of enhancement patterns or heuristics can be identified. We will return to this in more detail when discussing the quality of business process models in the next chapter, illustrating main patterns through examples.

1.2.2 Process Types and Process Maturity

In an organization, many processes are performed on different levels of dynamicity and need for flexibility, knowledge creation, and emergence. Whereas some processes can be viewed as static such that they can be fully automated with limited human intervention, others must be adapted for each process instance.

In Ross et al. (2006), the operational model of an organization is classified by the degree of business process standardization and the degree of business process integration as illustrated in Fig. 1.3.

Fig. 1.3 Characteristics of
four operational models
(inspired by Ross et al.
(2006))

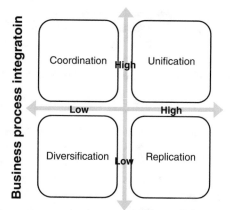

Business process standardization

However, owing to the different dynamicity of processes within the same organization, it is often not ideal to have the same approach to all processes. Whereas unification is a good idea for the administrative processes within a university, for instance, for research processes in different research groups and departments across different disciplines such as engineering, humanities, social science, and medicine, a unification strategy is bound to fail. In other cases, international companies have found that it is very difficult to standardize fully because of differences in both compliance rules and culture (Krogstie et al. 2004).

In manufacturing companies, the so-called lean principles are viewed as beneficial for guidance process design by supporting both effectiveness (doing the right thing) and efficiency (doing the thing right).

There are five main lean principles:

1. Identify customers and specify a value—The starting point is to recognize that only a small fraction of the total time and effort in any organization actually adds value for the end customer. By clearly defining value for a specific product or service from the end customer's perspective, all non-value activities—or waste —can be targeted for removal.
2. Identify and map the value stream—The value stream is the entire set of activities across all parts of the organization involved in jointly delivering the product or service. This represents the end-to-end process that delivers value to the customer. Once you understand what your customer wants, the next step is to identify how you are delivering that to them (or not).
3. Create flow by eliminating waste—Typically, when you first map the value stream, you will find that only 5 % of activities add value; this can rise to 45 % in a service environment. Eliminating this waste ensures that your product or service "flows" to the customer without any interruption, detour, or waiting.
4. Respond to customer pull—This is about understanding the customer demand for your service and then creating your process to respond to this. You should produce only what the customer wants when the customer wants it.

5. Pursue perfection—Creating flow and pull starts with radically reorganizing individual process steps, but the gains become truly significant as all the steps link together. As this happens, more and more layers of waste become visible, and the process continues toward the theoretical end point of perfection, where every asset and every action add value for the end customer.

There are several forms of waste that can be attacked in different ways as described in Table 1.3.

In many areas, including software development processes, maturity levels have been defined. Process improvement has long been viewed as an important way to address problems within information systems development, and similar thinking is found in other areas of the organization. Although the overall ideas have gained much support, it has often proved difficult in practice to implement the methodology across organizations as a basis for long-term process improvement, and it is challenging to find an efficient way—in IT, for instance—to integrate development, maintenance, and operations (Iden et al. 2013). Many of the conventional process maturity frameworks view work from a somewhat mechanistic point of view, being oriented top-down in the sense that a manager evaluates the current status of the processes and decides on the improvement actions to perform. As indicated above, the useful level of formality of a process will differ across processes. Whereas you would like to optimize some processes, others are best to not overconstrain.

Process maturity measures the level of sophistication of each process on a scale from zero to five, where five represents the highest degree of maturity. If a process is caught between two categories, it can be assigned a half-point (e.g., 2.5). If a process does not consistently rest at a specific level, it is rated at the lowest common denominator. Definitions of these rating levels are as follows:

0. Not recognized—This process is not done even when it is acknowledged that it should be. (It is not necessarily the case that all processes in a reference process framework should be performed.)
1. Ad hoc—An "ad hoc" rating indicates that the process is performed on a "memory bases" each time (CMM: Initial (Paulk et al. 1993)).
2. Repeatable—This rating refers to how consistently a unit has implemented the process. To qualify as having a "repeatable" process, a function or task must be performed as an iterative set of steps consistently used by the people involved in the process. If a policy or checklist also governs the process, it may be rated at 2.5 (CMM: Repeatable).
3. Deployed—The process has been formally documented and communicated and is used consistently (CMM: Defined).
4. Metrics and continuous improvement—To achieve a rating of "4", a process must be documented, be fully and consistently implemented, and have result and process metrics that are used as bases for continuous improvement (CMM: Managed).

Table 1.3 Reduction of waste in lean approaches

Waste form	Description	Primary performance dimension(s)	How waste can be reduced
Divergence	Wasted efforts due to politics, mismatch of goals	Effectiveness	Unification (Hansen and Nohria 2004)
Misunderstanding	Disconnect in understanding	Effectiveness	In-context collaboration. Semantic GUIs supporting aggregated knowledge representations
Undercommunicating	Excess or not enough time spent in collaboration	Effectiveness efficiency	Piloting aggregated knowledge representations
Interpreting	Time spent interpreting communication or artifacts	Efficiency	Activity-centric GUIs improving (collaborative) task identification and task execution Semantic GUIs supporting aggregated knowledge representations Interactive access to expertise that can transfer knowledge
Searching	Time spent searching for information, relationships	Efficiency	New search capabilities Broad knowledge discovery functionalities searching both knowledge and information, and the people behind the knowledge/information
Motion	Handover of artifacts or communications	Efficiency	Make decisions as soon as possible; using notification mechanisms to flag decision items to relevant stakeholders
Extra processing	Excess creation of artifacts or information	Effectiveness efficiency	Knowledge briefs, A3, aggregated knowledge, and information views reducing need for additional artifacts
Translation	Time spent conforming objects to new inputs	Efficiency	Semantic, activity-centric GUIs improving (collaborative) task identification and task execution

(continued)

Table 1.3 (continued)

Waste form	Description	Primary performance dimension(s)	How waste can be reduced
Waiting	Delays due to reviews, approvals, and bottlenecks	Efficiency	All relevant stakeholders directly involved in decisions Transparent processes highlighting items that have reached "definition of ready" state for further processing
Misapplication	Incorrect use of methods and technologies	Effectiveness	Collaborative approaches imply rapid feedback loops that to some extent prevent incorrect use or at minimum incorrect sustained use

5. Business results—To qualify for a rating of "5", a process must be measured and improved, and the process and its measurements and improvements must demonstrably contribute to the overall strategic goals and objectives of the client's organization (CMM: Optimized).

Not all processes are beneficial or possible to achieve a level higher than 3 or 4.

1.3   BPM in the Large and in the Wild

Whereas early work on business processes primarily considered processes internally in an organization, the technological possibilities over the last two decades have made it possible and necessary to also consider processes across organizations in more or less well-structured collaborations.

Based on globalization trends, new challenges pop up, particularly when multinational companies must coordinate their local business units to serve other multinational companies in an integrated fashion. In a certification company (Krogstie et al. 2004), there was a need to standardize the processes of the company's national branches to build a common image of the organization (both inward and outward) and support the certification of the cross-national processes of their multinational customers while adhering to national and cultural rules and expectations. This case is treated in more detail in Chap. 4.

In addition to process integration, the integration of common technologies such as mobile devices, techniques from the ubiquitous computing context, and the increasing use of sensor network technologies/IoT for the collection of process-relevant data and the application of service-oriented architectures (SOAs) in addition to Web 2.0 and cloud technologies can improve the flexibility of intercorporate BPM (Vanderhaeghen et al. 2010) and thus increase the effectiveness and efficiency of business processes in intercorporate value chain networks.

Furthermore, there is an increase in the options for action by the human actors involved. Figure 1.4 illustrates a collaborative scenario in a value chain network in which the mentioned technologies are applied. Scenarios such as these are important not only in business but also in the public administration area as described in the EU Ministerial Declaration on e-Government (EU 2009), which emphasizes the need to develop and improve cross-border e-Government services, making it easier for businesses and citizens to operate in and across any EU member state. Similarly, the digital transformation influences all areas of organized activity.

The above scenario illustrates four important trends:

1. Processes are *increasingly interconnected*, and it often makes little sense to look at a single process in isolation;
2. The *number of processes* with which an organization must cope *is rapidly increasing* (large organizations have hundreds to thousands of processes to be managed);
3. Modern technology is generating unprecedented streams of event data representing the states of different processes (sensor data, RFID data, remote logging, remote services, etc.); and
4. Different devices are used to access the BPM system (BPMS) in different situations, necessitating a flexible multichannel support that influences which parts of the workflow are available in which manner depending on the context of use.

Based on these trends and the application of the mentioned technologies, the enterprises' agility and handling of more and more dynamic business conditions can be improved. On the other hand, business process management becomes increasingly complex. The *reasons for this complexity* are manifold (Houy et al. 2010):

1. the range of intercorporate collaborative business processes,
2. the number of organizational units involved in a business process,
3. the need to manage and control mobile actors in business processes,
4. the need to control person–machine and machine–machine interactions,
5. the interdependencies in sensor networks, and
6. the need to manage services in a business process applying SOA, etc.

From the reasonably structured collaboration in supply chains depicted in Fig. 1.4, we see a development in the direction of systems being supported to a larger degree by *virtual communities* of nomadic, human/organizational *actors*, coworking on partially shared digital artifacts (Jansen et al. 2009). New ICT solutions are not created from scratch, but are based on building upon a large number of existing and evolving systems and services hosted in the cloud. Because the subsystems are not under any centralized control and exhibit emergent features, the term "digital ecosystems" has been proposed to describe such systems. A digital ecosystem is a metaphor inspired by natural ecosystems to describe a distributed, adaptive, and open socio-technical system. A wide range of individuals and organizations use and provide data, content, and services to the digital ecosystem, as

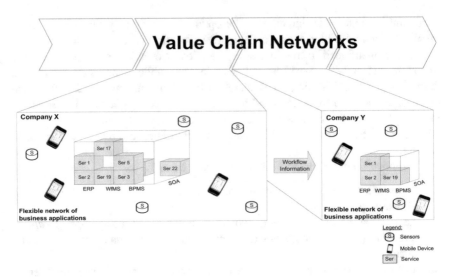

Fig. 1.4 Collaborative scenario in value chain networks (Houy et al. 2010)

shown in Fig. 1.5. Such systems are ideally characterized by self-organization, autonomous subsystems, continuous evolution, scalability, and sustainability, aiming to provide both economic and social values. However, as these systems grow organically, they become exposed to a number of threats to the overall dependability and thus trustworthiness of the system.

There are three partly related variants of digital ecosystems: software ecosystems, data-oriented ecosystems, and infrastructure ecosystems.

Software ecosystems are *"a set of businesses functioning as a unit and interacting with a shared market for software and services, together with relationships among them. These relationships are frequently underpinned by a common technological platform and operate through the exchange of information, resources, and artifacts"* (Jansen et al. 2009). For instance, within open source systems (OSS), hundreds of thousands of coevolved software "components" are freely available. Their quality and documentation are rather variable. However, OSS components are integrated into many applications, and some organizations and individuals also contribute back (Hauge et al. 2010). Conventional customers—such as municipalities—cooperate to provide improved e-services for their inhabitants. End users, even children, are becoming developers of components for the potential use of others.

Data-oriented ecosystems: In recent years, an increasing amount of data and metadata have been made available for common use, representing the basis for an ecosystem of services being developed based on shared online data. Of particular interest is the explosion of linked open data that make it possible to access, interpret, and share heterogeneous and dynamically changing data across the Web with limited knowledge of how the data were produced. Because applications do not require any ownership of these data or access to an appropriate infrastructure for

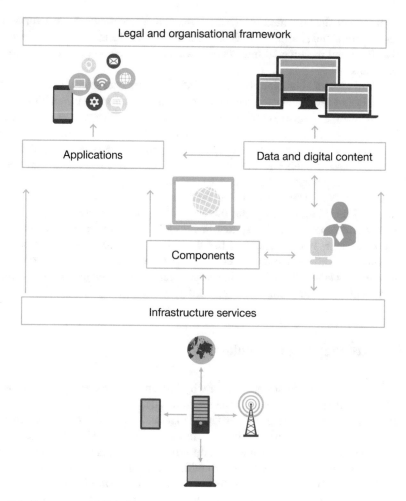

Fig. 1.5 Components of digital ecosystems

local management of large-scale data, the provision of linked open data enables a new breed of data-driven applications that are more cost-effective to develop and can combine data in new and innovative ways. Moreover, anyone can contribute to the total data model by publishing their own definitions, ensuring that the data model is dynamically adapted and is relevant for outside use. It is in the nature of such data to be both heterogeneous and distributed. This creates new challenges, as these data often cannot be transferred owing to volume or legal constraints. In addition to data in the traditional sense, also models (including data and process models) are becoming first-class citizens in the digital ecosystems.

A variant of data-oriented ecosystems are content ecosystems—networks that address creation and sharing of artistic or intellectual artifacts. The Web allows for highly visual and multimodal interactions, which will become represented through richer means.

The third type of ecosystem is the ICT infrastructure ecosystem. It consists of a huge number of interconnected networks, computing, and storage facilities owned and operated by a number of autonomous market actors (Veenstra et al. 2012). In addition, it has infrastructure services, such as positioning, and infrastructure information, such as maps, on which a range of end user services rely. The organization of these systems is mostly based on bilateral commercial agreements between market actors; hence, it is a techno-economic ecosystem rather than an engineered system. There may be regulations that place requirements on these systems and their interworking, but these are of a general nature.

In summary, there is no entity that has a global view and control of how this system of systems is organized and has the ability to address events "across systems" that may threaten the ecosystem's role as the critical infrastructure on which our modern societies to an increasing degree rely. This openness also influences how we deal with and model the supported processes (Krogstie 2012b).

1.4   Introduction to Modeling

One can argue that an important reason why humans have excelled as a species is our ability to represent, reuse, and transfer knowledge across time and space. Based on our mental models, we grow our knowledge and wisdom through experiences and participative learning. Whereas in most areas of human conduct, one-dimensional natural language is used to express and share knowledge, we see the need for and use of two- and multidimensional representational forms to increase. One such representational form is called a *conceptual model*.

A *conceptual model* is historically defined as a description of the phenomena in a domain at some level of abstraction, which is expressed in a semiformal or formal visual (diagrammatical) language. Conceptual models include business process models, in addition to other types such as data and object models.

In this book, similarly to Krogstie (2012a), we apply the following limitations when we talk about conceptual models:

- The languages for conceptual modeling are primarily diagrammatic with a limited vocabulary. The main symbols of the languages represent *concepts* such as states, processes, entities, and objects. The diagrams typically consist of general (often directed) graphs containing nodes and edges between nodes and edges representing the different phenomena and phenomena classes.
- Conceptual models are used either as an intermediate representation or as a directly used representation in the process of development and evolution of

enterprise information systems (including the non-automated parts of the enterprise).

- The conceptual modeling languages presented in this text are meant to have general applicability; that is, they are not made specifically for the modeling of a limited area. We realize that the interest in and application of so-called domain-specific languages (DSM (Kelly and Tolvanen 2008)) have increased over the last decade, but in this book, we will concentrate on generally applicable languages that can be further tailored to specific usage areas if they are deemed useful.

One important type of modeling and of particular focus in this book is *(business) process modeling.* A well-known language for business process modeling that can be used to illustrate the kind of models we are focusing on is BPMN Silver 2012). BPMN is described in more detail in Sect. 1.5.3. A simple example is depicted in Fig. 1.6. The model depicts the main tasks relative to submitting a scientific paper for a conference. Based on receiving a CFP (call for papers), a paper is written and submitted; after a review, accepted papers are then worked into a final version, which is then submitted. Although we have shown a process model in this example, we use the term "conceptual modeling" much more broadly than for business process modeling, including data modeling, enterprise modeling, object-oriented modeling, rule modeling, organizational modeling, and business modeling. As is clear from the title, the emphasis in this book will be business process models.

Models are assembled from different *signs*; thus, many in the field (Krogstie 2001; Price and Shanks 2004; Stamper 1987) base their modeling work on theories from semiotics. The study of signs has been associated with philosophical and linguistic enquiry into language and communication from the time of the Greek philosophers. Modern semiotics, as proposed by Pierce (1931–1935) and later developed by among others (Morris 1938), describes the study of signs in terms of their logical components. These are a sign's actual *representation*; its *referent* or intended meaning; and its *interpretation* or received meaning. Relations among these three aspects of a sign were further described by Morris as syntactic (between sign representations), semantic (between a representation and its referent), and pragmatic (between the representation and the interpretation) semiotic levels. The process of interpretation at the pragmatic level necessarily results from and depends on the use of the sign. This process can be viewed in terms of its potential influence on the interpreter's subsequent actions or, in cases where the sign representation

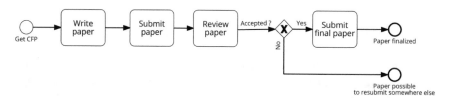

Fig. 1.6 Simple process model in BPMN

was deliberately generated by a sender, as a means of communication. In either case, the actual interpretation of the sign depends both on the interpreter's general sociolinguistic context (e.g., societal and linguistic norms) and on his/her individual circumstances (e.g., personal experience or knowledge).

In the FRISCO report (Falkenberg et al. 1996), a semiotic ladder is proposed, extending the triad of Morris to include all key aspects to consider in information systems models:

1. Physical: use of various media for modeling—documents, wall charts, computer-based modeling tools, and so on; physical size and amount and effort to manipulate them.
2. Empirical: variety of elements distinguished; error frequencies when being written and read by different users; coding (shapes of boxes); and ergonomics of human–computer interaction (HCI) for documentation and modeling tools.
3. Syntactic: languages—natural, constrained, or formal; and logical and mathematical methods for modeling.
4. Semantic: interpretation of the elements of the model in terms of the real world; ontological assumptions; operations for arriving at values of elements; and justification of external validity.
5. Pragmatic: roles played by models—hypothesis, directive, description, and expectation; responsibility for making and using the model; and conversations needed to develop and use the model.
6. Social: communities of users; the norms governing use for different purposes; and organizational framework for using the model.

The lists under each level are indicative rather than exhaustive, and we will provide more detail in Chaps. 2–5 on how this influences our thinking on quality in business process modeling. An issue when discussing a problem area such as modeling is that people, when using multilayer-related terms, frequently fail to mention the layer on which they are focusing, which may result in severe misunderstandings.

These 6 layers can be divided into two groups to reveal the technical versus the social aspect. Physics, empirics, and syntactical aspects comprise an area in which pure technical and formal methods are adequate. However, semantics, pragmatics, and the social sphere cannot be explored using those methods unmodified. This underscores that one must include human judgment when discussing the higher semiotic layers (layers 4–6).

1.4.1 Abstraction Mechanisms and Levels of Modeling

Hierarchical abstraction mechanisms are a central mechanism found in most modeling languages. There are a vast number of hierarchies that one might want to model, and these have rather diverse properties.

Original work in the field of semantic data modeling (Hull and King 1987; Peckham and Maryanski 1988; Potter and Trueblood 1988), ontologies (Leppänen 2005), and semantic networks (Findler 1979) has led to the identification of four standard hierarchical relations:

- Classification,
- Aggregation,
- Generalization,
- Association.

The four relations have the following definitions, based on the definitions originally provided by Potter and Trueblood (1988):

- Classification: Specific instances are considered as a higher level object type (a class) via the *is-instance-of* relationship (e.g., "Barbara Pernici" and "Keng Siau" are specific instances of "Professors," "CAiSE'2016" is an instance of "Conference").
- Aggregation: An object is related to the components that compose it via the *is-part-of* relationship (e.g., a bicycle has wheels, a seat, a frame, handlebars, etc.; a conference might have keynote sessions, paper sessions, workshops, tutorials, panels, etc.). Leppänen (2005) called this relation composition.
- Generalization: Similar object types are abstracted into a higher level object type via the *is-a* relationship (e.g., an employee is a person, a male singer is a singer, and a conference is an event).
- Association: Several object types are considered as a higher level set object type via the *is-a-member-of* relationship (e.g., the sets "men" and "women" are members of the set "sex groups" and "CAiSE'1989" and "CAiSE'2015" are members of the set "Held CAiSE conferences"). Association can also be found under the names of membership (e.g., Potter and Trueblood 1988), grouping (e.g., Hull and King 1987; Leppänen 2005), or collection (e.g., Hagelstein and Riau 1987).

For a long time, there have been approaches to support the development of new modeling languages (the so-called meta-modeling) rather than the use of existing, defined languages. In particular, this is exploited in domain-specific modeling and domain-specific languages (DSM/DSL). The use of meta-modeling is also found in MDA (model-driven architecture) and enterprise modeling. The term "meta" indicates that something is after something; that is, a meta-model is a model after (of) a model. This meta-level discussion uses the classification abstraction described above. It can be argued that the term "meta-model" is most correctly used when it is the model used for designing the database structure of a model repository (i.e., so that the instances in the meta-model constitute a model). Often, the term is also used for the related (but at times somewhat different) model that results when describing the modeling concepts and relationships of a modeling language (below termed "language model"). The meta-model for defining the storage of the model and the language model usually are quite similar, but the meta-model typically covers additional technically oriented aspects. We will use both terms below and distinguish them according to how we have defined the difference here.

In principle, it is possible to apply an infinite number of meta-levels. In practice, one normally views this at no more than four levels. The generally accepted conceptual framework for meta-modeling explains the relationships between meta-meta-model, meta-model, model, and (now somewhat misleading) "user data." Together, they form four layers on top of each other, illustrated in meta-object facility (MOF) in OMG (which again is based on the work on CDIF in the 1980s) as depicted in Fig. 1.7.

- M0: The user object layer comprises the information that we wish to describe. This information is what one in a database world typically called "data," but this is just as much a model as what we find on the other levels. More precisely, it is a model on the *instance* level representing physical or virtual individual phenomena in the world. Whereas instance-level modeling is quite common within enterprise modeling, software modeling is typically performed on the next layer (M1). Note that, contrary to the figure, an M0 model can also be an instance of an M2 concept (when the language includes instance-level concepts in addition to type-level concepts, something often found in enterprise modeling, for instance).

Fig. 1.7 Meta-levels as defined in OMG MOF

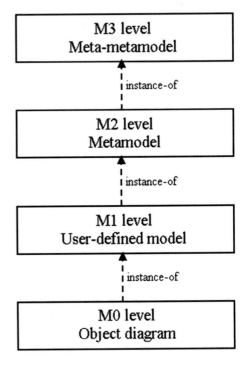

- M1: The model layer comprises the metadata that describe information. Metadata are informally aggregated as models.
- M2: The meta-model layer comprises the descriptions (i.e., meta-metadata) that define the structure and semantics of metadata. Meta-metadata is informally aggregated as meta-models. A meta-model can also be considered as a "language" for describing different kinds of data.
- M3: The meta-meta-model layer comprises the description of the structure and semantics of meta-metadata. In other words, it is the "language" for defining different kinds of metadata (modeling languages), in simple cases consisting of "nodes" and "edges" between "nodes."

Note that these levels are conceptual; that is, in a technical system, implementing these levels does not have to be strictly followed. Often, we also see approaches that mix aspects of the two sublevels at the same level (e.g., mix process instances and process types—i.e., levels M0 and M1).

1.4.2 Perspectives of Modeling

Modeling is performed using a modeling language. Any modeling language is biased toward a particular way of perceiving the world:

- The languages have constructs that force analysts, domain experts, and users to emphasize some aspects of the world and largely neglect others.
- The more the analysts and users work with one particular language, the more their thinking will be influenced by this, and their awareness of aspects of the world that do not fit in may consequently be diminished. This is a similar phenomenon to that presented in the Sapir–Whorf hypothesis, which states that a person's understanding of the world is influenced by the (natural) language he/she uses (Stamper 1987).
- For the types of problems that fit well with the particular language used, neglecting features that are not covered can have a positive effect, because it becomes easier to concentrate on the relevant issues. However, it is often difficult to know what issues are relevant in the given case. In addition, different issues may be relevant for different people at the same time.

Modeling languages can be divided into classes according to the core phenomena classes (concepts) that are represented and focused on in the language. We have called this the *perspective* of the language. Another term that can be used is *structuring principle*. Generally, we can define a structuring principle as some rule or assumption concerning how a model should be structured. We observe that

- A structuring principle can be more or less detailed: On a high level, for instance, one has the choice between structuring the information hierarchically or in a general network. Most approaches take a far more detailed attitude toward structuring: deciding what is going to be decomposed and how. For instance, structured analysis (Gane and Sarson 1979) implies that the things primarily to be decomposed are processes, and an additional suggestion might be that the hierarchy of processes should not be deeper than 4 levels and that the maximum number of processes in one diagram is 7.
- A structuring principle might be more or less rigid: In some approaches, one can override the standard structuring principle if one so chooses; in others, this is impossible.

A central structuring principle is the aggregation principle. Aiming for a certain aggregation principle thus implies decisions concerning:

- What kind of components to aggregate.
- How other kinds of components (if any) will be connected to the hierarchical structure.

Some possible aggregation principles are the following:

- Object orientation,
- Process orientation,
- Actor orientation,
- Goal orientation.

Objects are the things subject to processing, processes are the actions performed, and actors are the ones who perform the actions. Goals are the reasons why the actions are performed in the first place. Clearly, these four approaches concentrate on different aspects of the perceived reality, but it is easy to be mistaken about the difference. It is not which aspects they capture and represent that are relevant. Instead, the difference is one of focus, representation, dedication, visualization, and sequence, in the sense that an oriented language typically prescribes the following (Opdahl and Sindre 1997):

- Some aspects are promoted as fundamental for modeling, whereas others are covered mainly to provide the context and additional information relevant to the promoted ones (focus).
- Some aspects are represented explicitly and others only implicitly (representation).
- Some aspects are covered by dedicated modeling constructs, whereas others are less accurately covered by general ones (dedication).
- Some aspects are visualized in diagrams; others are recorded only textually (visualization).
- Some aspects are captured before others during modeling (modeling sequence).

An alternative term to perspective is "view," and approaches such as ARIS (Scheer 1999) differentiate between the control view, data view, and organization view.

Based on the existing work on modeling as summarized by Krogstie (2012a), to give a broad overview of the different perspectives accommodated by conceptual modeling approaches, we have identified the following perspectives:

- Behavioral perspective: Languages in this perspective go back to at least the early 1960s, with the introduction of Petri nets (Petri 1962). In most languages with a behavioral perspective, the main phenomena are states and transitions between states. State transitions are triggered by events (Davis 1988). A finite state machine (FSM) is a hypothetical machine that can be in only one of a given number of states at any specific time. In response to an input, the machine generates an output and changes its state.

- Functional perspective: The main phenomena class in the functional perspective is the *transformation*: A transformation is defined as an activity that, based on a set of phenomena, transforms them to another (possibly empty) set of phenomena. Other terms used for this phenomenon are function, process, activity, and task. A well-known conceptual modeling language with a functional perspective is dataflow diagrams (DFDs) (Gane and Sarson 1979).

- Structural perspective: Approaches within the structural perspective concentrate on describing the static structure of a system. The main construct of such languages is the "entity." Other terms used with some differences in semantics are object, concept, thing, and phenomena. Note that objects as used in object-oriented approaches are discussed further under the object perspective below. The structural perspective has conventionally been handled by languages for data modeling. Whereas the first data modeling language was published in 1974 (Hull and King 1987), the first with a major impact was the entity-relationship language of Chen (1976).

- Goal and rule perspective: Goal-oriented modeling focuses on structures of goals and rules. A rule is something that influences the actions of a set of actors. A rule is either a rule of necessity or a deontic rule (Wieringa 1989). A rule of necessity is a rule that must always be satisfied. A deontic rule is a rule that is only socially agreed upon among a set of persons and organizations. A deontic rule can thus be violated without redefining the terms in the rule. A deontic rule can be classified as being an obligation, recommendation, permission, discouragement, or prohibition (Krogstie and Sindre 1996). The general structure of an individual rule is "if condition, then expression," where condition is descriptive, indicating the scope of the rule by designating the conditions in which the rule apply, and the expression is prescriptive for what should happen. According to Twining and Miers (1982), any rule can be analyzed and restated as a compound conditional statement of this form. In the early 1990s, one began to relate rules in the so-called rule hierarchies, linking rules on different abstraction levels.

- Object perspective: The basic phenomena of object-oriented modeling languages are similar to those found in most object-oriented programming languages:

- Object: An object is an "entity" that has a unique and unchangeable identifier and a local state consisting of a collection of attributes with assignable values. The state can be manipulated only with a set of methods defined on the object. The value of the state can be accessed only by sending a message to the object to call on one of its methods. The details of the methods may not be known except through their interfaces. The occurrence of an operation triggered by receiving a message is called an event.
  - Process: The process of an object, also called the object's life cycle, is the trace of the received events during the existence of the object.
  - Class: A set of objects that share the same definitions of attributes and operations compose an object class. A subset of a class, called a subclass, may have special attribute and operation definitions, but still share (usually all) definitions of its superclass through inheritance.

- Communication perspective: Much of the work within this perspective is based on language/action theory from philosophical linguistics. The basic assumption of language/action theory is that persons cooperate within work processes through their conversations and mutual commitments taken within them. Speech act theory which was initially developed by Austin and Searle (Austin 1962; Searle 1969, 1979) starts from the assumption that the minimal unit of human communication is not a sentence or other expression, but rather the performance of certain types of language acts. Illocutionary logic (Dignum and Weigand 1995; Searle and Vanderveken 1985) is a logical formalization of the theory and can be used to formally describe communication structures.
- Actor and role perspective: The main phenomena of languages within this perspective are actors (alternatively using the term "agent") and roles. The background for modeling of the kind described in this perspective comes from organizational science, work on programming languages (e.g., actor languages (Thomlinson and Scheevel 1989)), and work on intelligent agents in artificial intelligence (e.g., Genesereth and Ketchpel 1994; Shoham 1994).
- Topological perspective: This perspective relates to the topological ordering between the different phenomena. The best background for conceptualization of these aspects comes from the cartography and CSCW fields, differentiating between space and place (Dourish 2006; Harrison and Dourish 1996). "Space" describes geometrical arrangements that might structure, constrain, and enable certain forms of movement and interaction; "place" denotes the ways in which settings acquire recognizable and persistent social meaning in the course of interaction.

Many modern frameworks and approaches to modeling combine several perspectives in integrated approaches. However, we have experienced this as a useful way to order the presentation of modeling approaches.

Another way to classify languages is according to their level of formality. Conceptual modeling languages can be classified as semiformal (having a formal syntax, but no formal semantics) or formal (having logical and/or executable semantics). The logical semantics used can vary (e.g., first-order logic, description logic, and modal logic). Executional or operational semantics enable that a model in the language can be executed on a computing machine if it is complete. They can also be used together with descriptions in informal (natural) languages and non-linguistic representations, such as audio and video recordings.

Finally, it is important to differentiate the level of modeling; are we modeling types or instances?

1.5 Business Process Modeling

The first process modeling language was described as early as 1921 (Gilbreth and Gilbreth 1921). Other important early attempts toward conceptual modeling occurred in the late 1950s and early 1960s with the work of Young and Kent (1958) and early work on Petri nets (Petri 1962). Process modeling approaches as we know them today within the information systems field were introduced on a large scale approximately 40 years ago, with the development and adoption of such techniques as DFDs. The interest in process modeling has undergone phases with the introduction of different approaches, including structured analysis in the 1970s (Gane and Sarson 1979), business process reengineering in the late 1980s/early 1990s (Hammer and Champy 1993), and workflow management in the 1990s (WfMC 2000). Lately, with the proliferation of BPM (business process management) (Havey 2005), interest in and use of process modeling has increased even further.

Models of work processes have long been utilized to learn about, guide, and support practice in other areas as well. In software process improvement (Derniame 1998), enterprise modeling (Fox and Gruninger 2000), and quality management, process models describe methods and standard working procedures. Simulation and quantitative analyses are also performed to improve efficiency. In process-centric software engineering environments (Ambriola et al. 1997) and workflow systems (Weske 2007), model execution is automated.

1.5.1 Goals of Process Modeling

According to the general model theory (Stachowiak 1973), there are three common characteristics of models: *representation, simplification,* and *pragmatic orientation* (or in German, Abbildungsmerkmal, Verkürzungsmerkmal, Pragmatisches Merkmal).

- *Representation*: Models represent something else than the model itself.
- *Simplification*: Models possess a reductive trait in which they represent only a subset of attributes of the phenomenon being modeled.

Table 1.4 Types of models according to temporal aspects and purpose

Type of model	Past	Present	Future
Ideal model	Ideal model of the past	Reference model	Ought-to-be model
Simulated model (what-if)	Possible model of the past	Possible model	Possible model of the future
Model espoused	As-was-planned	Should-have been model	To-be model
Model in use	Actual as-was model	As-is model	Work-around model
Motivational model	Past burning platform model	Burning platform model	Burning platform model

- *Intentionality*: Models have a substitutive function in which they substitute a certain phenomenon as being conceptualized by a certain subject in a given temporal space with a certain *intention* or operation in mind.

Thus, a model is not just a representation of something else; it is a conscious construction to achieve a certain goal beyond the making of the model itself.

In Table 1.4, we list relevant situations along the temporal and purpose axes.

First of all, models can represent past situations, the present, or a potential future situation. Here, we primarily consider the present and future, noting that in several areas, it is also important to keep track of the processes used in the past—e.g., in areas where compliance is important and one can get into situations in which, for instance, the authorities question adherence to compliance rules in the past. At all temporal stages, models can be viewed as:

- Ideal: A model of an ideal situation in the area, ignoring contextual restrictions such as current legacy systems and practices.
- Simulated: A model that differs in some way from the actual state of things— e.g., to be able to perform what-if analysis and other simulations.
- Espoused: The official model in a restricted area.
- In use: How the situation actually is (or was). This difference between model espoused and model in use is parallel to the notions in Argyris and Schön (1978) on theory espoused versus theory in use. The model in use should ideally not be so different from the model espoused; but in practice, we often find that these differ.
- Motivational: A simulation that depicts a defensive approach—i.e., what happens if nothing is done. Another term for such models is a burning platform scenario (Conner 1992).

In total, this gives 15 model types, the most important being depicted below along with an overview of the main goals of modeling. However, it is first important to realize that the to-be situation (both ideal and actual) is a moving target. When one implements a new solution (the to-be), both the ought-to-be and to-be have moved further. We will look below particularly at the interplay between the actual as-is model, the ought-to-be ideal model, and the to-be model, where contextual constraints are considered.

Process modeling is usually performed in some organizational setting. It is important to develop both corporate future goals and a target architecture in the form of a "Future Operating Model" (cf. ought-to-be model above) along with detailed workflows with both as-is and to-be activities. To achieve this, we need a combined top-down and bottom-up approach. The Future Operating Model is a top-down model describing the best practice of how we want to operate in the future (ought-to-be). Process modeling often combines a best practice model with detailed workflow models, making the process move from as-is to to-be easier, more structured and more efficient—e.g., to achieve a common understanding of the present and the future (target model). By linking the best practice with as-is and to-be models, it will be possible to analyze how close (or far) the current practice is to (from) the best practice.

As illustrated in Fig. 1.8, an organization can at a point in time be viewed as being in a state (the current state, often represented as a descriptive "as-is" model) that is to be evolved to some future wanted state (conventionally represented as a "to-be" model prescribing a wanted future organizational state). In practice, looking only at as-is and to-be models is insufficient; one also must have the possibility to experiment with could-be models (different scenarios) and ought-to-be models (the perceived ideal scenario).

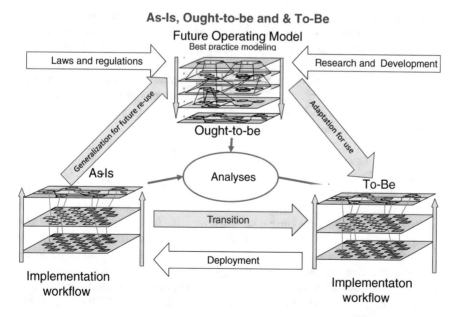

Fig. 1.8 Interplay among as-is, to-be, and ought-to-be models

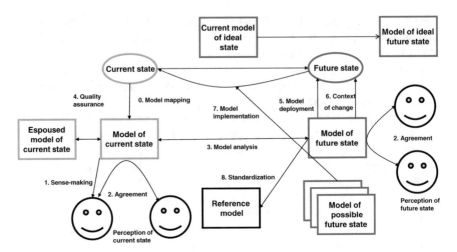

Fig. 1.9 Application of business process modeling

An organizational state includes the existing processes, organization, and computer systems of the enterprise. These states are often modeled, and the state of the organization is perceived (differently) by different persons through these models. This opens up different *usage areas*, and thus, different goals for the use of business process models as extensions of similar overview found in, e.g., Krogstie (2012a) are further illustrated in Fig. 1.9:

0. Model mapping: Representation of the current situation as it actually is (not as it was planned to be). This can be accomplished for several actual model objectives (thus listed as objective 0). Model mapping can be performed manually or be supported by tools—e.g., in process mining of event logs of running systems (van der Aalst et al. 2011).

1. Human sense-making (Weick 1995): The development and use of a model of the current state can be useful for people to make sense of and learn about the current situation, models (perceived as) representing organizational reality. This includes models made for training purposes.

2. Communication to establish agreement among people in the organization: As discussed already by Bråten (1973), models are important in human communication. Thus, in addition to supporting the sense-making process for the individual, a model can act as a common framework supporting communication, potentially ending up in agreement. This relates to communication for agreement relative to both the current state and possible future states and scenarios—e.g., agreeing on the new procedures or requirements for new systems. In connection with the current state, the different stakeholders involved in the communication are often skewed by higher initial knowledge among some parts than others. In certain settings—e.g., for training purposes—this is to be expected. In other cases, this might be more problematic as in the case of model monopoly (Bråten 1973).

3. Model analysis: The goal is to gain knowledge about the organization through simulation or deduction, often by comparing a model of the current state with a model of a future, potentially better state. Moreover, by analyzing the model instead of the business area itself, one might deduce properties that are difficult if not impossible to perceive directly because the model enables one to concentrate on a limited number of aspects at a time. Several situations might be compared, but one situation is typically better than the other; this is a basis for gap analysis to determine how to move from the current to a future state. In connection with implementation—e.g., of ERP solutions, which come with an explicit reference process model that is supported in the system—an important task is to perform *fit analysis*—i.e., how well do the reference process fit the current situation and what must change when implementing the new system: the organizational processes or the ERP system?

4. Quality assurance: This ensures, for instance, that the organization acts according to a certified process typically represented as an espoused model achieved through an ISO certification project resulting in a process model. As indicated above, compliance checking might need to relate to a number of versions of the model espoused.

5. Model deployment and activation: The model of the future state is integrated into an information system directly and thus actively takes part in the actions of the organization. Models can be activated in essentially three ways:

   a. Through people guided by process "maps," in which the system offers no active support, but makes the model available only as a manual checklist.

   b. Automatically, in which the system plays an active role as in automated workflow systems.

   c. Interactively, in which the computer and the users cooperate in interpreting the model. The computer makes decisions about prescribed parts of the model, while the users resolve ambiguities and incomplete models. This approach can be found, e.g., in the use of active knowledge models (AKM) (Lillehagen and Krogstie 2008) and emergent workflow (Krogstie and Jørgensen 2004), supporting interaction machines, not only algorithmic machines (Wegner 1997).

6. To give the context for a conventional system development project without being directly activated: This is the conventional usage of process models in information systems development, in which the model represents the wanted future state and acts as a prescriptive model, including requirements, as a basis for design and implementation of an information system, acting in the end as documentation of the developed system (i.e., turning into an espoused model of the current state when the system is put in production) that can be useful in the future evolution of the system.

7. Model implementation: The purpose of both usage areas 5 and 6 is to change the situation in the organization. In addition, one often must also perform other tasks to make this an actual reality—i.e., have people work according to the new processes, e.g., by using the system as envisaged. In connection with this,

motivational models showing the negative effects of what will happen if the situation does not change can be important. Although depicting unwanted behavior, work-around models (Alter 2015) can also depict likely deviations, both for risk analysis and for the ability to quickly catch work-arounds because this is a symptom that the new model is not properly implemented.

8. Standardization relates to not only making changes internally in the organization but also influencing reference models external to the organization that others might need to relate to.

The different approaches to the business process described above are appropriate for supporting different types of processes—from static, to very dynamic, even emergent processes. Often we see that an overall process has both static and more dynamic aspects; thus, many examples exist in which it is proposed to combine perspectives (e.g., hybrid models, in which knowledge-intensive tasks are modeled with a declarative (rule-oriented) language and the static part is modeled by a more conventional functional or behavioral language). Moreover, a mixed use of behavioral and speech act models is an example of this.

The different process types decide the extent to which the underlying process implementation and support technology can be based on hard-coded, predefined, evolving, or implicit process models. This gives a number of development approaches as illustrated in Fig. 1.10. On one extreme, process support systems are manually coded on top of a conventional runtime environment, and on the other, enterprise models are used directly to generate and evolve solutions. Between these, we have approaches including the use of BPM and workflow technology for the partly automated execution of the process solution.

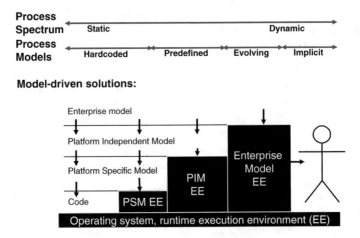

Fig. 1.10 Overview of different execution environments for different process models

1.5.2 Perspectives to Business Process Modeling

Looking back at Sect. 1.4.2, process modeling has primarily been accomplished according to a functional or behavioral perspective. On the other hand, one finds examples of process modeling following all the described perspectives (except structural modeling) in the literature (Krogstie 2012a). We will here first refer briefly to work of this kind before describing in more detail some functional and behavioral modeling languages that will be used in examples and cases later in the book.

1.5.2.1 Declarative Process Modeling—Process Modeling According to the Goal and Rule Perspective

The relationships among the tasks, choices for gateways, etc., represent different (business) rules. In the workflow area, focusing on representing the rules is conventionally termed declarative workflow. Constraint-based languages (Dourish et al. 1996; Glance et al. 1996) do not prescribe a course of events; rather, they capture the boundaries within which the process must be performed, leaving the actors to control the internal details. Instead of telling people what to do, these systems warn about rule violations and enforce constraints. Thus, common problems with unwarranted or premature overserialization can be avoided (Glance et al. 1996).

A wide variety of declarative modeling approaches has been specified in business process management, from the use of basic event–condition–action (ECA) rules (Kappel et al. 1998) to declarative process modeling languages such as DecSerFlow (Aalst and Pesic 2006), BPCN (Lu et al. 2009), and ConDec (Pesic and Aalst 2006). Goedertier and Vanthienen (2009) present an overview of the most common declarative process modeling languages.

Languages representing rule-based process modeling can potentially provide a higher expressiveness than diagrammatic languages (e.g., the ability to specify temporal requirements) (Lu et al. 2007), but this might result in process models that are less comprehensible (Fickas 1989) owing to large, essentially flat rule models.

Declarative process enactment guarantees high runtime flexibility for declarative process specifications that contain only the strictly required mandatory constraints. An individual execution path that satisfies the set of mandatory constraints can be dynamically built for a specific process instance. Process compliance is ensured when all mandatory rules are correctly mapped onto mandatory business constraints. During the construction of a suitable execution path, little support is provided to the end user (Weske 2007), which could affect the process effectiveness. Krogstie and Sindre (1996) proposed the idea of differentiating constraints by modality, in which recommendations would guide the user, whereas mandatory constraints would ensure compliant behavior. The guidance provided by the deontic constraints might depend on explicit domain knowledge or be learned through process mining (Schonenberg et al. 2008). Finally, the increased size and complexity of contemporary process models might reduce the potential for process automation because current declarative workflow management systems might have limited efficiency in these cases according to van der Aalst et al. (2009).

A graphic depiction of these models is difficult because it would correspond to a visualization of several possible solutions to the set of constraint equations constituting the model. The support for articulation of planned and ongoing tasks is limited. Consequently, constraints are often combined with transformational models (Bernstein 2000; Dourish et al. 1996). Alternatively, one can link the operational rules to goal hierarchies as in Tempora (Krogstie et al. 1991), EEML (Krogstie 2008), and other approaches for goal-oriented modeling (Kavakli and Loucopoulos 2005).

1.5.2.2   Process Modeling Following an Object Perspective

UML (Booch et al. 2005) has become the official and de facto standard for object-oriented analysis and design. People also apply UML to model other things, including business processes. Object orientation offers a number of useful modeling techniques such as encapsulation, polymorphism, subtyping, and inheritance. UML integrates these capabilities with, e.g., requirements capture in use case descriptions and behavior modeling in state, activity, and sequence diagrams. On the other hand, UML is designed for software developers, not end users. A core challenge thus remains in mapping system-oriented UML constructs to user- and process-oriented concepts (Hommes and Reijswoud 1999). To this problem, no general solution exists (Loos and Allweyer 1998; Störle 2001). UML process languages utilize associations, classes, operations, use cases, interaction sequences, or activity diagrams. The lack of a standardized approach reflects the wide range of process modeling approaches in business and software engineering. One approach is PML (Anderl and Raßler 2008), which uses object-oriented techniques based on viewing classes in a particular way. Whereas a class conventionally is defined by class name, attributes, and methods, in this approach, the class is defined with process name, methods, and resources. The PML process class describes the process generically. This allows one to define all methods with assurances and resources needed for the process. The instantiation of a process is a project. This means that the instance of a process defines the current occurrence of resources, data models used, etc. With regard to connections and dependencies between single process classes, PML features the standard UML concepts of inheritance and associations.

1.5.2.3   Process Modeling Following a Communication Perspective

The communication perspective, often termed as the language action perspective, was brought into the workflow arena through the COORDINATOR prototype

(Winograd and Flores 1986) and was later succeeded by the action workflow system (Medina-Mora et al. 1992).

The main strength of this approach is that it facilitates analysis of the communicative aspects of the process. It highlights that each process is an interaction between a customer and a performer, represented as a cycle with four phases: preparation, negotiation, performance, and acceptance. The dual-role constellation is a basis for work breakdown; e.g., the performer can delegate parts of the work to other people. This explicit representation of communication and negotiation, especially the structuring of the conversation into predefined speech act steps, has also been criticized (Button 1995; De Michelis and Grasso 1994; Suchman 1994). Minimal support for situated conversations, the danger that explication leads to increased external control of the work, and a simplistic one-to-one mapping between utterances and actions are among the weaknesses. On the other hand, it has been reported that the action workflow approach is useful when people act pragmatically and do not always follow the encoded rules of behavior (De Michelis and Grasso 1994)—e.g., when the communication models are interactively activated.

Some later approaches to workflow modeling include aspects of both the functional and language action modeling. In Krogstie and Carlsen (1997), speech act information was added to dataflow in extended DFDs. In WooRKS (Ader et al. 1994), functional modeling is used for processes and speech acts for exceptions, and thus, these perspectives are not used in combination. TeamWare Flow (Swendson et al. 1994) and Obligations (Bogia 1995), on the other hand, can be said to be hybrid approaches but use radically different concepts from those found in conventional conceptual modeling.

1.5.2.4 Process Modeling According to the Actor/Role Perspective

Role-centric process modeling languages have been applied for workflow analysis and implementation since the 1990s. Role interaction nets (RIN) (Singh and Rein 1992) and role activity diagrams (RAD) (Ould 1995) use roles as their main structuring concept. The activities performed by a role are grouped in the diagram, either in swimlanes (RIN) or inside boxes (RAD). The use of roles as a structuring concept makes very clear who is responsible for what. RAD has also been merged with speech acts for interaction among roles (Benson et al. 2000). Also the RIS method (Iden 2009) and the specialized BPMN notation used in the case presented in Sect. 4.2 have specific mechanism for supporting the modeling of collaboration between roles. The role-based approach also has limitations—e.g., making it difficult to change the organizational distribution of work. It primarily targets analysis of administrative procedures, in which formal roles are important. The use of swimlanes in BPMN and UML activity diagrams as described below might also have this area of use. Some other approaches worth mentioning on this level are REA and e³Value.

The REA language was first described by McCarthy (1982) and was then developed further by Geerts and McCarthy (1999). REA was originally intended as a basis for accounting information systems and focuses on representing increases and decreases of value in an organization. REA has subsequently been extended to enterprise architectures (Hruby 2006) and e-commerce frameworks (UMM 2007). The core concepts in the REA language are *resource*, *event*, and *agent*. The intuition behind this language is that every business transaction can be looked upon as an event in which two agents exchange resources. Some newer approaches including BPCM (Gao and Krogstie 2012) look at combining this approach with reference process models such as SCOR.

E^3Value (Gordijn et al. 2006) is an actor-/role-oriented modeling language for interorganizational modeling. The purpose of this modeling language is to represent how actors of a system create, exchange, and consume objects of economic value. E^3Value models give a representation of actors, value exchanges, and value objects of a business system.

1.5.2.5   Process Modeling Following the Topological Perspective

The concept of place can be related to a process, given that a place focuses on the typical behavior in a certain setting (also known as a habitat—e.g., a meeting room or a movie theater) rather than where it physically is located. Whereas some processes are closely related to place (e.g., what can be done in a certain, specialized factory), more and more tasks can be accomplished in more or less any setting owing to the pervasive mobile information infrastructure that has been established in the last decade, thus making it useful to be able to differentiate topological from transformation-oriented modeling. In certain representations, aspects of space and place are closely interlinked (e.g., in the representation of the agenda of a conference, also considering time). Some approaches allow the place-oriented aspects to be considered—e.g., work on extending UML activity diagrams and BPMN with place-oriented aspects (Gopalakrishnan et al. 2010, 2012).

Conventional representations of space such as a map have to a limited degree been oriented toward representation of process knowledge. Some recent approaches do consciously consider these aspects, as exemplified by Nossum and Krogstie (2009), and Krogstie and Nossum (2014).

1.5.2.6   Process Modeling According to the Functional Perspective

Most process modeling languages take a functional (or transformational/input –process–output) approach, although some of the most popular also include behavioral aspects as will be discussed below. Processes are divided into activities, which may be divided further into subactivities. Each activity takes inputs, which it transforms into outputs. Input and output relations thus define the sequence of work. Whereas the dataflow diagram (DFD) (Gane and Sarson 1979) is a paradigm

Fig. 1.11 Main components
of IDEF0

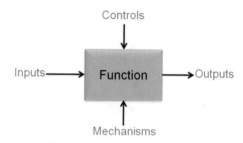

example of this perspective, we will briefly describe another approach, IDEF0, because it is used in one of the case studies we present later in the book.

IDEF0 (IDEF0 2015) is a process modeling language and a method for using this language to model the decisions, actions, and activities of an organization or system. IDEF0 was derived from the structured analysis and design technique (SADT). In December 1993, the Computer Systems Laboratory of the National Institute of Standards and Technology (NIST) released IDEF0 as a standard for function modeling in FIPS Publication 183.

IDEF0 makes it possible to represent the functions that are performed and what is needed to perform those functions. *Originally*, IDEF0 was developed to enhance communication among people trying to understand the system. *Now*, IDEF0 is being used for documentation, understanding, design, analysis, planning, and integration.

A model of a function at the highest level of inputs, outputs, controls, and mechanisms is depicted in Fig. 1.11.

The inputs and outputs are known as ICOMs:

- **Input**: Can be a trigger and is an input that is transformed to output in the function.
- **Control**: Guide or regulating activity. A main distinction between input and control is that inputs are transformed (change), whereas controls remain unchanged.
- **Outputs**: Results of a performing the activity.
- **Mechanism**: Resources needed to perform the activity. These can be people or roles, equipment, IT, or financial resources.

IDEF0 is regarded as a best practice for logical/generic/conceptual process models with a process breakdown structure. IDEF0 also can be used to model all variants of value chains, value shops, and value networks (Stabell and Fjeldstad 1998).

IDEF0 provides hierarchical breakdown/decomposition of the functional structure. When combined with other modeling perspectives in enterprise modeling environments, the ICOMs can also be decomposed; i.e., this top-down model can represent not only the process breakdown but also the breakdown of information structure (input/output), the logical applications, and role and control structure shown in Fig. 1.12.

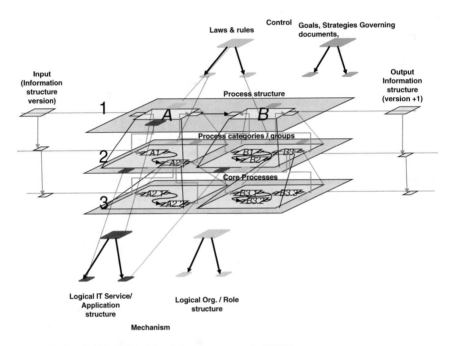

Fig. 1.12 Parallel hierarchical breakdown structures in IDEF0

Given the extensive use of transformational languages, a number of analyses focus on this category (Conradi and Jaccheri 1998; Curtis et al. 1992; Green and Rosemann 2000; Lei and Singh 1997). The expressiveness of these languages typically includes decomposition and dataflow, whereas organizational modeling and roles are often integrated (see also role-oriented process modeling above). In approaches that integrate behavioral and functional aspects, we also see a support for control flow. Aspects such as timing and quantification, products and communication, or commitments are better supported by other perspectives. User-orientedness is a major advantage of transformational languages. Partitioning the process into steps matches well the descriptions that people use elsewhere. Graphical input–process–output models are comprehensible given some training, but you can also build models by simply listing the tasks in plain text or in a hierarchical work breakdown structure. Hence, the models can be quite simple, provided that incomplete ordering of steps is allowed.

1.5.3   Combined Behavioral and Functional Approaches

A number of the recent process modeling notations add control flow aspects to a transformational approach—i.e., can be said to somehow combine the functional and behavioral perspectives. Some examples of this are ARIS EPC (Keller et al. 1992), UML activity diagrams (Booch et al. 2005), YAWL (Aalst and Hofstede 2005), and BPMN (Silver 2012). We focus here on the latter because it is used in examples and cases later in the book.

The Business Process Modeling Notation (BPMN version 1.0) was proposed in May 2004 and adopted by OMG for ratification in February 2006. Since then, BPMN has been evaluated in different ways by the academic community (Aagesen and Krogstie 2010, 2015) and has become widely supported in the industry with a large number of tools supporting (parts of) the notation (Evoquoz and Sterren 2011).

The first BPMN version was followed by BPMN 1.1 (OMG 2008), and the current version (BPMN 2.0) was released in 2011 (OMG 2011). BPMN is based on the revision of other notations and methodologies, especially UML activity diagram, UML EDOC business process, IDEF0 (above), ebXML BPSS, activity-decision flow (ADF) diagram, RosettaNet, LOVeM, and event-driven process chains.

The original goal of BPMN was to provide a notation that is readily understandable by all business users, from the business analysts who create the initial draft of the processes, to the technical developers responsible for implementing the technology that will support the performance of those processes, and, finally, to the business people who will manage and monitor those processes (White 2004).

Another factor that drove the development of BPMN is that, historically, business process models developed by business people have been technically separated from the process representations required by systems designed to implement and execute those processes. Thus, it was necessary to manually translate the original process models to execution models. Such translations are subject to errors and make it difficult for the process owners to understand the evolution and the performance of the processes they have developed. To address this, a key goal in the development of BPMN was to create a bridge from a visual notation to execution languages.

BPMN 2.0 consists of four diagrams: process, choreography, collaboration, and conversation diagrams.

- Process diagrams: The traditional workflow diagram in BPMN. This is described in more detail below.
- Choreography diagrams: Choreography diagrams are new in BPMN 2.0 and focus on between-processes interactions and message flows. Another way to look at choreography is to view it as a type of business "contract" between two or more organizations. Choreography is a type of process, but differs in purpose and behavior from a standard BPMN process. A standard (orchestration) process defines the flow of activities of a specific participant or organization. In contrast, choreography formalizes the way participants coordinate their interactions. Thus, the focus is not on orchestrations of the work performed within these participants, but rather on the exchange of information (messages) between

these participants. A choreography diagram can be used to analyze how participants exchange information to coordinate their interactions.

- Collaboration diagrams: Collaboration diagrams represent interactions between two or more processes, where each individual process represents a person, role, or a system. A collaboration diagram is quite commonly used and is easily recognized because it consists of more than one pool. A pool may be empty, may be a black box, or may show a process within.
- Conversation diagrams: Conversation diagrams have been introduced in BPMN 2.0 and represent a particular usage of and an informal description of a collaboration diagram. In general, a conversation diagram is a simplified version of a collaboration diagram. A conversation diagram provides an overview of which partners of a certain domain cooperate on which tasks. The conversation diagram "view" of a collaboration diagram includes two additional graphical elements that do not exist in other BPMN views: conversation node elements (hexagon) and a conversation link (double line). It is also possible to combine the message flows from two or more conversations in one diagram. Collaboration and conversation diagrams can also be combined on a single diagram.

In this book, process diagrams are regarded as the most important since variants of this is what are the most used in practice and in our cases. Thus, we will focus on this here. The graphical notation of the core process diagrams of BPMN 2.0 is very similar to earlier versions of the standard and so are the facilities for model analysis.

BPMN allows the creation of end-to-end business processes and is designed to cover many types of modeling tasks constrained to business processes. The structuring elements of BPMN will allow the viewer to differentiate between sections of BPMN diagrams using groups, pools, or lanes. Basic types of submodels found within a BPMN model are *private business processes* (internal) and *public processes* (public).

Private business processes are internal to a specific organization and are the types of processes that have been generally called workflow or BPM processes.

Public processes depict the interactions between two or more business entities. These interactions are defined as a sequence of activities that represent the message exchange patterns between the entities involved.

The number of concepts in BPMN has become quite large; thus, three levels of use have been defined (Silver 2012):

- Level 1: Descriptive modeling—geared toward simply documenting the process flow, primarily for sense-making and communication and also for manual deployment. Most use of BPMN is at this level (Silver 2012).
- Level 2: Analytical modeling—enables more accurate modeling with respect to exceptions and complex events and supports qualitative and quantitative analyses with regard to key performance indicators. The additional features are particularly relevant to include when performing computer-assisted analysis or

Fig. 1.13 Core flow object elements in BPMN: activity, events (start, intermediate, and end), and gateway

supporting quality assurance and when the models are meant to be used as context for change through a conventional development project.

- Level 3: Executable modeling—graphical models that can be transformed into XML-based specifications that drive process engines. These make it possible to support automatic activation of the models.

The language constructs of BPMN are grouped into four basic categories of elements: flow objects, connecting objects, swimlanes, and artifacts. The notation is further divided according to the 3 levels described above. The group of *flow objects* (Fig. 1.13) contains events, activities, and gateways.

Activities are divided into processes, subprocesses, and tasks and denote the work that is done. According to Silver (2012), a BPMN activity is an action that is performed repeatedly by a performer as part of an organized activity. Each instance of the activity represents more or less the same action on a different case (e.g., handling an order). The activity is a discrete action with a well-defined start and end. Thus, functions that are performed continuously (e.g., management) are not activities in the BPMN sense. A process in BPMN is a sequence of activities leading from an initial state of the process instance to one of the defined end states. Different types of tasks have been defined and are distinguished through the use of icons in the upper-left corner of the activity symbol. Defined types of tasks are as follows:

- User task: Manual task performed by a human (e.g., an approval);
- Send task: Sends a message;
- Receive task: Waits for a message;
- Script task: Logic encoded in a programming or scripting language;
- Service task: Calls a Web service;
- Reference task: Uses the definition of another task in the process; shares the process definition (rather than duplicating it).

Tasks can be indicated to be a singular instance or a loop (sequential execution of instances) of multiple instances (parallel execution of instances). Activities can be decomposed into subactivities (subprocesses).

Events are defined as things that happen in a process and how the process responds to them (if it is a catching event), or how the process generates a signal that something has happened (if it is a throwing event). *Events* are either start events, intermediate events, or end events.

The full range of event types is described in Silver (2012). A brief description is provided below.

- Empty—works as a placeholder (one does not know yet what type of event it is),
- Message—receiving or sending a message,
- Timer—a scheduled event or a delay that triggers flow,
- Error—throw or catch an error,
- Escalation—a non-interrupting counterpart of an error event; an escalation boundary event signifies a non-interrupting exception inside an activity,
- Cancel—cancellation of the process,
- Compensation—trigger and perform compensation handling when the process does not succeed,
- Conditional—a condition is met or exception raised,
- Link event—a visual shortcut within or between diagrams (i.e., not actually an event in the conceptual sense),
- Signal—a broadcasted event. Whereas an error and escalation event can be thrown only to the parent of a subprocess and messages can be thrown only to another pool, signals do not have this limitation,
- Terminate—kill the process,
- Multiple—several triggers; only one is needed or several results are required.

The most frequently used event types are message, timer, and error events. A new feature of BPMN 2.0 is non-interrupting events (as boundary event on an activity—i.e., when they are thrown, the activity continues).

Gateways are used for determining branching, forking, merging, or joining of paths within the process. Markers can be placed within the gateway to indicate the behavior of the given construct (*or*, *exclusive-or*, *and*, and *complex*).

Connecting objects (Fig. 1.14) are used for connecting the flow objects. *Sequence flow* defines the execution order of the activities within a process, whereas *message flow* indicates a flow of messages between business entities or roles prepared to send and receive them. *Association* is used to associate both text and graphical non-flow objects. Sequence flows can be described as unguarded, guarded (conditional—fires when the condition is met), or default (chosen when no conditional flows fire).

Swimlanes (Fig. 1.15) are constructs that are used to denote a participant (roles or actors) in a process and act as graphical containers for a set of activities taken on

Fig. 1.14 BPMN connection objects: sequence flow, message flow, and association

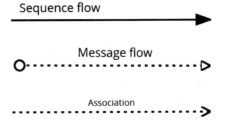

Sequence flow

Message flow

Association

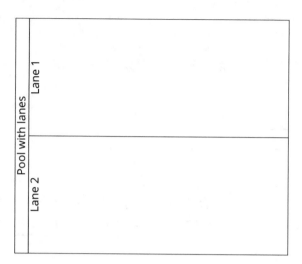

Fig. 1.15 BPMN pool and lanes

Fig. 1.16 BPMN model showing the main steps in a paper process

by that participant. By dividing *pools* into *lanes* (thus creating subpartitioning), activities can be organized and categorized according to the part of the organizations performing them.

Artifacts are data objects, data stores, groups, and annotations. *Data objects* are not considered as having any other effect on the process than information on resources required or produced by activities. The *group* construct is a visual aid used for documentation or analysis purposes, whereas the *text annotation* is used to add additional information about certain aspects of the model.

Figure 1.16 shows a simple example of a BPMN paper process. It is the "happy path" of the paper process depicted in Fig. 1.6, in which the paper is written, submitted, reviewed, and accepted (because this is the happy path). The final step is that the final updated paper is submitted to be published.

A more comprehensive model of the same situation is shown in Fig. 1.17. Here, we also have included pools and lanes. One pool is for the author, and the other is for the reviewer. The author writes the paper and sends it to the reviewer. This is depicted with a message flow because it is dataflow between pools. The paper is reviewed, and a verdict is sent as a message to the author. As we can see, the behavior of both the author and the reviewer is influenced by the verdict (accept or

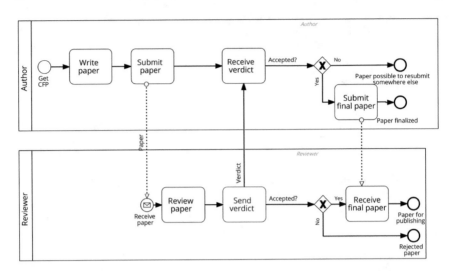

Fig. 1.17 BPMN model showing the paper process in more detail

reject). If it is accepted, the reviewer (representing the conference organization) waits for the final version of the paper, which is written and submitted by the author.

Because it is not actually the reviewer that further works with the submitted paper, a more comprehensive process would depict the program committee chair, at which point the production of the proceedings and the reviewers separate. Thus, a more complete model, also using some other parts of BPMN, is depicted in Fig. 1.18. First, it shows how the overall process starts: The PC chair is triggered by a time event when it is time to issue the CFP. Many reviews are provided per paper (⫴), and many verdicts are sent simultaneously. The model also shows an example of the use of databases and the possibility of activity decomposition (shown with the "+" on review paper).

A basis for the expressiveness of BPMN is the possibility to catch and throw a number of different events, being either interrupting or non-interrupting. In Fig. 1.19, we see an example of an interrupting timer event, where one stops working on writing the paper when the deadline is reached. A non-interrupting variant of this would be that one a bit before the deadline arrives asks for an extension (and that it is first if such extension request is rejected that one stop working on the paper).

Figure 1.20 shows the situation when plagiarism is detected (here after that a paper is sent to review). This situation will result in specific actions, but also that for instance already performed reviews of this paper are rolled back (the actual compensation task is not shown in Fig. 1.20).

The following is part of the modeling palette when modeling on level 1 (descriptive modeling):

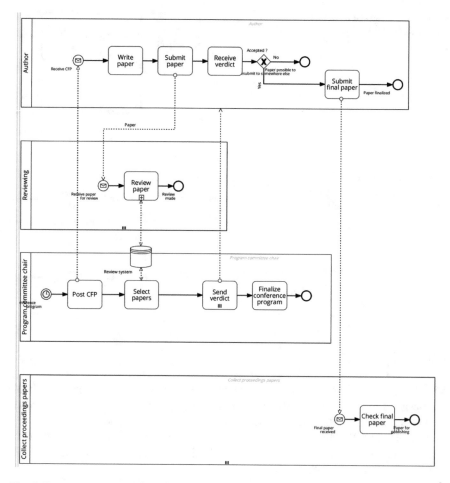

Fig. 1.18 A more complex BPMN example from the conference domain

- Pool and lane,
- User task and service (automated) task,
- Subprocess, collapsed and expanded,
- Start event (none, message, timer),
- End event (none, message, terminate),
- Exclusive and parallel gateways,
- Sequence flow and message flow,
- Data object, data store, and message,
- Text annotation,
- Link event pair (off-page connectors).

As we will see later in the book, even narrower subsets of BPMN are used for process modeling in some organizational settings.

Fig. 1.19 Example of use of timer to model time-out

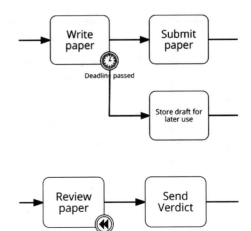

Fig. 1.20 Example of situation where compensation action might be necessary

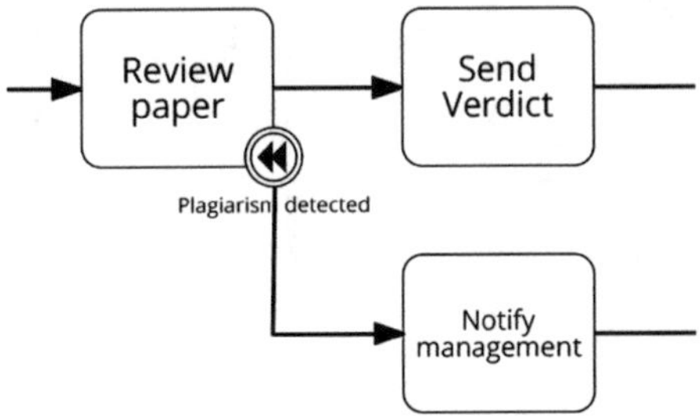

1.6   Summary

We have provided an overview of the main basis areas and terminology of the book —business processes and business process modeling—ending with an overview of process modeling notations and approaches. A main focus in the last part has been on IDEF0 and BPMN, because variants of these notations are used in the case studies and detailed examples of quality in business process modeling that we will present later in the book.

In the next chapter, we will look in more detail at aspects of quality of models in general and of business process model quality in particular.

References

Aagesen, G., Krogstie, J.: Analysis and design of business processes using BPMN. In: vom Brocke, J., Rosemann, M. (eds.) Handbook on Business Process Management. Springer, Berlin (2010)

Aagesen, G., Krogstie, J.: BPMN 2.0 for modeling business processes. In: vom Brocke, J., Rosemann, M. (eds.) Handbook on Business Process Management. Springer, Berlin (2015)

Ader, M., Lu, G., Pons, P., Monguio, J., Lopez, L., De Michelis, G., Grasso, M.A., Vlondakis, G.: WOOrks, an object-oriented work flow system for offices. Technical report, ITHACA technical report (1994)

Alter, S.: A workaround design system for anticipating, designing, and/or preventing workarounds. In: Proceedings of EMMSAD 2015, Stockholm, Sweden (2015)

Ambriola, V., Conradi, R., Fuggetta, A.: Assessing process-centered software engineering environments. ACM Trans. Softw. Eng. Methodol. **6**(3), 283–328 (1997)

Anderl, R., Raßler, J.: PML an object-oriented process modelling language. In: IFIP International Federation for Information Processing, vol. 277, pp. 145–156. Computer-Aided Innovation (CAI), Gaetano Cascini, Boston, Springer (2008)

Andersen Consulting Process Excellence Handbook. http://www.scribd.com/doc/31730974/ Process-Excellence-Handbook#scribd. Last Accessed 8 Jan 2016 (1997)

Argyris, C., Schön, D.: Organizational Learning: A Theory of Action Perspective. Addison Wesley, Reading (1978)

Austin, J.L.: How to Do Things with Words. Harvard University Press, Cambrige (1962)

Benson, et al.: Mathematical structure for reasoning about emergent organizations. In: CSCW2000 Workshop: Beyond Workflow Management: Supporting Dynamic Organizational Processes, Philadelphia, USA (2000)

Bernstein, A.: How Can Cooperative Work Tools Support Dynamic Group Processes? Bridging the Specificity Frontier, ACM CSCW Conference, Philadelphia, USA (2000)

Bogia, D.P.: Supporting flexible, extensible task descriptions in and among tasks. PhD thesis, University of Illinois, Urbana-Champaign (1995)

Booch, G., Rumbaugh, J., Jacobson, I.: The Unified Modeling Language: User Guide Second Edition. Addison-Wesley (2005)

Bråten, S.: Model monopoly and communications: systems theoretical notes on democratization. Acta Sociol. J. Scand. Social. Assoc. **16**(2), 98–107 (1973)

Button, G.: What's wrong with speach act theory. Comput. Support. Cooper. Work **3**(1), 39–42 (1995)

Chen, P.P.: The entity-relationship model: towards a unified view of data. ACM Trans. Database Syst. **1**(1), 9–36 (1976)

Conner, D.: Managing at the Speed of Change. Random House, New York (1992)

Conradi, R., Jaccheri, M.L.: Process modelling languages. In: Software Process: Principles, Methodology and Technology. Lecture Notes in Computer Science 1500. Springer, Berlin (1998)

Curtis, B., Kellner, M.I., Over, J.: Process modeling. Commun. ACM **35**(9), 75–90 (1992)

Davis, A.M.: A comparison of techniques for the specification of external system behaviour. Communications of the ACM, **31**(9), 1098–1115 (1988)

De Michelis, G., Grasso, M.A.: Situating conversations within the language/action perspective: the Milan conversation model. In: Proceedings of the ACM 1994 Conference on Computer Supported Cooperative Work (CSCW'94), pp. 89–100. Chapel Hill, NC, 22–26 Oct (1994)

Derniame, J.C. (ed.): Software Process: Principles, Methodology and Technology. Lecture Notes in Computer Science 1500. Springer, New York (1998)

Dignum, F., Weigand, H.: Modelling communication between cooperative systems. In: Iivari, J., Lyytinen, K., Rossi, M. (eds.) Proceedings of the 7th International Conference on Advanced Information Systems Engineering (CAiSE'95), Jyväskylä, Finland, 12–16 June 1995, pp. 140–153. Springer, Berlin (1995)

Dourish, P.: Re-spaceing place: "place" and "space" ten years on proceedings of ACM conference. In: Computer-Supported Cooperative Work CSCW'06, Banff, Canada, pp. 299–308. ACM, New York (2006)

Dourish, P., Holmes, J., MacLean, A., Marqvardsen, P., Zbyslaw, A.: Freeflow: Mediating between representation and action in workflow systems. In: ACM CSCW Conference, Boston, USA, (1996)

Dumas, M., La Rosa, M., Mendling, J., Reijers, H.: Fundamentals of Business Process Management. Springer, Berlin (2013)

EU: Ministerial Declaration on eGovernment, Malmø, Sweden 5th Ministerial eGovernment conference (2009)

Evéquoz, F., Sterren, C.: Waiting for the miracle: comparative analysis of twelve business process management systems regarding the support of BPMN 2.00 Palette and Export Technical report IIG-TR 2011-.03 (2011)

Falkenberg, E.D., Hesse, W., Lindgreen, P., Nilsson, B.E., Oei, J.L.H., Rolland, C., Stamper, R. K., Assche, F.J.M.V., Verrijn-Stuart, A.A., Voss, K.: A Framework of information system concepts—The FRISCO Report, IFIP WG 8.1 Task Group FRISCO (1996)

Fickas, S.: Design issues in a rule-based system. J. Syst. Softw. **10**(2), 113–123 (1989)

Findler, N.V. (ed.): Associative Networks: Representation and Use of Knowledge by Computer. Academic, New York (1979)

Fox, M.S., Gruninger, M.: Enterprise modeling. AI Mag. **19**(3), 109–121 (2000)

Gane, C., Sarson, T.: Structured Systems Analysis: Tools and Techniques. Prentice Hall, Englewood Cliffs (1979)

Gao, S., Krogstie, J.: Capturing process knowledge for multi-channel information systems: a case study. Int. J. Inf. Syst. Model. Des. **3**(1), 78–98 (2012)

Geerts, G.L., McCarthy, W.E.: An accounting object infrastructure for knowledge-based enterprise models. IEEE Intell. Syst. **14**, 89–94 (1999)

Genesereth, M.R., Ketchpel, S.T.: Software agents. Commun. ACM **37**(7), 48–53 (1994)

Gilbreth, F.B., Gilbreth, L.M.: Process Charts. American Society of Mechanical Engineers (1921)

Glance, N.S., Pagani, D.S., Pareschi, R.: Generalized process structure grammars (GPSG) for flexible representation of work. In: ACM CSCW Conference, Boston, USA (1996)

Goedertier, S., Vanthienen, J.: An overview of declarative process modeling principles and languages. Commun. Syst. Inf. World. Netw. **6**, 51–58 (2009)

Gopalakrishnan, S., Krogstie, J., Sindre, G.: Adapting UML activity diagrams for mobile work process modelling: experimental comparison of two notation alternatives. In: Proceedings of PoEM 2010. Springer, Berlin (2010)

Gopalakrishnan, S., Krogstie, J., Sindre, G.: Capturing location in process models: comparing small adaptations of mainstream notation. Int. J. Inf. Syst. Model. Des. **3**(3), 24–45 (2012)

Gordijn, J., Yu, E., van der Raadt, B.: e-service design using i* and e3 value. IEEE Softw. **23**(3), 23–33 (2006)

Green, P., Rosemann, M.: Integrated process modeling: an ontological evaluation. Inf. Syst. **25**(3), 73–87 (2000)

Hagelstein, J., Rifaut, A.: A comparison of semantic models for collections. Technical Report, Philips Research Lab, Brussels, Belgium (1987)

Hammer, M., Champy, J.: Reengineering the Corporation: A Manifesto for Business Revolution. Harper Business, New York (1993)

Hansen, M.T., Nohria, N.: How to build collaborative advantage. MIT Sloan Manag. Rev. **46**(1), 22–30 (2004)

Harrison, S., Dourish, P.: Re-placeing space: the roles of space and place in collaborative systems. In: Proceedings of ACM Conference on Computer-Supported Cooperative Work CSCW'96, Boston, MA, pp. 67–76. ACM, New York (1996)

Hauge, Ø., Ayala, C., Conradi, R.: Adoption of open source software in software-intensive industry—a systematic literature review. Inf. Softw. Technol. **52**(11), 1133–1154 (2010)

Havey, M.: Essential Business Process Modelling. O'Reilly, Cambridge (2005)

Heggset, M., Krogstie, J., Wesenberg, H.: Ensuring quality of large scale industrial process collections: Experiences from a case study. In: The Practice of Enterprise Modeling, pp. 11–25. Springer, Berlin (2014)

Hommes, B.-J., van Reijswoud, V.: The quality of business process modelling techniques. In: Conference on Information Systems Concepts (ISCO). Leiden, Kluwer (1999)

Houy, C., Fettke, P., Loos, P., van der Aalst, W.M.P., Krogstie, J.: BPM-in-the-large—towards a higher level of abstraction in business process management. Paper presented at GISP under WCC, Brisbane, Australia (2010)

Hruby, P.: Model-Driven Design Using Business Patterns. Springer, New York (2006)

Hull, R., King, R.: Semantic database modeling: survey, applications, and research issues. ACM Comput. Surv. **19**(3), 201–260 (1987)

IDEF0: http://www.idef.com/IDEF0.htm. Last Accessed 1 July 2015

Iden, J.: Business Process Management. The RIS Methodology. Bergen, IPAAS (2009)

Iden, J., Tessem, B., Paivarinta, T.: Problems in the interplay of IS development and IT operations: an alignment analysis. In: Pooley, R., Coady, J., Schneider, C., Linger, H., Barry, C., Lang, M. (eds.) Information Systems Development. Springer, New York (2013)

Jansen, S., Finkelstein, A., Brinkkemper, S.: A sense of community: a research agenda for software ecosystems. In: 31st International Conference on Software Engineering (ICSE), New and Emerging Research Track—Companion (2009)

Kappel, G., Rausch-Schott, S., Retschitzegger, W.: Coordination in workflow management systems: a rule-based approach. In: Coordination Technology for Collaborative Applications, pp. 99–119. Springer, Berlin (1998)

Kavakli, E., Loucopoulos, P.: Goal modeling in requirements engineering: analysis and critique of current methods in information modeling methods and methodologies. In: Krogstie, J., Siau, K., Halpin, T. (eds.) information Modeling Methods and Methodologies. Idea Group Publishing, Hershey (2005)

Keller, G., Nüttgens, M., Scheer, A.W.: Semantische Prozeßmodellierung auf der Grundlage Ereignisgesteuerter Prozeßketten (EPK). Wirtschaftsinformatik 89 (1992)

Kelly, S., Tolvanen, J.-P.: Domain-Specific Modelling: Enabling Full Code Generation. Wiley, Hoboken (2008)

Kolata, G.: A Sea Change in Treating Heart Attacks. New York Times, June 19 (2015). http://www.nytimes.com/2015/06/21/health/saving-heart-attack-victims-stat.html?_r=0

Krogstie, J.: A semiotic approach to quality in requirements specifications. Paper presented at the IFIP 8.1. Working Conference on Organizational Semiotics (2001)

Krogstie, J.: Integrated goal, data and process modeling: from TEMPORA to model-generated work-places. In: Johannesson, P., Söderstrøm, E. (eds.) Information Systems Engineering from Data Analysis to Process Networks, pp. 43–65. IGI, Hershey (2008)

Krogstie, J.: Model-Based Development and Evolution of Information Systems: A Quality Approach. Springer, London (2012a)

Krogstie, J.: Modeling of digital ecosystems: challenges and opportunities. IFIP Adv. Inf. Comm. Technol. **380**, 137–145 (2012b)

Krogstie, J., Sindre, G.: Utilizing deontic operators in information systems specifications. Requir. Eng. J. **1**, 210–237 (1996)

Krogstie, J., Carlsen, S.: An integrated modelling approach for process support. Paper presented at the Hawaii International Conference on System Sciences (HICSS-30), Maui, Hawaii (1997)

Krogstie, J., Jørgensen, H.: Interactive models for supporting networked organisations. Paper presented at the 16th conference on advanced information systems engineering (CAiSE 2004), Riga, Latvia, 9–11 June (2004)

Krogstie, J., Nossum, A.: A semiotic approach for guiding the visualizing of time and space in enterprise models. In: Proceedings ICISO 2014, Shanghai, China (2014)

Krogstie, J., McBrien, P., Owens, R., Seltveit, A.H.: Information systems development using a combination of process and rule based approaches. Paper presented at the third international conference on advanced information systems engineering (CAiSE'91), Trondheim, Norway (1991)

Krogstie, J., Dalberg, V., Jensen, S.M.: Harmonising business processes of collaborative networked organisations using process modelling. In: PROVE'04. Toulouse, France (2004)

Lei, Y., Singh, M.P.: A comparison of workflow metamodels. In: ER Workshop on Behavioral Modeling, Lecture Notes in Computer Science 1565 (1997)

Leppänen, M.: An ontological framework and a methodical skeleton for method engineering: a contextual approach. PhD thesis, University of Jyväskylä (2005)

Lillehagen, F., Krogstie, J.: Active Knowledge Modeling of Enterprises. Springer, Berlin (2008)

Loos, P., Allweyer, T.: Process Orientation and Object-Orientation—An approach for Integrating UML with Event-Driven Process Chains (EPC). University of Saarland, Germany (1998)

Lu, R., Sadiq, S., Governatori, G.: On managing business processes variants. Data Knowl. Eng. **68** (7), 642–664 (2009)

McCarthy, W.E.: The REA accounting model: a generalized framework for accounting systems in a shared data environment. Account. Rev. **57**, 554–578 (1982)

Medina-Mora, R., Winograd, T., Flores, R., Flores, F.: The action workflow approach to work flow management technology. In: Proceedings of CSCW'92, Toronto (1992)

Morris, C.: Foundations of the theory of signs. In: International Encyclopedia of Unified Science, vol. 1. University of Chicago Press, London (1938)

Nossum, A., Krogstie, J.: Integrated quality of models and quality of maps. Paper presented at the EMMSAD (2009)

OMG: BPMN v1.1 specification. Technical report, OMG. http://www.omg.org/, http://www.omg.org/spec/BPMN/1.1/. Accessed Jan 2008

OMG: Business Process Model and Notation (BPMN 2.0). http://www.omg.org/spec/BPMN/2.0 (2011)

Opdahl, A.L., Sindre, G.: Facet modeling: an approach to flexible and integrated conceptual modeling. Inf. Syst. **22**(5), 291–323 (1997)

Ould, M.A.: Business Processes—Modeling and Analysis for Re-engineering and Improvement. Wiley, Beverly Hills (1995)

Paulk, M.C., Weber, C.V., Curtis, B., Chrissis, M.B.: Capability maturity model for software (Version 1.1). Technical Report, Software Engineering Institute, Carnegie Mellon University, Pittsburgh, PA. *CMU/SEI-93-TR-024* ESC-TR-93-177 (1993)

Peckham, J., Maryanski, F.: Semantic data models. ACM Comput. Surv. **20**(3), 153–190 (1988)

Petri, C.A.: Kommunikation mit automaten (In German). Schriften des Rheinisch-Westfalischen Institut für Instrumentelle Mathematik an der Universität Bonn, (2) (1962)

Potter, W.D., Trueblood, R.P.: Traditional, semantic and hyper-semantic approaches to data modeling. IEEE Comput. **21**(6), 53–63 (1988)

Pierce, C.S.: Collected Papers. Harvard University Press, Cambridge, MA (1931–1935)

Price, R., Shanks, G.: A semiotic information quality framework. In: IFIP WG8.3 International Conference on Decision Support Systems (DSS2004), Prato, Italy, pp. 658–672, 1–3 July 2004

Recker, J.: Green, greener, BPM? BPTrends **5**(7), 1–8 (2011)

Reijers, H.A., Mansar, S.: Best practice in business process redesign: an overview and qualitative evaluation of successful redesign heuristics. OMEGA **33**, 283–306 (2005)

Rosemann, M., Recker, J.: Systemic ideation: a playbook for creating innovative ideas more consciously 3600. Bus. Transform. J. **13**, 34–45 (2015)

Ross, J.W., Weill, P., Robertson, D.C.: Enterprise Architecture as a Strategy. Harvard Business School Press (2006)

Scheer, A.W.: ARIS, Business Process Framework, 3rd edn. Springer, Berlin (1999)

Schonenberg, H.B., Weber, B., van Dongen, B., van der Aalst, W.M.P.: Supporting flexible processes through recommendations based on history. In: Proceedings of the 6th International Conference on Business Process Management. Springer, Berlin (2008)

Searle, J.R.: Speech Acts. Cambridge University Press, Cambridge (1969)

Searle, J.R.: Expression and Meaning. Cambridge University Press, Cambridge (1979)

Searle, J.R., Vanderveken, D.: Foundations of Illocutionary Logic. Cambridge University Press, Cambridge (1985)

Shoham, Y.: Agent oriented programming: an overview of the framework and summary of recent research. In: Masuch, M., Polos, L. (eds.) Knowledge Representation and Reasoning under Uncertainty: Logic at Work, pp. 123–129. Springer, Berlin (1994)

Silver, B.: BPMN Method and Style. Cody-Cassidy Press (2012)

Singh, B., Rein, G.L.: Role interaction nets (RINs); a process description formalism. Technical Report CT-083-92, MCC, Austin (1992)

Stabell, C.B., Fjeldstad, Ø.D.: Configuring value for competitive advantage: on chains, shops, and networks. Strateg. Manag. J. **19**, 413–437 (1998)

Stachowiak, H.: Allgemeine Modelltheorie. Springer, Wien (1973)

Stamper, R.: Semantics. In: Boland Jr., T.J., Hirschheim, R.A. (eds.) Critical Issues in Information Systems Research, pp. 43–78. Wiley, Englewood Cliffs (1987)

Störle, H.: Describing process patterns with UML. In: EWSPT 2001. Lecture Notes in Computer Science 2077. Springer, Berlin (2001)

Suchman, L.: Do categories have politics? Comput. Support. Cooper. Work **2**(3), 177–190 (1994)

Swenson, K.D., Maxwell, R.J., Matsymoto, T., Saghari, B., Irwin, I.: A business process environment supporting collaborative planning. J. Collab. Comput. **1**(1), 15–34 (1994)

Tomlinson, C., Scheevel, M.: Concurrent programming. In: Kim, W., Lochovsky, F.H. (eds.) Object-Oriented Concepts, Databases and Applications. Addison-Wesley, New York (1989)

Twining, W., Miers, D.: How to Do Things with Rules. Weidenfeld and Nicholson, London (1982)

UN/CEFACT: Modeling Methodology (UMM) User guide. Project report. http://www.unece.org/fileadmin/DAM/cefact/umm/UMM_userguide-nutshell.pdf (2007)

van der Aalst, W.M.P., ter Hofstede, A.H.M.: YAWL: yet another workflow language. Inf. Syst. **30**(4), 245–275 (2005)

van der Aalst, W.M.P., Pesic, M.: DecSerFlow: towards a truly declarative service flow language. Web Serv. Form. Method. **4814**, 1–23 (2006)

van der Aalst, W.M.P., Pesic, M., Schonenberg, H.: Declarative work flows: balancing between flexibility and support. Comput. Sci. Res. Dev. **23**(2), 99–113 (2009)

van der Aalst, W.M.P., et al.: Process Mining manifesto. Business Process Management Workshops 2011. Lecture Notes in Business Information Processing, vol. 99. Springer, Berlin (2011)

Vanderhaeghen, D., Fettke, P., Loos, P.: Organizational and technological options for business process management from the perspective of web 2.0—results of a design oriented research approach with particular consideration of self-organization and collective intelligence. Bus. Inf. Syst. Eng. **2**, 15–28 (2010)

Veenstra, A.F., Aagesen, G., Janssen, M., Krogstie, J.: Infrastructures for public service delivery: complexities of governance and architecture in service infrastructure development. e-Serv. J. (2012)

Von Brocke, J., Rosemann, M.: Handbook on Business Process Management, 2nd edn. Springer, Berlin (2015)

Wegner, P.: Why interaction is more powerful than algorithms. Comm. ACM **40**(5) (1997)

Weick, K.: Sensemaking in Organisations. Sage, London (1995)

Weske, M.: Business Process Management: Concepts, Languages, Architectures. Springer, New York (2007)

WfMC Workflow Handbook 2001: Workflow Management Coalition, Future Strategies Inc., Lighthouse Point, Florida, USA (2000)

White, S.A.: Introduction to BPMN. IBM Cooperation (2004)

Wieringa, R.: Three roles of conceptual models in information systems design and use. In: Falkenberg, E., Lindgren, P. (eds.) Information Systems Concepts: An In-Depth Analysis, pp. 31–51. North-Holland, Amsterdam (1989)

Willoch, B.E.: Business Process Reengineering – En praktisk innføring og veiledning. Fagbokforlaget Vigmostad og Bjorke AS, Bergen (1994)

Winograd, T., Flores, F.: Understanding Computers and Cognition. Addison-Wesley, Reading (1986)

Young, J.W., Kent, H.K.: Abstract formulation of data processing problems. J. Ind. Eng. 471–479 (1958)

Chapter 2
Quality of Business Process Models

Figure 2.1 illustrates main frameworks for discussing quality of IT-relevant artifacts described in this chapter. As we will see, there is quite a bit of overlap in the notions used in quite different fields. In Sect. 2.1, we start with a brief description of general system quality notions, exemplified with ISO9000 and ISO9126 and related material. We then discuss data quality (Sect. 2.1.1) and model quality for different types of models (requirements models in Sect. 2.1.2, data models in Sect. 2.1.3, and enterprise models in Sect. 2.1.4). Section 2.2 describes more generic, comprehensive frameworks, such as SEQUAL (Sect. 2.2.1) and the work of Nelson et al. (Sect. 2.2.2). Aspects of quality of business process are described in detail in Sect. 2.3.1, whereas in other parts of Sect. 2.3, we describe particular work on quality of business process model, such as GoM (Sect. 2.3.2) and 7PMG (Sect. 2.3.3).

A specialization of the SEQUAL framework for discussing and assessing the quality of business process models taking all this into account is presented in Chap. 3.

2.1 Quality in Information Systems Development and Evolution

"Quality" is a difficult notion, and within the field of information systems, many approaches to quality have been proposed. Whereas some take a very subjective approach to the quality of models (e.g., (Rumbaugh et al. 1991) states: "*A good model feels right and does not appear to have extraneous detail*"), a standard approach to quality among engineers claims that a product has high quality if it is according to its specification. For example, the ISO 9000 quality standard was

© Springer International Publishing Switzerland 2016
J. Krogstie, *Quality in Business Process Modeling*,
DOI 10.1007/978-3-319-42512-2_2

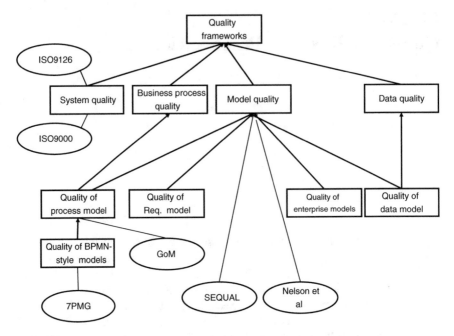

Fig. 2.1 Frameworks for discussing quality

originally developed according to this philosophy. ISO (2005) states that quality is the "degree to which a set of inherent characteristics fulfils requirements." ISO-9000:2005 defines the requirement as the needs or expectations of a customer (and no longer as the necessarily explicit *specifications* of such needs). In ISO-9000, one defines a number of quality characteristics, with subcharacteristics, and metrics to be able to measure the different subcharacteristics. The following quality characteristics are listed for software products in ISO/IEC 9126:

- Functionality: A set of attributes that bear on the existence of a set of functions and their specified properties. The functions are those that satisfy stated or implied needs.
- Reliability: A set of attributes that bear on the capability of software to maintain its level of performance under stated conditions for a stated period of time.
- Efficiency: A set of attributes that bear on the relationship between the level of performance of the software and the amount of resources used, under stated conditions.
- Usability: A set of attributes that bear on the effort needed for use, and on the individual assessment of such use, by a stated or implied set of users. Portability: How easy is it to transfer the software to another (technical) environment?
- Maintainability: A set of attributes that bear on the effort needed to make specified modifications.

ISO/IEC 9126 further divides these characteristics into 24 quality subcharacteristics, which are measured by 113 quality metrics. Denning (1992) goes beyond the original ISO 9000 thinking, observing that if a product is in "accordance with the specification," this is only the first level of quality. A second level is achieved if there are no negative side effects of the installed information system. The highest (third) level of quality is achieved if, in addition to achieving the first two levels, the information system enables additional information systems support to its users that was not initially conceived, i.e., actually giving users *more* of what they need than what was promised in the specification. It can be argued that the newest ISO definitions also take these levels into account. The three-level distinction is parallel to the differentiation of software requirements in the Kano model (Kano 1984; Krogstie 1999), where requirements are classified into three categories: normal, expected, and exciting.

1. Normal requirements are what stakeholders communicate during traditional facilitated sessions or in interviews. They cover the basic functionality expected of the application. These requirements proportionally contribute to customer satisfaction and expectations.
2. Expected requirements are those aspects that users assume developers already know. Missing an expected requirement represents the greatest risk to user satisfaction. There is little benefit to implementing these requirements. However, there is a heavy price if they are omitted. An example could be that it should be possible to print the text from a text editor.
3. Exciting requirements are aspects that the users do not expect and first find useful when they see them. Oftentimes, exciting requirements involve innovation of the business process or new methods of handling functionality. Stakeholder satisfaction with the application can be dramatically improved through the implementation of a few exciting requirements. Failure to implement these requirements does not adversely affect overall satisfaction.

A number of detailed overviews of quality characteristics in the IT field are provided in the literature, and as a background for the notions typically noted in relation to the quality of models in general, we briefly describe these in the subsections below.

2.1.1   Data and Information Quality

There are a number of approaches to defining the dimensions of data quality. We have based this section on the framework presented in Batini and Scannapieco (2006) where the aspects listed in Table 2.1 are discussed in relation to the data values in a relational database.

When examining data quality in isolation, the underlying data model can be viewed as part of the context (i.e., a preexisting model that this model should relate

Table 2.1 Dimensions of data quality from (Batini and Scannapieco 2006)

Dimension name	Subcategory	Definition
Accuracy	Syntactic Semantic	Distance between v (the correct value) and v' (the incorrect value)
Completeness		Degree to which all values are present in a data collection
Time-related aspects	Currency	Degree to which the data are up-to-date
	Volatility	Frequency with which data vary with time
	Timeliness	How current the data are for the task at hand
Consistency		Coherence of the same datum, represented in multiple copies, or different data to respect the same integrity constraints and rules
Interpretability		Concerns the documentation including the data model and other metadata that are available to correctly interpret the meaning of the data
Accessibility		Data are accessible for those needing access to the data in a format that can be understood
Quality of information source	Believability	Are the data provided experienced to be true, real, and credible?
	Reputation	Is the source normally credible?
	Objectivity	Is the source believed to be objective?

to). Clearly, how the data are meant to be and actually are used influences the perceived quality of the data. To also capture the use of data, (Price and Shanks 2004, 2005) use the term *information quality* to combine a product-based and service-based view of data quality. The product-based perspective, covered by traditional data quality properties as descried above, has an internal information systems view. From this view, quality is defined in terms of the degree to which the data meet the initial requirements specifications or the degree to which the data correspond to the relevant real-world phenomena that they represent. The limitation of this view is that even if data correspond to a requirements specification or the real world, there can still be quality deficiencies with respect to actual use-related data requirements, which may differ from the planned uses catered for in the initial specifications. This leads to a service-based perspective of data quality, called *information quality,* which focuses on the information consumer's response to his/her task-based interactions with the IS. Building on semiotic theory as described in Sect. 1.4, Price and Shanks define this area as follows:

Syntactic Criteria (based on rule conformance)

- *Conforming to metadata, i.e., integrity rules.* Data follow specified database integrity rules.

Semantic Criteria (based on external correspondence)

- *Mapped completely.* Every real-world phenomenon is represented.
- *Mapped unambiguously.* Each identifiable data unit represents at most one specific real-world phenomenon.
- *Phenomena mapped correctly.* Each identifiable data unit maps to the correct real-world phenomenon.
- *Properties mapped correctly.* Non-identifying (i.e., non-key) attribute values in an identifiable data unit match the property values for the represented real-world phenomenon.
- *Mapped consistently.* Each real-world phenomenon is represented either by at most one identifiable data unit or by multiple but consistently identifiable units or by multiple identifiable units whose inconsistencies are resolved within an acceptable time frame.
- *Mapped meaningfully.* Each identifiable data unit represents at least one specific real-world phenomenon.

Pragmatic Criteria (use-based consumer perspective)

- *Accessible (easy, quick).* Data are easy and quick to retrieve.
- *Suitably presented (suitably formatted, precise, and measured in appropriate units).* With respect to format, precision, and units, data are presented in a manner appropriate for their use.
- *Flexibly presented (easily aggregated; format, precision, and units easily converted).* With respect to aggregating data and changing the data's format, precision, or units, data can be easily manipulated, and the presentation customized.
- *Timely.* The currency (age) of the data is appropriate to their use.
- *Understandable.* Data are presented in a manner that makes them easy to comprehend.
- *Secure.* Data are appropriately protected from damage, tampering, or abuse (including unauthorized access, use, or distribution).
- *Type sufficient.* The data include all of the types of information important for their use.
- *Allowing access to relevant metadata.* Appropriate metadata are available to define, constrain, and document data, e.g., how data have been produced and refined, and by whom.
- *Perceptions of the syntactic and semantic criteria defined above.*

A more complete overview, including metrics, is found in Batini et al. (2009). Note that many of the metrics are subjective, given that they have to be collected through user questionnaires.

2.1.2 Quality of Requirements Specifications

In Davis et al. (1993), the work on the quality properties for a software requirements specification (SRS) is summarized. The paper also includes proposals for
metrics and weights for the different properties.

An SRS can be viewed as being either a model of the perceived future IS or the
perceived future computerized IS without locking it to one specific implementation.
Regardless, one can identify three interrelated "domains":

1. Everything the software is supposed to do (for the moment ignoring the different
   views of the software to be produced that stakeholders have).
2. Constraints imposed by earlier baselined models such as system-level requirements specifications, statements of work, and earlier versions of the SRS to
   which the new SRS must be compatible.
3. Constraints imposed by the fact that one wants to produce a software system
   based on the SRS under the given time and resource constraints.

We will refer to these 3 subdomains when relevant below. It is important to note
that the quality properties have been suggested under the assumption of an
objectivistic worldview by Davis and others, i.e., that objective requirements agreed
by all stakeholders can be developed.

Unambiguous: An SRS is unambiguous if and only if every requirement stated
therein has only one possible interpretation. Note that this can be looked upon as
being inconsistent with the characteristic "design independent", but even if you can
design a solution in several ways, you should be able to say if it has achieved the
requirement.

Complete: An SRS is complete if:

1. Everything that the software is supposed to do is included in the SRS.
2. Responses of the software to all realizable classes of input data in all recognizable classes of situations are included.
3. All pages are numbered; all figures and tables are numbered, named, and referenced; all terms are defined; all units of measure are provided; and all referenced material is present.
4. No sections are marked «To be determined».

   Correct: An SRS is correct if and only if every requirement represents something required of the system to be built.
   Understandable: An SRS is understandable if all types of SRS readers can
   easily comprehend the meaning of all of the requirements with a minimum of
   explanation.
   Verifiable: An SRS is verifiable if there are finite, cost-effective techniques that
   can be used to verify that every requirement stated therein is satisfied by the
   system to be built. Testable is another term often found for this.
   Internally Consistent: An SRS is internally consistent if and only if no subset
   of individual requirements stated therein conflicts. Davis suggests using

languages with formal syntax and semantics to be able to detect and remove inconsistency.

Externally Consistent: An SRS is externally consistent if and only if no requirement stated therein conflicts with any already baselined project or organizational documentation.

Achievable: An SRS is achievable if and only if there could exist at least one system design and implementation that correctly implements all of the requirements stated in the SRS.

Concise: An SRS is concise if it is as short as possible without affecting any other quality of the SRS.

Design-independent: An SRS is design-independent if and only if there are more than one system design and implementation that correctly implements all of the requirements stated in the SRS.

Traceable: An SRS is traceable if and only if it is written in a manner that facilitates the referencing of each individual statement, e.g., to be able to trace back from the implementation to assure that it addresses all requirements.

Modifiable: An SRS is modifiable if its structure and style are such that any changes can be made easily, completely, and consistently. Requirements to a system will always evolve, and one should be able to control the necessary evolution of the SRS.

Electronically Stored: An SRS is electronically stored if and only if the entire SRS is in a word processor, it has been generated from a requirements database, or it has been otherwise synthesized from some other electronic form.

Executable/Interpretable/Prototypable: An SRS is executable, interpretable, or prototypable if and only if there exists a software tool that is capable of providing a dynamic behavioral model based on (relevant parts of) the SRS.

Annotated by Relative Importance: An SRS is annotated by relative importance if a reader can easily determine which requirements are of the most importance to customers and which are the next most important, etc.

Annotated by Relative Stability: An SRS is annotated by relative stability if a reader can easily determine which requirements are most likely to change and which are the next most likely to change.

Annotated by Version: An SRS is annotated by version if a reader can easily determine which requirements will be satisfied in which version of the implemented system.

Not Redundant: An SRS is redundant if the same requirement is stated more than once.

At Right Level of Detail: Requirements can be stated at many levels of abstraction. What is the right level of detail is a function of how the SRS is being used. Generally, the SRS should be sufficiently specific so that any system built that satisfies the requirements in the SRS satisfies all user needs and sufficiently abstract so that all systems that satisfy all user needs also satisfy all requirements.

Precise: An SRS is precise if and only if (a) numeric quantities are used whenever possible and (b) the appropriate levels of precision are used for all numeric quantities. Precise requirements are often useful to assure that the SRS is verifiable.

Reusable: An SRS is reusable if and only if its sentences, paragraphs, and sections can be easily adopted and adapted for use in a subsequent SRS if this is for a similar system.

Traced: An SRS is traced if and only if the origin of each of its requirements is clear. This can be other higher level requirements specifications or other documents, but can also be the human source of the requirement or the requirements specification session that produced the requirement.

Organized: An SRS is organized if and only if its contents are arranged so that readers can easily locate information and logical relationships among adjacent sections are apparent. One method is to follow any of the many SRS standards, e.g., group by class of user, common stimulus, common response, feature, or object.

Cross-referenced: An SRS is cross-referenced if and only if cross-references are used in the SRS to relate sections containing requirements to other sections containing identical (i.e., redundant) requirements, more abstract or more detailed descriptions of the same requirements, and requirements that depend on them or on which they depend.

2.1.3 Quality of Data Models

One type of model that has been used for a long period of time is data models. Data models are a type of structural model. Going back to ANSI SPARC (Tsichritzis and Klug 1978), one differentiates between three levels of data models:

- Conceptual models (e.g., ERER models)
- Logical models (e.g., in the form of relational tables)
- Physical models (e.g., a physical implementation of a relational database).

There are typically well-defined methods of going between models on these levels, although often automatic mappings are not sufficient in practice to obtain the ideal database performance based on the conceptual and logical models.

Much work in this field concentrates on the conceptual level, although often with the goal of producing logical/physical models as part of running information systems.

Additionally, some of the early work on the quality of models focused on data models (Moody and Shanks 1994), work that was extended in Moody (1998, 2003) based on empirical investigations on its use.

Moody (2003) contains the following desired characteristics and metrics for data model quality:

- Correctness is defined as whether the data model conforms to the syntax and other rules of the modeling language used for data modeling (i.e., whether it is a valid data model). This characteristic includes diagramming conventions, naming rules, definition rules, the rules of composition, and normalization. The proposed metrics are as follows:

  1. Number of violations of data modeling standards,
  2. Number of instances of entity redundancy,
  3. Number of instances of relationship redundancy,
  4. Number of instances of attribute redundancy.

- Completeness refers to whether the data model contains all of the information required to support the required functionality of the system.

  5. Number of missing requirements,
  6. Number of superfluous requirements,
  7. Number of inaccurately defined requirements,
  8. Number of inconsistencies of the data model with the process model.

- Integrity is defined as whether the data model defines all of the business rules that apply to the data.

  9. Number of missing business rules,
  10. Number of incorrect business rules,
  11. Number of business rules that are inconsistent with the process model,
  12. Number of business rules redundantly defined in process model rules.

- Flexibility is defined as the ease with which the data model can cope with business and/or regulatory change.

  13. Number of data model elements that are subject to change,
  14. Probability adjusted cost of change,
  15. Strategic impact of change.

- Understandability is defined as the ease with which the concepts and structures in the data model can be understood.

  16. User rating of understandability,
  17. Proportion of user interpretation errors,
  18. Application developer rating of understandability,
  19. Subject area–entity class ratio,
  20. Entity class-attribute ratio.

- Simplicity means that the data model contains the minimum possible entities and relationships.

  21. Number of entity classes (E),
  22. Model complexity (E+R): The total number of entity classes and relationship classes,

23. Total complexity (aE+bR+cA): The total number of entity classes, relationship classes, and attributes, weighted, typically to put higher weight on entity classes and relationship classes than attributes.

- Integration is defined as the consistency of the system data model with the rest of the organization's data models and data.

24. Number of conflicts with the corporate data model,
25. Number of data model conflicts with existing systems,
26. Number of data items duplicated in existing systems or projects,
27. Rating of ability to meet corporate needs.

- Implementability is defined as the ease with which the data model can be implemented within the time, budget, and technology constraints of the project.

28. Development cost estimate,
29. Technical risk rating.

Based on an empirical investigation (Moody 2003) (which perceived only metrics 22, 26, and 28 as being cost beneficial to keep track of in the context of the particular case investigated), two additional metrics were proposed:

- Metric 30. Reuse Level. This metric is the inverse or "positive" of the level of duplication metric (Metric 26) and measures the number of existing data items reused as part of the new model.
- Metric 31. Number of Issues by Quality Factor. Each quality issue raised as a result of quality reviews can be classified by the quality factor it relates to. The number of issues raised and their severity by quality factor provide a "defect frequency" that can be used for purposes of comparison over time.

Although one lesson from (Moody 2003) is that one may want to limit the number of metrics, this study does not provide what metrics are best to include; thus, generic frameworks such as this framework would often need to include a large set of potentially useful metrics.

Another overview of data model (schema) quality is presented in Batini and Scannapieco (2006), which contains the following areas:

- Correctness with respect to the model concerns the correct use of the concepts in the data modeling language. The negative example is representing FirstName as an entity and not as an attribute (because FirstName does not have a unique existence in the real world),
- Correctness with respect to requirements,
- Minimalization, where no requirement is represented more than once,
- Completeness,
- Pertinence that measures how many unnecessary conceptual elements are included,
- Readability through aesthetics,

- Readability through simplicity,
- Normalization.

Whereas the last applies first on the logical level, the others apply on the conceptual level.

2.1.4   Quality of Enterprise Models

Larsson and Segerberg (2004) have investigated whether the quality criteria for data models defined by Moody and Shanks (1994) are applicable to enterprise models, and they have proposed several modifications to their original criteria. The resulting quality criteria for enterprise models (EM) are as follows:

- Completeness—the degree to which all relevant facts of the problem domain are included in the enterprise model.
- Correctness—refers to how well the enterprise model conforms to the rules of the modeling technique.
- Flexibility—is defined as the ease with which the enterprise model can cope with changes in the modeling domain.
- Integration—refers to the degree of consistency between the different submodels that constitute the overall enterprise model. An enterprise model often contains different submodels, e.g., a process model, a goal model, an organizational model, and a systems model focusing on different modeling perspectives.
- Simplicity—refers to the degree of minimal use of modeling constructs for presenting knowledge in the enterprise model.
- Understandability—is defined as the ease with which the concepts and structures in the enterprise model can be understood by stakeholders.
- Usability—is defined as the ease with which the enterprise model can be used for its intended purpose. Just as with a business process model, an enterprise model can be used for achieving different goals as illustrated in Sect. 1.5.

In Sandkuhl et al. (2014), the authors build on this proposal and suggest several guidelines for quality improvements of enterprise modeling and enterprise modeling languages.

- Reducing ambiguity: Ambiguous models are hard to understand. In Sandkuhl et al. (2014), they give several concrete suggestions relative to the 4EM language, e.g., starting goal formulation with "The goal is…" Another aspect of ambiguity is lack of concrete detail and aspects that can be taken up and implemented. One solution is to identify concrete actions that need to be carried out connected to the models and who will be responsible for them.

- Identifying areas of stability and flexibility: A small change in the domain should not force to make large changes in the model. It should be possible to add or remove some statements from the model without major changes or restructuring the rest of the model.
- Having homogeneity of concepts (such that they do not cover too many things). A modeling concept is said to have a high degree of homogeneity if the phenomena it represents are very similar to one another and display the same kinds of properties and relationships. Homogeneity contributes to factors such as flexibility, simplicity, understandability, and usability.
- Clarifying the scope of the model and working for completeness within the selected scope. An enterprise model should always have a well-defined scope. The scope serves to decide what is important for modeling and what is not. Determining the scope precisely may, however, be difficult:

  - The stakeholders might not know or recognize what the real problem is (blurred scope).
  - There could be disagreement among stakeholders about what the scope is (multiple scopes).
  - Because of hidden agendas, the real scope might be covered.
  - The scope may change during modeling because the participants acquire new knowledge and want to extend, narrow, or shift the scope.

Another challenge for reaching completeness is that there might not be enough time and/or stakeholder interest to develop the model to the required level of completeness.

- Having integration between submodels. Enterprise models address an area from different perspectives. Integration of the submodels of different perspectives significantly contributes to understandability and usability of the model. Each submodel should be connected internally and with other submodels. Detailed guidelines for how to do this will depend on the concrete sublanguages in the language to be integrated.
- Striving for simplicity: Simple models are more understandable. They are also easier to improve, maintain, and reuse. The guiding principle recommends using as few modeling constructs as possible, something that must be balanced by the requirement for complete models.

2.2   Comprehensive Frameworks for the Quality of Models

Whereas the quality thinking presented in the previous section examines specific types of data, model, and system quality, a number of more comprehensive generic quality frameworks have been developed, of which two will be presented in this section.

2.2.1 SEQUAL—Semiotic Quality Framework

Work on SEQUAL can be traced back to at least 1993 (Lindland 1993). In particular, Sindre and Lindland collaborated on the next step, which ended up in a widely cited article (Lindland et al. 1994). Although it was an elegant framework that was easily applicable for understanding important aspects of the quality of models, several other works pointed to the need to extend the framework. In this regard, important inspirations were the work on the three dimensions of requirements engineering (Pohl 1993), work related to the semiotic ladder presented in early versions of the IFIP 8.1 FRISCO framework (Lindgren 1990), and work on the social construction of "reality" and models thereof of the domain, which are typically not as ideal and objectively given in practice as the original framework took as a basis (Berger and Luckmann 1966). Thus, SEQUAL, the SEmiotic model QUALity framework, is based on theories from the field of semiotics, the science of *signs*, and what they refer to. The application of semiotic theory is similar to what was described in the Framework for Information Systems Concepts (FRISCO) report (Falkenberg et al. 1996), which was also described in Chap. 1.

In SEQUAL (Krogstie 2012a, b), we describe in much more detail what the different semiotic levels entail in regard to model quality to be able to have a more precise understanding of the issues at stake at each level and how deliberations on the different levels can be combined. In addition to acting as a generic framework for discussion and assessment of quality of models, specialization of the frameworks has been made relative to a number of different types of modeling, including quality of maps (Nossum and Krogstie 2009), data (Krogstie 2013b, 2015), ontologies (Hella and Krogstie 2010), data models (Krogstie 2013b, 2015), object-oriented models (Krogstie 2003), rule and goal models (Krogstie 1999, 2008), actor models (Krogstie et al. 2012), requirements specifications (Krogstie 2001), enterprise models (Krogstie 2012a), interactive models (Krogstie and Jørgensen 2002), and early work on business process model (Lin et al. 2006; Krogstie 2012b).

Compared with the early work on the quality of models, SEQUAL had three unique properties:

- It distinguishes between the quality characteristics (goals) and means to potentially achieve these goals by separating what one is attempting to achieve from how to achieve it.
- It is based on a constructivistic worldview, recognizing that significant models are typically created as part of a dialogue between the many stakeholders involved in modeling, whose knowledge of the modeling domain changes as modeling occurs.
- It is closely linked to linguistic and semiotic concepts. In particular, the core of the framework, including the discussion on syntax, semantics, and pragmatics, is parallel to the use of these terms in the semiotic theory. Additionally, the work in FRISCO on the semiotic ladder takes the work of Morris as its starting point

but extends it with physical, empirical, and social aspects. The differentiation between empirical quality (on comprehensibility) and pragmatic quality (on actual human comprehension) is motivated by empirical investigation on the applicability of the framework (Moody et al. 2002) and the utility of distinguishing between technical and social aspects. The inclusion of the semiotic levels enables us to address quality at different levels. A term such as "quality" is used on all of the semiotic levels. We include physical, empirical, syntactical, semantical, pragmatic, social, and deontic qualities. The inclusion of deontic quality is to be able to better take into account the overriding goals of modeling in a modeling task, which is often decided in a wider organizational setting.

The main concepts and their relationships are shown in Fig. 2.2. The quality types for a conceptual model are indicated in the figure with solid lines, indicating relationships between sets in Fig. 2.2, which are depicted as ellipses. We take a set-theoretic approach to the discussion of the different quality types and characteristics. Sets are written using *SLANTED BOLDFACE UPPERCASE* letters, whereas the elements of sets are written in normal UPPERCASE letters. The different sets are described first, whereas the quality types, including the goals and means to achieve quality at each level, are described next.

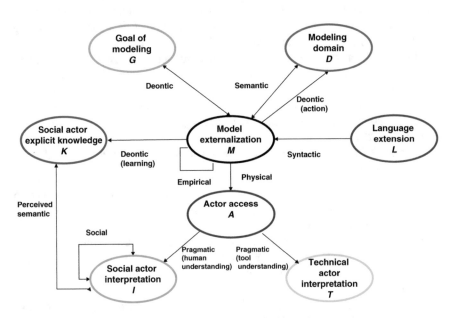

Fig. 2.2 SEQUAL framework for discussing the quality of models

Quality has been defined referring to the correspondence between statements belonging to the following sets:

- **G**, the set of goals of the modeling task. Typical types of goals of modeling were described in Sect. 1.5.1
- **L**, the language extension, i.e., the set of all statements that are possible to make according to the rules of the modeling languages used.
- **D**, the domain, i.e., the set of all statements that can be stated about the situation.
- **M**, the externalized model itself represented on some physical medium.
- **A**, the part of the model that can be accessed by one or more actor, with potential actors being both persons and tools.
- **K**, the explicit knowledge about the domain that is relevant to the audience.
- **I**, the social actor interpretation, i.e., the set of all statements that the audience interprets that an externalized model consists of.
- **T**, the technical actor interpretation, i.e., the statements in the model as "interpreted" by modeling tools.

The main quality types as illustrated as relationships in Fig. 2.2 are as follows:

1. Physical quality: The basic quality goal is that the relevant parts of the externalized model **M** are available to the relevant actors and not to others (**A**).
2. Empirical quality addresses comprehensibility when a visual model **M** is read by different social actors. Before evaluating empirical quality, physical quality should be addressed.
3. Syntactic quality is the correspondence between the model **M** and the language extension **L**. Before evaluating syntactic quality, physical quality should be addressed.
4. Semantic quality is the correspondence between the model **M** and the domain **D**. It includes both validity and completeness. Before evaluating semantic quality, syntactic quality should be addressed. Domains can be divided into two parts, exemplified with a software requirements model:

   (a) Everything the computerized information system (CIS) is supposed to do (for the moment ignoring the different views on the CIS to be made that stakeholders have).
   (b) Constraints on the model because of earlier baselined models, such as system-level requirements specifications, enterprise architecture models, statements of work, and earlier versions of the requirements specification to which the new requirements specification model must be compatible.

5. Pragmatic quality is the correspondence between the available part of the model **M** (i.e., **A**) and the actor interpretation (**I** and **T**) of it. One differentiates between social pragmatic quality (to what extent people understand the model) and technical pragmatic quality (to what extent tools can be made that can interpret the model). Before evaluating pragmatic quality, empirical quality should be addressed. Good syntactic quality may also be beneficial, especially when the audience is familiar with the modeling language used.

6. Perceived semantic quality is the similar correspondence between the social actor interpretation I of a model M and his or her current knowledge K of domain D. Before evaluating the perceived semantic quality, pragmatic quality should be addressed.
7. The goal defined for social quality is agreement among the social actor's interpretations (I). Before evaluating social quality, the perceived semantic quality should be addressed.
8. The deontic quality of the model is related to the notion that all of the statements in the model M contribute to fulfilling the goals of modeling G and that all of the goals of modeling G are addressed through the model M. In particular, under deontic quality, one often includes the extent that, after interpreting the model, the participants learn based on the model (increase K) and that the audience is able to change the domain D if doing so is beneficially to achieving the goals of modeling (if the model is prescriptive).

For all layers of model quality, specific quality characteristics are identified as described briefly above. The means to achieve these quality characteristics can be related to the modeling method, including the order of addressing the different quality characteristics, the use of particular modeling techniques, modeling tools, and the choice of an appropriate modeling language.

Language quality goals are thus viewed as means in the framework. Seven areas of language quality are differentiated, as illustrated in Fig. 2.3.

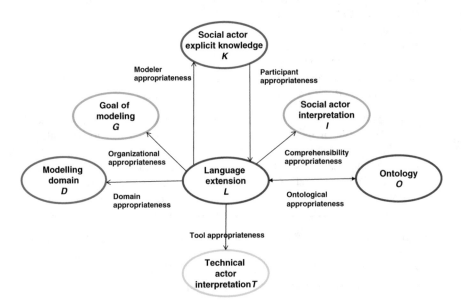

Fig. 2.3 Quality of modeling languages

1. Domain appropriateness. This area relates to the language and the domain. Ideally, the conceptual basis must be sufficiently powerful to express anything in the domain, not having what (Wand and Weber 1993) term construct deficit. However, one should not be able to express things that are not in the domain, i.e., what is termed construct excess (Wand and Weber 1993). Domain appropriateness is primarily a means of achieving semantic quality.
2. Ontological appropriateness. Although domain appropriateness discusses the appropriateness of languages in relation to a specific domain, when discussing expressiveness in general, one may want to do so in relation to some general framework or *ontology* developed for the field. Any modeling approach or perspective taken includes some level of ontological commitment, and general discussions on construct deficit and construct excess are typically done in relation to some existing ontology.
3. Comprehensibility appropriateness relates the language to the social actor interpretation. The goal is that the participants in the modeling effort using the language understand all of the possible statements of the language. Comprehensibility appropriateness is primarily a means of achieving empirical and pragmatic quality.
4. Participant appropriateness relates to the social actors' explicit knowledge of the language (i.e., do the participants know the language being used). Participant appropriateness is primarily a means of achieving semantic and pragmatic quality.
5. Modeler appropriateness: This area relates the language extension to the knowledge of the modeler. The goal is that there are no statements in the explicit knowledge of the modeler that cannot be expressed in the language. Modeler appropriateness is primarily a means of achieving semantic quality.
6. Tool appropriateness relates the language to the technical audience interpretations. For tool interpretation, it is especially important that the language lends itself to automatic reasoning, which requires formality (i.e., both formal syntax and formal semantics being operational and/or logical). However, formality is not necessarily sufficient because the reasoning must also be efficient to be of practical use. This issue is covered by what we term analyzability (being able to exploit any mathematical semantics efficiently) and executability (being able to exploit any operational semantics efficiently). Different aspects of tool appropriateness are means of achieving syntactic, semantic, and pragmatic quality (through formal syntax, mathematical semantics, and operational semantics, respectively).
7. Organizational appropriateness relates the language to standards and other organizationally imposed constraints on modeling. Organizational appropriateness is expected to support achieving deontic quality.

2.2.2 Quality of Models According to Nelson et al

Nelson et al. (2011) extend the coverage of model quality of an earlier version of SEQUAL and the work by Wand and Weber (1993) on the Bunge–Wand–Weber ontology (BWW). An important differentiation in their framework is between physical aspects (things in the world) and cognitive aspects (in the mind). This is also an important area of differentiation in SEQUAL and the semiotic levels. In Fig. 2.4, we find the physical aspects on the left and the cognitive aspect on the right; they are further described below, where we also describe the relationships.

- Physical Domain. The physical domain is the real-world universe of discourse, meaning the things and/or phenomena that are of interest to users and modelers. It corresponds to the SEQUAL modeling domain.
- Domain Knowledge. The domain knowledge is the human understanding of the real-world universe of discourse by both the users and modelers involved in the process. It corresponds to the social actor's knowledge and the modeler's knowledge created by their perception of the application domain in SEQUAL. This view consists of those elements shaped by the user's and/or modeler's context that they consider meaningful to the situation at hand.
- Physical Model. In other works, one would use the term ontology on this level. An ontology focuses on the things that are regarded as important to the problem at hand and discards those things that have nothing to do with the problem. The physical model is the ontological construct in the BWW framework, shown as ontology in the language quality figure in SEQUAL (Fig. 2.3). This model is preferably represented in a formal language.
- Model Knowledge. This aspect is the ontology as understood by the users and modelers who are involved in the modeling process. It is their mental model, as shaped by the physical model.
- Physical Language. The language consists of the grammar and the vocabulary that are used in combination with the model. This cornerstone corresponds to the language extension element in SEQUAL.
- Language Knowledge. This aspect is the language, as understood by the modelers who are actively involved in the modeling process. It is the same as the modeler knowledge as a basis for modeler appropriateness in SEQUAL.
- Physical Representation. The physical representation corresponds to the SEQUAL model externalization
- Representation Knowledge. This is the users' cognitive interpretation of the physical representation. It corresponds to the social actors' interpretation in SEQUAL.

The arrows between concepts in Fig. 2.4 indicate the different quality types in Nelson et al. (Table 2.2).

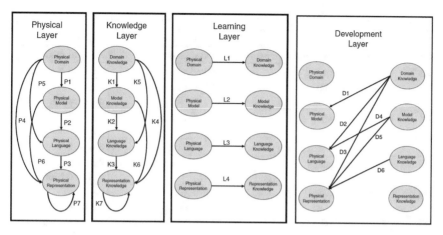

Fig. 2.4 Categories and relationships in Nelson et al. (2011)

The physical layer has seven quality types, described below.

- P1: Model-Domain Appropriateness. The physical model (ontology) must be appropriate to the domain being modeled and for the ultimate use of the physical representation. For example, the entity-relationship model is appropriate for conceptualizing a data-oriented domain, but is not appropriate for a more process-oriented domain.
- P2: Ontological Quality. The physical, external language (the grammar and the vocabulary of the language) must be appropriate for expressing the concepts of the physical model and for ultimately encoding the concepts in the physical representation (cf. ontological appropriateness of SEQUAL).
- P3: Syntactic Quality. All of the elements in the final physical representation must be able to be derived from the vocabulary and the grammar of the physical language (cf. syntactic quality in SEQUAL).
- P4: Semantic Quality. The final representation must accurately and completely capture the meaning of the physical domain, within the constraints of the modeling task at hand (cf. semantic quality in SEQUAL).
- P5: Language-Domain Appropriateness. The language must be sufficiently powerful to express anything in the physical domain (cf. domain appropriateness in SEQUAL).
- P6: Intentional Quality. The physical representation should remain true to the mind-set and the meanings defined by the physical model. For example, the ontological foundations for the use of relationships, and what a relationship actually is, are found in the physical model.
- P7: Empirical Quality. This is a measure of the readability of a conceptual representation. The physical representation is both the object of interest and the quality reference (cf. empirical quality in SEQUAL).

Table 2.2 Quality types and their associated quality cornerstones (From Nelson et al. (2011))

Label	Quality type	Quality reference	Object of interest
P1	Model-domain appropriateness	Physical domain	Physical model
P2	Ontological quality	Physical model	Physical language
P3	Syntactic quality	Physical language	Physical representation
P4	Semantic quality	Physical domain	Physical representation
P5	Language-domain appropriateness	Physical domain	Physical language
P6	Intentional quality	Physical model	Physical representation
P7	Empirical quality	Physical representation	Physical representation
K1	Perceived model-domain appropriateness	Domain knowledge	Model knowledge
K2	Perceived ontological quality	Model knowledge	Language knowledge
K3	Perceived syntactic quality	Language knowledge	Representation knowledge
K4	Perceived semantic quality	Domain knowledge	Representation knowledge
K5	Perceived language-domain appropriateness	Domain knowledge	Language knowledge
K6	Perceived intentional quality	Model knowledge	Representation knowledge
K7	Perceived empirical quality	Representation knowledge	Representation knowledge
L1	View quality	Physical domain	Domain knowledge
L2	Pedagogical quality	Physical model	Model knowledge
L3	Linguistic quality	Physical language	Language knowledge
L4	Pragmatic quality	Physical representation	Representation knowledge
D1	Applied domain-model appropriateness	Domain knowledge	Physical model
D2	Applied domain-language appropriateness	Domain knowledge	Physical language
D3	Applied domain knowledge quality	Domain knowledge	Physical representation
D4	Applied model-language appropriateness	Model knowledge	Physical language
D5	Applied model knowledge quality	Model knowledge	Physical representation
D6	Applied language knowledge quality	Language knowledge	Physical representation

The knowledge layer of quality types parallels the physical layer of quality types. However, where the physical layer exists in the "real world," the knowledge layer exists only cognitively, in the minds of the stakeholders involved in the conceptual modeling process and in the process of using the physical representation. The knowledge layer quality types refer to the quality of the model, language, and representation, but not to the quality of the knowledge itself (for which there are the learning layer quality types). Although the physical layer quality types of model, language, and representation quality are defined objectively, i.e., independent of the stakeholder involved in evaluating quality, the corresponding knowledge layer quality types recognize a subjective notion of quality, i.e., quality as perceived by the user or modeler. When an objective measurement of some physical layer quality type is not possible, the corresponding knowledge layer quality type may be assessed as an approximation.

Any examination of the qualities of the knowledge layer must explicitly note the source of the knowledge. The knowledge layer parallels the physical layer described above; thus, the individual quality types will not be described in detail. However, one example can serve to illustrate the layer: The perceived semantic quality (K4) of a physical representation is the correspondence between the stakeholder's knowledge concerning the domain as derived from the real-world domain itself and the knowledge concerning the domain as derived from the real-world representation (see also the description of this concept in SEQUAL).

The learning quality layer measures how well learning, interpretation, and/or understanding occurs. The stakeholder's first exposure to anything in the physical world begins with his/her perception of that world's artifacts, although noting that what we already know often influences what we look for (and thus perceived context drives the stakeholder's perceptions). It determines which things are meaningful and which things will fade into the background. Each of the quality types in the learning layer is, to a greater or lesser extent, grounded in perception. What is perceived, and how it is learned, depends on the quality cornerstone. The quality types of the learning layer are described more fully below.

- L1: View Quality. The stakeholder must have a complete and valid understanding of the real-world domain as it relates to the problem at hand. Whether the real-world physical domain exists or whether the domain knowledge is a product of perception or is a social construction (Wand and Weber 2002), the quality of a stakeholder's domain knowledge is based on the quality of his/her learning. In earlier versions of SEQUAL, this was termed "knowledge quality."
- L2: Pedagogical Quality. The stakeholder must have the proper mind-set, as defined by the physical model's paradigm.
- L3: Linguistic Quality. The stakeholder must have a mastery of the modeling language (the vocabulary and the grammar). Linguistic quality is of primary concern to modelers, but users of conceptual representation also need to master the basics of the employed modeling language to understand the conceptual representation (participant appropriateness in SEQUAL).

- L4: Pragmatic Quality. This type addresses the comprehension of the final physical representation by the stakeholders: the analysts who must use the representation to create the information system and other users who must understand what the representation is modeling. Pragmatic quality captures the extent to which the stakeholder completely and accurately understands the statements in the representation that are relevant to them (cf. the use of this term in SEQUAL).

The development layer: The elements of the physical layer have their developmental roots in the knowledge layer. A developer's knowledge is used to create the subsequent physical artifacts. For example, a domain expert's knowledge is used to create the physical model, the physical language, and the physical representation. A modeler's knowledge can be used to develop the language and the representation. The development layer's quality types measure how well this knowledge has been used to create the physical elements.

- D1: Applied Domain-Model Appropriateness. The physical model (ontology, mind-set) being developed must be appropriate to the modeler's conceptual understanding of the domain. This quality type is especially relevant to, for example, the development of domain ontologies.
- D2: Applied Domain-Language Appropriateness. Any modeling language being developed must be appropriate to the modeler's knowledge of the real-world domain (cf. domain appropriateness in SEQUAL).
- D3: Applied Domain Knowledge Quality. Knowledge of the domain is fundamental to all disciplines. The quality of the final representation is directly dependent on the accurate communication and application of that knowledge.
- D4: Applied Model-Language Appropriateness. The modeling language being developed must be appropriate to the developer's knowledge of the particular mind-set or ontology it will be based on.
- D5: Applied Model Knowledge Quality. Knowledge of the model that underlies the language and the domain is important to the quality of the final representation. For example, an incomplete or incorrect understanding of the object-oriented model (misinterpreting object-oriented concepts as procedural programming concepts) can lead to an object-procedural code hybrid in the final representation.
- D6: Applied Language Knowledge Quality. The modeler uses the modeling language, the vocabulary, and the grammar to create the physical representation. Although the modeler's knowledge of the language may be incomplete (he or she may not be familiar with some of the language's constructs), accurate knowledge of the language and its application is critical to the quality of the physical representation (cf. modeler appropriateness in SEQUAL).

Thus, the framework includes many of the same concepts as SEQUAL and also looks upon additional aspects of the relationships between the sets. It does not cover social and deontic aspects though.

2.3 Quality of Business Process Models

Although we have described above the quality aspects of different types of system representations, many of which are also relevant for process models, we will herein present the relevant work that particularly examines the quality of (business) process models. First, however, we examine the aspect of the quality of business processes.

2.3.1 Quality of Business Processes

As discussed in Chap. 1, a good business process is one that optimizes one or more of the following:

- Time,
- Quality,
- Cost,
- Flexibility,
- Resource usage,
- Unwanted side effects,
- Operations according to regulations.

The aspects that are to be emphasized also influence the quality evaluation of the supporting business process models, e.g., that the models particularly include the representation of the information needed to evaluate these aspects. It is not possible to optimize according to all these dimensions simultaneously; thus, as part of the goal of the business and, secondarily, as a goal of the model of a future improved situation reflecting the business, one must select what type of improvement to focus on. This improvement strategy is often linked to the overall image that the organization attempts to establish for its products and services; thus, there is no standard answer on how to optimize. Because different patterns of improvement optimize different dimensions, one must select which patterns apply in which cases.

Based on Andersen Consulting (1997), Dumas et al. (2013), Rosemann and Recker (2015), and Willoch (1994), a number of enhancement patterns and heuristics can be identified. We will here structure these according to the seven Rs described in Chap. 1 and use examples from the conference organizing domain on each heuristic. In doing so, it should be clear that different optimizations are good based on different goals. We will also observe that improvements in practice are often a combination of different Rs, as also illustrated in the first case from the healthcare sector presented in Chap. 1. As for the conference domain, Fortnow (2011) lists a number of reasons for having conferences:

1. To rate publications and researchers.
2. To disseminate new research results and ideas.

3. To network, gossip, and recruit.
4. To discuss controversial issues in the community.

In most fields, items 2, 3, and partly 4 are most important, although also the first is relevant, in particular in the IT area.

Rethinking (Why is the process there at all)
Rethinking is about clarifying and challenging the rationale and assumptions behind processes and their outcomes. This area is different from the other six because challenging an assumption does not necessarily lead to a solution. However, it does allow for more creative thinking. The other six areas can then be used to generate new process designs that address the new goals.

This area is a reminder to ask essential questions, such as the following:

- What is the root cause of the problem? Example: A conference may have a problem with obtaining detailed reviews on papers and thus have a limited basis for choosing the papers to be accepted. A root cause of this problem may be that the reviewers receive too many papers to review in a limited amount of time or the papers do not fit the interest and expertise of the program committee members. This issue relates not to the actual review process, but possibly to the process of organizing the program committee (with too few people familiar with the area of the conference).
- What are the reasons for doing it in this manner? Oftentimes, the exercise of articulating *why* the organization does the things it does quickly reveals reasons that are unknown, not compelling, easily changeable, or no longer valid; additionally, the reasons may be valid, but not relevant because the desired outcome can be achieved in some other manner. Once the reasons are articulated, they can be probed and challenged and either discarded or accepted as explicit constraints to innovation efforts. Example: A conference may have as a focus to publish the best technical papers and reject paper with novel ideas that are yet not fully validated. However, if one only focuses on the good technical papers, then one obtains fewer submissions because, instead, researchers will have these papers published in journals. Additionally, allowing papers with novel ideas that are evaluated according to slightly different criteria may make attending the conference more worthwhile because conferences are regarded as good places to discuss new ideas.
- Is this process sufficiently valuable to continue? Should the process be fixed or eliminated? Example: If the interest in a conference is reduced with fewer papers submitted and fewer people participating, one may do things to increase interest or perhaps instead join forces with another conference (as an accompanying event/workshop), piggybacking on the interest and organizational efforts of the other event.

To be able to reason about this, the *goal* of the process model should be captured in some manner as part of or related to the main process model.

Reconfiguring the Process (What)

Reconfiguring focuses on what work is being done. Some heuristics for this area with examples are described below.

Eliminating an activity, e.g., eliminating intermediaries and non-value-adding work: When submitting a paper, one should also enter certain metadata, e.g., keywords according a predefined classification. Rather than checking this after submission, one can automate the control of this in the user interface of the conference system.

Inserting a new activity: When using a conference system, one has user identification through, e.g., the username and password. Even if login to the system is then introduced as an extra step when, for instance, entering a review, it ensures that the right person enters the assigned review (and not, e.g., the author himself).

Consolidating activity: If a process consists of sequential tasks performed by many different people with special competences, two problems often arise:

1. The tasks take up too much specialist time.
2. It is difficult to track the status of the process because there are many persons involved.

One solution to this problem is to give one person or a group the main responsibility for the process. This person or persons can execute smaller tasks between the specialist tasks. In this manner, the specialists can release time for other more important duties, and the customer has one contact point where he or she can have all of the desirable information. The role of a PC chair in controlling the overall review process is an example of such a strategy.

Dividing a practice into two subsequent practices (decoupling horizontally): A task can be divided into two subsequent tasks, e.g., because the different parts are better undertaken by different persons. When writing a paper, one typically conducts a language check at the end. If the main author is not good at writing in English, one may choose to have another person (or organization, e.g., a professional proofreading company) conduct the language check.

Buffering: Instead of requesting information from an external source, one should buffer it and subscribe to updates. Instead of starting from scratch when organizing a program committee, one maintains a database of potential PC member candidates, inviting a selection of these to the program committee. If one needs more PC members (e.g., due to more submitted papers than expected), one has a reserve of additional potential PC members and reviewers readily available.

Dividing a practice into two parallel elements (decoupling vertically): When writing a paper, one may accelerate the process by having different people write different parts in parallel. For example, one might write the background part in parallel to someone else writing the contribution part.

Integrating two subsequent practices: When a final version of a paper is to be delivered, one also has to provide a copyright transfer form. Although, logically, there are two different processes that can be done sequentially, one can ensure that both are done simultaneously, e.g., when using a paper submission tool.

Reducing reconciliation by putting quality at the source: One should also mandate that the submission of original papers is done according to the final format and length limitations by sharing these guidelines with people who want to submit a paper. Although it is not strictly necessary to enforce these guidelines before papers are accepted, having done so will mean fewer problems for the authors of accepted papers in terms of getting a (possibly much too long) paper in the right format and length and simultaneously address comments by reviewers.

Specializing the process according to the case type: In a conference, one may want to have different processes for different paper types, e.g., having more reviewers for certain types of papers.

Having specific ways of treating exceptions: Business processes should be designed for typical cases, addressing exceptions outside the normal flow. In a conference, one should be able to address cases of plagiarism but not have this ability as part of the normal flow. If plagiarism becomes a large problem, then one may include a system to check for plagiarism as a standard part of the review process (which is often done in journals).

Reducing the number of inputs and outputs in a process: High numbers of input and output flows between different departments and groups within an organization increase organizational complexity. The chances of misunderstandings and errors are high, and the many parallel flows can also delay the process execution. A large number of input flows can result in a bottleneck. For example, when developing and submitting the final version of a paper, one needs the information on acceptance/rejection, the comments to be addressed, a description of the format/length of the final paper, and information on a copyright transfer form. In some cases, the last may not be ready when the acceptance is ready to be sent. Because the main work to be performed is updating the paper, one can send the acceptance and comments as soon as they are available, whereas the copyright transfer form, which basically has to be signed, can be sent later (although before the deadline for the submission of the final version of the paper). A process with many outputs can similarly act as a bottleneck if everything has to be ready before anything can proceed. For example, one may send out rejection letters later than acceptance letters because the timing issue (from the perspective of the organizers of the conference) is not as acute for a rejection (for the author, rejection information may actually be more time-critical because it may enable them to rework the rejected paper to submit it to another venue).

Making a previously obligatory activity optional: A conference may require that all accepted papers should include a description of the changes the authors have made when delivering the final paper. A change in this situation would be to only do so in the case of borderline and shepherded papers.

Borrowing and improving on best practices from other industries: In recent years, many companies have improved their processes by benchmarking across industry lines. For example:

- In a large conference, one may provide guidance for which session to attend by using recommendations similar to what is done in the recommender systems of Amazon, Netflix, etc.
- A mobile phone company learns delivery management techniques from a leading pizza delivery company.
- An office equipment company improves its warehouse productivity by analyzing the methods employed by a US-based catalog retailer.
- An international manufacturer obtains ideas for cost-cutting and improving customer service from a computer parts wholesaler and a major auto company.
- A medical center, realizing that patients judge their hospital experience not only based on the quality of care but also based on how much time, hassle, and paperwork are involved, uses an international hotel operator to help redesign its admitting process.
- An airline uses the best practices of an Indianapolis 500 pit crew to help develop faster turnaround in its maintenance processes.

Reassigning (Who)

Reassigning is concerned with the following question: Who does the work? Today, there are a large number of possible answers to this question. In nearly every industry, organizations are turning to suppliers, customers, strategic partners, outsourcing partners, subsidiaries, temporary workers, and others to do work previously done in-house.

Pulling instead of pushing: Instead of the papers being distributed to the reviewers, the reviewers select (or bid for) the papers themselves. The papers that no one selects are then distributed to those having selected the fewest papers.

Letting workers perform as many steps as possible for a single case: To avoid too many handovers between people, this idea can be good. In a two-level structure, a program board (PB) member should facilitate the discussion among the reviewers of the proposed verdict of the paper, present this verdict in the PB meeting, and perform the necessary shepherding of the paper if needed.

Having a flexible assignment: One should assign work such that maximal flexibility is preserved for the near future. If a PC member has indicated skills in very few areas, then papers should be assigned to him first because it will most likely be easier to assign later papers to people who have indicated a larger variety of knowledge areas.

Dividing responsibilities: One should avoid shared responsibilities for tasks by people from different functional units. Although the program chair is responsible for the selection of papers, one may have a separate proceedings chair from the conference organizer responsible for communication in relation to the final proceedings with the publisher because he has to address monetary aspects (whereas the PC chair is often with another organization than the main conference organizer).

Assigning a case manager: One person is made responsible for handling each type of case. An example of such a policy would be when a program board member is responsible for following up one paper.

Customer team: One should compose a work team across different departments that will completely address the handling of specific cases. One could imagine that the general chair, proceedings chair, and publisher compose a joint team to ensure the smooth production of the proceedings.

Minimizing the number of partners in a task: One could imagine, for instance, that all of the people on the organizing committee of a conference work at the same place (and at the same place as the conference is being held).

Involving extra resources: If more papers than expected are submitted, one should attempt to recruit more program committee members or reviewers to avoid a workload that is too large for each reviewer.

Empowering the worker: One should give workers most of the decision-making authority. In many conferences with a two-level structure, one can follow this principle by removing the extra layer and inviting all PC members to participate in the final selection of papers instead of a separate program board.

Outsourcing the activity: Instead of having the organizing committee do all of the participant handling, one involves a professional conference organizing company that, for a fixed fee per participant, will do all of the participant handling, including payments and reimbursements and agreements with hotels.

Using a trusted third party: This action is related to that above. For example, rather than arranging for payment services oneself, the conference organizer uses standard payment and banking services.

Having customers and supplier share information: When registering for a conference, information on who else will attend can be made available. By giving access to this information (which needs to be accepted by the participant), one can make the conference more attractive and make it easier for conference participants to plan who they would particularly like to talk to during the conference.

Having the customer perform the activity: A publisher may have had a process for checking the final manuscript in detail before publication. By providing a good template and mandating that the conference proceedings editor ensure adherence to its standard use (and return manuscripts with too many errors), they may have to do less work themselves.

Integrating the business processes of customers and suppliers: When a paper is published, the paper is to be registered in the national publication database. If the publisher makes it possible to directly import all of the publication information into this national system, then the reporting work of the author will be eased.

Facilitating interfacing: One should improve coordination by having a standardized interface between customers and partners. When organizing a conference, one mandates a certain paper format (e.g., Springer LNCS), even in conferences not being published by Springer, because it is a well-known format with available style guides and templates.

Making the organization perform an activity that the customer is currently performing: Although the formatting of references was previously done by the author, this is by Springer done by them, to ensure that papers and citations are correctly referenced and thus correctly indexed.

Resequencing (When)

This heuristic centers on the question of when work is done: sequencing, timing, and interdependencies. When activities have been performed in a certain manner for many years, it is easy to assume that some steps simply must be performed before others. However, there may be fewer real dependencies than what is written in the procedures. Varying the timing and sequence of work can be a powerful lever for designing not only a faster process but also a process that enables greater customization, lower cost, and fewer errors. Once process performance requirements are known, one should check whether resequencing the work can help achieve them.

Using predicting to increase efficiency: One should use statistics from submissions to earlier conferences to estimate at an early time how many papers one will end up with. If the number seems to indicate fewer submissions than usual, one should intensify the marketing activities to attract more papers.

Changing the decision moment: Earlier decisions will make it easier to continue the process and make it more efficient. Later decisions will provide time to evaluate and choose between the alternatives and therefore provide more flexibility. For example, one should use a knockout approach. If a paper is clearly not relevant for the conference, then the program committee chair removes this paper ("desk reject") from the papers to be reviewed and thus decreases the number of reviewing tasks.

Increasing flexibility with postponement: When one receives all of the reviews of a paper, one possibility would be to decide on the acceptance/rejection of this paper immediately. By waiting until all of the reviews are received on all of the papers, it is possible to view the selection of the overall program and perhaps accept a somewhat weaker paper because it fits with some other accepted papers in a session.

Minimizing the number of interconnections and dependencies: In many conferences, one has one call for papers and then decides on the paper sessions based on the overall accepted papers. If one places great focus on having not only good papers but also coherent sessions, then the selection of papers may end up depending on too many other reviews. In some conferences, one has predefined tracks with separate submissions from the start, which makes the selection within the session independent of what is done in other tracks.

Changing the number of alternatives: A number of alternatives that are too large can result in complexity and inefficiency. If the selection of alternatives is too small, then one risks that none of the solutions are appropriate for the special case. For example, a conference may have ten different paper types. In this case, one may end up with ten parallel decision processes that must then be coordinated. If the conference has only one paper type, then it may end up with only standard technical papers and not include other types of papers (e.g., novel ideas and experience papers) at all.

Resequencing the work: Typically, in a conference, the papers are first published at the conference. A different model could consist of having the papers published well ahead of the conference so that participants can have the time to read the papers and prepare for the conference upfront.

Reorganizing partial processes: It may be possible to organize sequential partial processes in parallel. If it is possible, in most cases, doing so will decrease the execution time of a process. For instance, in the case of a conference, reviews are performed by several people in parallel and not sequentially.

Another possibility is merging two or more partial processes or dividing one partial process into various smaller processes. Merging can be an effective tool for improvement if the processes are tightly bound. Desirable consequences of merging and dividing partial processes include the better use of resources and faster process accomplishment.

A thorough analysis of the partial processes and their internal dependency can also uncover parts that are useless for the entire process. These parts are only a waste of time and resources and should therefore be eliminated (cf. the discussion on lean principles in Chap. 1).

Relocating (Where)

This heuristic focuses on the question of where work is done; it concerns location, distance, and physical infrastructure. There may be some correlation with the heuristics for reassigning. The idea is to minimize distance and maximize communication between the people involved in a process, thereby reducing the costs associated with travel time, handoffs, late error detection, rework, and quality problems.

Moving the activity closer to the customer or supplier: When deciding on the conference location, oftentimes, one criterion is that it is close to one of the universities where some main researchers within the community reside, making it more likely that it will attract more participants.

Moving the activity closer to related activities to improve communication: When deciding on the venue of a conference, oftentimes, one possibility is to have it at a hotel because all of the participants also need accommodation and food. Thus, a total package with one supplier of conference facilities, lunches, accommodation, and potentially a conference dinner can be negotiated.

Decreasing time by reducing travel time and distance: Another criterion for conference location can be that it is at a place that is convenient to travel to for most participants. An extreme variant of this would be to have a virtual conference where everyone participates remotely. Although this would be good from a resource usage point of view, only parts of goals of the conference can be achieved in such setting.

Creating a geographically virtual organization: Before the arrival of general e-mail services and the Internet made arranging such an organization easier, the organizing of a scientific conference is a good example.

Centralization: One should treat geographically dispersed resources as though they were centralized. When everyone uses the same review systems, the international program committee can work as though it was centralized.

Reducing (How often)

This set of heuristics concerns frequencies, volumes, the amount of resources, information and quality levels, and determining how much of each is actually necessary and appropriate. Despite its name, the heuristic of reducing encourages designers to explore what type of process improvements is possible if the frequency of activities varies up or down. Depending on the process outcomes desired, either direction may be the direction to go in.

Consolidating multiple practices into one: Subscription models consolidate the invoicing of individual services to larger, regular payments and consolidate at the end of the year based on actual use. One can also consider other methods of bundling payments. For example, in connection with a conference, one may have several subactivities that one can pay for individually. Being able to pay them in one transaction will typically make this task easier and entail fewer errors.

Individualizing: Breaking up a practice into multiple instances. In a conference, one may shepherd (some of) the accepted papers. Rather than sending out the reviews to all of the accepted papers from the program chair, the shepherds send out a personalized message for the papers he shepherds, starting the scientific discourse to ensure that the necessary changes and improvements are performed. Individualizing is performed to improve the quality of the final paper.

Reducing the number of customer contacts: When a paper is accepted, one must provide notification of this status and the deadline for the final version, send the review comments that should be addressed in the final version, and provide information on the format of the final version, the rules of copyright, the copyright form to be used, and how to register for the conference (and that it is mandated that at least one of the authors of the paper will register and come to the conference to present the paper). Sending all of the information at once is better than sending 3–4 individual e-mails.

Increasing quality through redundancy: One could have only one or two reviewers of each paper and still claim that all of the papers were peer-reviewed, but good conferences typically provide three or four reviews because if there is only one, much depends on the fact that the one reviewer knows the field of the paper well (which is difficult to guarantee) and that all of the reviewers use the reviewing scale in the same manner (something that never occurs). Additionally, having 4 and not 3 reviewers in case one wants to end up with at least 3 reviews is more robust because not all of the reviewers will manage to return the reviews in time. Providing several reviews will also be useful for the author to improve the paper (also if it is not accepted).

Using fewer controls to simplify and improve efficiency: This action could be used as an argument to reduce the number of reviewers. Additionally, not checking the submitted CRCs (if they are updated according to the comments from the reviewers) could be a method of improving efficiency (possibly jeopardizing quality).

Using critical resources more efficiently: One should understand which resources are the most critical to process success and find methods to make the most of them. What makes a resource critical?

- The process cannot operate without it.
- It is a high-cost item (either fixed or variable).
- It differentiates the company from competitors and drives competitive advantage in the marketplace.

In assembling the scientific program, the program committee chair has an important task. To allow the program committee chair to focus on this task, one may have others examine other parts of the program, the production of the proceedings, etc.

Enabling greater effectiveness through more information: Both having authors provide keywords and having keywords be automatically extracted using text mining techniques makes it easier to distribute papers to knowledgeable reviewers. Automatic keyword extraction using a similar technique based on the reviewers' publication over the last 5 years might be a way to improve the accuracy of the classification of the reviewer expertise.

Retooling (How)

This set of heuristics concerns how work is accomplished: the technologies, human capital, and competencies that enable organizations to do work. Few truly innovative processes are created without the extensive introduction of new technology and skills into an organization. Some examples include the following:

Transforming the process with the use of technology: Access to new technology will provide opportunities to change and improve the process execution. It is important for the enterprise to evaluate the time to perform the change so that it matches with, e.g., new releases of a software product. One should remember that introducing new technology may necessitate other processes that use resources; thus, one must examine the total resource consumption. For example, distributing papers to reviewers has historically been a manual task for the program committee chair. Instead, by having the program committee members bid for papers, this distribution can be performed automatically by a tool, making it more likely that a reviewer will receive a paper that fits his knowledge and interest. The evaluation of different subareas (e.g., novelty) could be improved by analyzing the age of the references.

Automating activity: One would like to avoid plagiarism. Traditionally, plagiarism needed to be checked manually (thus, cases of plagiarism were rarely discovered). In recent years, a number of tools for plagiarism detection have been developed so that one can now check for plagiarism on a routine basis.

Creating competitive advantage through technology: There are many methods of publishing the papers of a proceeding; thus, traditional publishers need to provide further services in addition to the actual publication and the reputation of the publisher. Thus, e.g., Springer is getting papers indexed very quickly, making references, etc., available through tools based on Google Scholar contributing to the citation statistics. Springer also has specific services in relation to download statistics, which makes it easier for authors and conference organizers to track the interest in their work.

Improving the process through up-skilling, down-skilling, or multiskilling: An increase in employees' skill levels can enable each individual to handle a wider range of integrated tasks, thereby reducing the need for handoffs. Thus, having the general chair of a conference handle most of the practical follow-up as part of his role can be more efficient than having separate people working to follow up all the different service suppliers.

At times, lower skill levels may be more cost-effective, e.g., Springer does typesetting and other tasks in India to use the cheaper cost of labor there.

Custom building or buying technology: As a rule, one should use packaged software for tactical processes and custom applications for strategic processes. Custom software lends itself to strategic processes in which flexibility is more important than fast implementation. Packaged software lends itself to tactical processes that require less flexibility and to situations where getting the system quickly installed and operational is more important. Twenty years ago, no Web-based review systems existed; thus, conferences had to create such a system themselves (Krogstie 1995). Over the last 15 years, a number of such services exist on the Web, and it is better to use (and configure) one of these services than it is to build the service oneself.

2.3.2   Guidelines of Modeling—GoM

The earliest approach to discussing the quality of process models in particular was GoM—Guidelines of Modeling (Becker et al. 1995, 2002). A number of basic principles of modeling addressing syntactic, semantic, and pragmatic demands on the proper creation of process models are proposed in Becker et al. (1995). They are also applicable to enterprise process models. There principles are as follows:

- The principle of accuracy: Subsequently renamed correctness, the model complies with the corresponding excerpt of the real world. As illustrated in Fig. 2.5, correctness has two aspects inspired by Batini's work on data quality described earlier: syntactic correctness and semantic correctness. A model is syntactically correct if it is consistent and complete in relation to the language on which the model is based. Semantic correctness entails that the structure and the behavior of the model are consistent with the real world. Consistency between different models is viewed as a part of the correctness of the model.
- The principle of relevance: Modeling constructs should be included in the model with a purpose; not everything should be represented in the model. Which information is relevant for a model depends on the intended use, i.e., the goal of the model, touching upon deontic quality using SEQUAL terminology.
- The principle of economic efficiency: The costs of modeling should not exceed the intended benefit, e.g., modeling should not be used for addressing trivial problems that can be resolved by other methods.

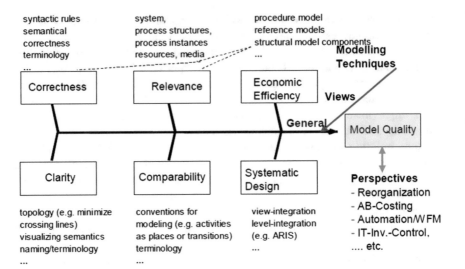

Fig. 2.5 Guidelines of Modeling (Becker et al. 2002)

- The principle of clarity: Models should be presented legibly and clearly, without more constructs than are necessary to be comprehensible for all stakeholders, supporting what in SEQUAL is termed empirical quality.
- The principle of comparability: Models created with different modeling techniques should be comparable at least to some extent.
- The principle of systematic design: If several models are created, then they should be connected in some structure to show how they contribute to the overall purpose of modeling.

In Becker et al. (2002), a specific version of these guidelines for (business) process models is presented. In addition to the six *general guidelines* (level 1), the GoM framework described there includes recommendations for different *views* (level 2, e.g., process models) and for different *modeling techniques* (level 3, e.g., event-driven process chains (EPCs) or UML activity diagrams), as indicated in Fig. 2.5.

These more detailed guidelines also take into account that there are different things that are important based on the goal of modeling (cf. Chap. 1), particularly aspects related to workflow models (usage area 5b, automatic activation) and model analysis/simulation (usage area 3).

2.3.3   Seven Process Modeling Guidelines (7PMG)

In Mendling et al. (2010c), the authors suggest seven process modeling guidelines (7PMG) in an attempt to provide a limited set of easily understandable guidelines.

- G1: Using as few elements in the model as possible. Larger models tend to be more difficult to understand (Mendling et al. 2007a) and have a higher probability of error than small models (Mendling et al. 2007a, 2010b).
- G2: Minimizing the routing paths per element. The higher the degree of an element in the process model is, i.e., the number of input and output arcs together, the more difficult it becomes to understand the model (Mendling et al. 2007a). As shown in Mendling et al. (2007b), there is a strong correlation between the number of modeling errors and the average or maximum degree of elements in a model.
- G3: Using one start event and one end event. The number of start and end events is positively connected to an increase in the probability of error (Mendling et al. 2007b). Additionally, most workflow engines require a single start and end node (van der Aalst et al. 2003). Moreover, models that satisfy this requirement are easier to understand and allow for all types of analysis (e.g., soundness checks). Note that these last aspects are primarily an issue when wanting to execute the process model.
- G4: Modeling as structured as possible. A process model is structured if every split connector matches a respective join connector of the same type. Structured models can be viewed as formulas with balanced brackets, i.e., every opening bracket has a corresponding closing bracket of the same type. Not only are unstructured models more likely to include errors (Mendling et al. 2007b), but people also tend to have larger problems with understanding them (Mendling et al. 2007a, b, c).
- G5: Avoiding OR routing elements. Models that have only AND and XOR connectors are less error-prone (Mendling et al. 2007b). Furthermore, there are some ambiguities in the semantics of the OR-join, which leads to paradoxes and potential implementation problems (Kindler 2006).
- G6: Using verb–object activity labels. A wide exploration of labeling styles that are used in actual process models reveals the existence of two popular styles (Recker and Mendling 2006). Based on these, people consider the verb–object style, such as "inform complainant," to be significantly less ambiguous and more useful than action-noun labels (e.g., "complaint analysis") or labels that follow neither of these styles (e.g., "incident agenda") (Mendling et al. 2007b).
- G7: Decomposing the model if it has more than 50 elements. For models with more than 50 elements, the probability of error tends to be higher than 50 % (Mendling et al. 2007b). The implication is that large models should be divided into smaller models. Note that the early guidelines for DFD were more restrictive, e.g., having no more than seven processes at a given decomposition level (based on the 7 ± 2 guideline for human short-term memory) (Gane and Sarson 1979).

It should be noticed that there are potential interaction effects between the seven proposed guidelines. For a given process model, many guidelines can be applicable at various places in a process model and conflicting to different degrees. In Mendling et al. (2010c), a suggested prioritization is G4, G7, G1, G6, G2, G3, and G5. The 7PMG guidelines primarily focus on aspects of empirical quality using the SEQUAL vocabulary. This suggestion should clearly also be held against other quality types (e.g., model completeness and validity). In Reijers et al. (2015), the 7PMG is placed as part of pragmatic quality means (using the original usage of this level from Lindland et al. (1994) before the split of pragmatic quality in SEQUAL into empirical and pragmatic qualities was done in 1995), and looking upon this in concert with syntactic and semantic goals and means to achieve these goals, although not discussing the interrelationship between quality of the different levels.

2.3.4   Pragmatic Guidelines for Business Process Modeling

Whereas 7PMG is meant to highlight the most important guidelines, the work by Moreno-Montes and Snoeck (2014) presents a comprehensive overview of such guidelines based on numerous sources (Arkilic et al. 2013; Becker et al. 2003; Cardoso et al. 2006; Claes et al. 2012; Davis 2001; Dijkman et al. 2008; Dumas et al. 2012; Effinger et al. 2010; Figl and Laue 2011; Gruhn and Laue 2007a, b; Gruhn and Laue 2011; Koehler and Vanatalo 2007; Lassen and van der Aalst 2009; Laue and Mendling 2008, 2010; Mendling 2007; Mendling et al. 2007a, b, c; Mendling and Reijers 2008a, b, c; Mendling et al. 2010a, b, c, 2012; Reggio et al. 2011a, b; Reijers and Mendling 2008, 2011; Reijers et al. 2010, 2011a, b; Rolón et al. 2007, 2009a, b; Sánchez-González et al. 2010; Sánchez-González et al. 2011a, b, 2012; Schrepfer et al. 2009; Sharp and McDerott 2001; Silver 2008, 2012; Vanderfeesten et al. 2008; Vanhatalo et al. 2007; Weber et al. 2011) that also include 7PMG. Their report presents an overview of the guidelines for undertaking business process modeling tasks. These guidelines can support practitioners and non-experts in modeling business process models. In particular, the guidelines focus on obtaining high-quality business process models in terms of their quality as a model, what we in SEQUAL place under empirical and syntactic qualities.

The guidelines which in particular are relevant for process models using languages like BPMN are structured into three groups:

1. Counting the number of different elements,
2. Composition of components,
3. Presentation.

We list all of the guidelines below, indicating the issue and the proposed guideline. In Moreno-Montes and Snoeck (2014), the authors discuss the problem, the rationale of the guideline, and how to use it in practice in more detail. Snoeck et al. (2015) provide an overview of how these guidelines are supported in different modeling tools.

2.3.4.1   Number of Elements

1. The model contains a high number of elements (i.e., gateways, activities, and events) -> Decompose models with more than 31 elements.
2. The model contains duplicate elements (e.g., identical start events, identical end events, and identical activities) or fragments, capturing the same control flow logic -> Avoid duplicate elements and fragments in the process models.
3. Models contain unnecessary elements (e.g., one empty arc between an AND split and an AND join) -> Avoid unnecessary elements.
4. A high number of events -> Avoid models with more than 7 events.
5. The model contains multiple start/end events -> Use no more than two start/end events in the top process level; use one start event in the subprocesses; and use two end events to distinguish success and fail states in the subprocesses.
6. Do not omit start and end events -> Have at least one start event and one end event in the process model.
7. A high number of intermediate events -> Avoid high numbers of intermediate events in the process model.
8. The model contains too many arcs -> Avoid models with more than 34 arcs.
9. The model contains too many gateways -> Avoid models with more than 12 gateways.
10. A high number of activities -> Minimize the number of activities.
11. A high number of routing paths per gateway -> Use no more than 3 routing paths per gateway. The associated metrics are as follows:

    i. Average connector degree (ACD),
    ii. Maximum connector degree (MCD),
    iii. Number of sequence flows from gateways (NSFG),
    iv. Control flow complexity for AND splits (CFCand split),
    v. Control flow complexity for inclusive OR splits (CFCor split),
    vi. Control flow complexity for XOR splits (CFCxor split).

12. Split/join gateways have more than one incoming and outgoing flows (i.e., two behaviors in the same gateway) -> Do not combine multiple inputs and multiple outputs in the same gateway.
13. There are too many outgoing sequence flows from an event -> Do not use more than 4 outgoing sequence flows from events.

2.3.4.2   Composition of Components

14 The model has deeply nested structured blocks -> Avoid deeply nesting structured blocks.
15 The model contains multiple cycles -> Avoid cycles in the process models, especially unstructured cycles (i.e., cycles with multiple exit points).

16 Badly formed cycles: The backward connection of a loop construct does not begin in an XOR split or does not lead back to an XOR join -> When modeling cycles, the backward connection should begin in an XOR split and lead back to an XOR join.
17 Multiple exit points per cycle -> Avoid multiple exit points per cycle.
18 A high level of parallelism (the sum of the output degrees of the AND and XOR gateways should be 8 at most) -> Avoid a high level of parallelism in the process models.
19 Bad parallelism: Parallel paths do not reach end events or do not synchronize -> Each parallel path must reach an end event or must be synchronized.
20 A high level of unstructuredness -> Every split gateway should match a respective join gateway of the same type.
21 The model contains a long path from the start node to the end node -> Keep the path from a start node to the end node as short as possible.
22 High gateway diversity -> Minimize gateway diversity.
23 Existence of inclusive OR gateways in the process models -> Avoid the use of inclusive OR gateways.
24 High complexity in the model -> Select the less complex alternative when modeling.
25 The model lacks modularity -> There should be no more than 31 nodes in a diagram (cf. guideline 1) and no less than 5 activities in a subprocess.

2.3.4.3 Presentation

26 The model is not readable because of a suboptimal layout -> In general: Keep the diagram as neat and consistently organized as possible by following the following list of advice:

- Minimize the number of unnecessarily crossing lines.
- Minimize the number of overlapping (connection) elements (edges should not overlap edges or other nodes.).
- Minimize the number of bends in connecting elements.
- Maximize the number of orthogonally drawn connecting objects.
- Make the models long and thin (instead of square): Maximize the number of connecting objects that respect the workflow direction.
- Place elements as symmetrically as possible.
- Minimize the drawing area.
- Place related elements close to each other.
- Adapt the size of objects such that elements have sufficient space.
- Consider the use of partitions, e.g., pools and swimlanes.
- Specify task types, especially user (human task) and service (automated task) tasks.
- Use a uniform style for the flow layout.

27 Labels are not correct/optimal.

- Labels do not follow the verb–object style.
- Labels are too long.
- Pools label is different from the process.
- Timer events are not labeled with the duration or date/time parameter.
- Gateways are not labeled.
- Black box pools are not labeled with the participant's name.
- There are constructions other than the send/receive task types that are labeled as send or receive.

2.3.5 Quality Through the Use of Reference Models

An important generic means often used primarily for improving semantic quality is the reuse of existing (good) models. The success of reuse is dependent on many factors at different quality levels:

- The model needs to be of good physical quality, i.e., it must be physically represented in a persistent form that is available to those who will potentially want to reuse it.
- For the reuse of semiformal and formal models, it is not always the model itself that is reused; rather, their presence will cause the next modeler to reuse the use of such modeling languages and do so correctly. For this usage to be successful, the original models should be syntactically correct.
- In cases where one actually wants to reuse the model as is (i.e., where the domains are very similar), the model should have a high semantic quality. For white box reuse, the model needs to be modifiable and should also be comprehensible and comprehended; thus, one must support techniques for achieving empirical and pragmatic qualities. The model should also be annotated with additional statements, making it easier to find the sought-for model, thus influencing what is an appropriate completeness.
- Where existing models need to be compared with models developed in a separate project, social means and techniques, such as model integration and conflict resolution, can be useful to investigate the extent to which the solutions based on the model to be reused should actually be reused.
- Successful reuse will influence the cost of modeling in a positive manner, addressing aspects of deontic quality. However, the reuse of, e.g., a reference model comes at a cost that itself should not be higher than the benefit gained.

Model reuse can be both within and between organizations. In regard to process models, a number of areas have developed "reference models" with what is established as good practices/best practices within a field. The right reuse of such models can be viewed as a particularly efficient method of improving the quality of business processes and business process models, especially when the processes are supported by a tool such as those found in SAP ERP.

In Frank (2007), a detailed overview of the relevant aspects for the evaluation of reference models is provided. First, he differentiates three usage settings:

1. Predevelopment, where the model is a basis for model activation or system implementation,
2. Post-development, where the reference model serves mostly as documentation,
3. Business redesign on an organizational/strategic level.

Four evaluation perspectives are described:

1. The economic perspective,
2. The deployment perspective,
3. The engineering perspective,
4. The epistemological perspective.

They all have their own detailed evaluation criteria, some of which are relevant for models in general, whereas others are specifically relevant for reference models, as detailed below.

2.3.5.1 Economic Criteria

These criteria address different aspects of the costs and benefits of using the reference model (cf. how reuse ties into the deontic quality level of SEQUAL). Although reference models are aimed at reducing costs, their use will also cause costs. Costs are in relation to the introduction (Table 2.3), transformation and analysis (Table 2.4), and maintenance of the reference models (Table 2.5).

Using a reference model promises a number of benefits. Two categories are proposed for this purpose: efficiency (Table 2.6) and flexibility (Table 2.7). The relevance of each point depends a lot on the goal of modeling.

As discussed in Chap. 1, one of the goals of all models should act to foster communication. An overview of aspects in this regard is found in Table 2.8.

Taking into account that using a reference model can cause substantial investments, the question of how these investments are protected is a core issue, as outlined in Table 2.9.

2.3.5.2 Deployment Criteria

The success of a reference model depends heavily on the ability and willingness of the users to address the model. Important aspects in this regard are outlined in Table 2.10.

Table 2.3 Cost of the introduction of the reference model

Aspect	Relevant for type of use	Criteria
Acquisition	1, 2, 3	Cost of purchasing, licensing model Cost of in-house development
Training	1, 2, 3	Familiarity of own staff with modeling language, terminology In-house modeling expertise Availability of training offers Overall complexity of the model
Adaptation	1, 2, 3	Concepts that support adaptation in a safe and convenient manner Availability of tools Cost of tools Cost of integrating with existing tools/systems
Strategic redesign	1, 2, 3	The model recommends/requires strategic adaptation Degree of change required
Organizational redesign	1, 2, 3	The model recommends/requires organizational adaptation Degree of change required
Integration	1, 2	Integration with existing models Integration with business partners Amount of integration required Compatibility of modeling concepts

Table 2.4 Cost of transformation and analysis

Aspect	Relevant for type of use	Criteria
Suitability	1, 2	Modeling concepts allow for automatic transformation into implementation-level documents Modeling concepts support required types of analysis If necessary: cost for adapting model for transformation/analysis
Tools	1	Availability of tools that feature transformation/analysis functions Cost of tools Cost of integrating tool with the existing software development environment
Training/support	1, 2	Skills required for performing transformation/analysis tasks available Cost of training Cost of external support

Table 2.5 Cost of maintenance of reference models

Aspect	Relevant for type of use	Criteria
Conceptual support	1, 2, 3	Concepts that support adaptation in a safe and convenient manner
Tools	1, 2, 3	Availability of tools that support model management (versions, users) Cost of tools
Skills	1, 2, 3	Cost of internal skills Cost of external skills

Table 2.6 Efficiency/effectiveness

Aspect	Relevant for type of use	Criteria
Software development and maintenance	1	Improvement in productivity Improvement in software quality Functionality and maturity of available tools Compatibility with existing abstractions Skills of software developers Willingness to use the reference model
Business/management	1, 2, 3	Increased efficiency of affected business processes Cost reduction in business processes Support for specific decision scenarios Familiarity with model-based decision making Willingness to use the model in decision scenarios Improved customer orientation

Table 2.7 Flexibility/integration

Aspect	Relevant for type of use	Criteria
Dependence on IT vendors	1, 2	Number of relevant IT vendors that support the model Number of users Degree of customization Standardization Level of industry commitment
Openness	1, 2	Compatibility with relevant standards Integration with further reference models Coverage of possible future business models
Expressive power	1, 2, 3	Degree of (ontological) completeness of the modeling language
Relationship with other IT artifacts	1, 2	Concepts that foster integration/transformation into other relevant representations

Table 2.8 Coordination/knowledge management

Aspect	Relevant for type of use	Criteria
Coordination	1, 2, 3	Helps overcome communication barriers within the company Fosters communication with external partners Improves coordination of business processes Fosters the establishment of interorganizational coordination

Table 2.9 Protection of investments

Aspect	Relevant for type of use	Criteria
Spreading/commitment	1, 2, 3	Number of organizations that use the model Number of vendors and service providers that support the model Standardization of the modeling language Standardization of the model
Technological change	1, 2	Independent of a particular technology Supports technologies that can be expected in the near future

Table 2.10 Deployment aspects of reference models

Aspect	Relevant for type of use	Criteria
Understandability	1, 2, 3	Elaborate structure for documentation (e.g., with design patterns) Comprehensive documentation Scenarios and examples Familiarity with the modeling language Familiarity with terminology Intuitive access to graphical representation Views for different groups of stakeholders
Appropriateness	1, 2	Amount of support for purposes relevant for users Supports technologies that can be expected in the near future
Attitude	1, 2, 3	"Not invented here" syndrome Reputation of model developers Resistance to organizational change Cultural barriers

Table 2.11 Engineering perspective on reference models

Aspect	Relevant for type of use	Criteria
Definition	1, 2, 3	Comprehensive description of intended application domains Comprehensive description of intended purposes
Explanation	1, 2, 3	Assigning model elements to requirements Justification/substantiation of design decisions Discussing design compromises and the resulting drawbacks Discussion of alternative approaches
Language features	1, 2, 3	Level of formalization, extensibility, supported conceptual views, integration of views, tool support, concepts to support the adaptation of models, and concept to foster model integrity
Technical model features	1, 2, 3	Formal correctness/consistency Model architecture Use of classes Use of generalization/specialization Use of modularization/encapsulation

2.3.5.3   Engineering Criteria

From an engineering perspective, two questions are important: Does the model fulfill the requirements to be taken into account? Is the specification appropriate for supporting the intended purposes of the model? These questions are detailed in Table 2.11.

2.3.5.4   Epistemological Criteria

This perspective serves to enrich the evaluation of reference models with epistemological considerations. Detailed aspects are described in Table 2.12.

2.3.6   Successful Business Process Modeling Projects

Sedera et al. (2003) have presented a process modeling success model where the identified success measures in their model are as follows:

1. Model use: How extensively the models are applied and utilized.
2. User satisfaction: The extent to which users believe that process modeling meets the fulfillment of the objectives that underlie the modeling project.

Table 2.12 Epistemological perspective on reference models

Aspect	Relevant for type of use	Criteria
Evaluation of theories	1, 2, 3	Precise description of core concepts with respect to the corresponding real-world concepts; precise description of underlying assumptions
Generic principles	1, 2, 3	Abstraction Originality Judgement
Critical distance	1, 2, 3	Subjective nature of underlying decisions Bias through familiarity with the modeling language High degree of spreading may be mistaken for high quality
Scientific progress	1, 2, 3	Discussion of long-term goals of the research Elaborate documentation of the model with respect to generic principles and long-term research goals Comparison with alternatives

3. Process impact: Measures the effects of modeling on process performance.
4. Process model quality: The extent to which all of the desirable properties of a model are fulfilled to satisfy the needs of the model users.

We will return to an application of these categories used in a case in Sect. 4.1.

2.4 Summary

We have in this paper provided description of thinking and framework on quality of IT artifact, including the quality of systems, data, and traditional conceptual models (including data, requirements, enterprise, and process models). Also aspects relative to business process quality and the area of reference models are touched upon. A main learning from these works and the work on more generic frameworks on quality of models (Nelson et al. and SEQUAL) is that although there are many similarities in the thinking on quality, comprehensive frameworks looking upon these holistically are useful. In the next chapter, we will extend the generic SEQUAL framework with aspects relative to quality of business processes and business process models and describing a framework for quality of business process models.

References

Andersen Consulting Process Excellence Handbook (1997). http://www.scribd.com/doc/31730974/Process-Excellence-Handbook#scribd

Arkilic, I.G., Reijers, H.A., Goverde, R.R.H.M.J.: How good is an as-is model really? In: Rosa, M., Soffer, P. (eds.) Business Process Management Workshops. Springer, Berlin, pp. 89–100 (2013)

Batini, C., Scannapieco, M.: Data Quality: Concepts, Methodologies and Techniques. Springer, Berlin (2006)

Batini, C., Cappiello, C., Francalanci, C., Maurino, A.: Methodologies for data quality assessment and improvement. ACM Comput. Surv. **41**(3) (2009)

Becker, J., Rosemann, M., Schütte, R.: Guidelines of Modelling (GoM). Wirtschaftsinformatik **37** (5), 435–445 (in German) (1995)

Becker, J., Rosemann, M., von Uthmann, C.: Guidelines of Business Process Modeling in Business Process Management Volume 1806 of the series Lecture Notes in Computer Science, pp. 30–49 (2002)

Becker, J., Kugeler, M., Rosemann, M.: Process Management: A Guide for the Design of Business Processes. Springer, Berlin (2003)

Berger, P., Luckmann, T.: The Social Construction of Reality: A Treatise in the Sociology of Knowledge. Penguin, London (1966)

Cardoso, J., et al.: A discourse on complexity of process models. In Business Process Management Workshops. Springer, Berlin (2006)

Claes, J., et al.: Tying process model quality to the modeling process: the impact of structuring, movement, and speed. In Business Process Management Conference, pp. 33–48 (2012)

Davis, R.: Business Process Modelling with Aris: A Practical Guide. Springer, Berlin (2001)

Davis, A.M., Overmeyer, S., Jordan, K., Caruso, J., Dandashi, F., Dinh, A., Kincaid, G., Ledeboer, G., Reynolds, P., Sitaram, P., Ta, A., Theofanos, M.: Identifying and measuring quality in a software requirements specification. In: Proceedings of the First International Software Metrics Symposium, Baltimore, pp. 141–152 (1993)

Denning, P.J.: What is software quality? Commun. ACM **35**(1), 13–15 (1992)

Dijkman, R.M., Dumas, M., Ouyang, C.: Semantics and analysis of business process models in BPMN. Inf. Softw. Technol. **50**(12), 1281–1294 (2008)

Dumas, M., et al.: Understanding business process models: the costs and benefits of structuredness. In Ralyté, J., et al. (eds.) Advanced Information Systems Engineering. Springer, Berlin, pp. 31–46 (2012)

Dumas, M, La Rosa, M, Mendling, J, Reijers, H.: Fundamentals of Business Process Management. Springer, Berlin (2013)

Effinger, P., Jogsch, N., Seiz, S.: On a study of layout aesthetics for business process models using BPMN. In: Mendling, J., Weidlich, M., Weske, M. (eds.) Business Process Modeling Notation. Springer, Berlin, pp. 31–45 (2010)

Falkenberg, E.D., Hesse, W., Lindgreen, P., Nilsson, B.E., Oei, J.L.H., Rolland, C., Stamper, R. K., Assche, F.J.M.V., Verrijn-Stuart, A.A., Voss, K.: A Framework of information system concepts—The FRISCO Report, IFIP WG 8.1 Task Group FRISCO (1996)

Figl, K., Laue, R.: Cognitive complexity in business process modeling. In: Advanced Information Systems Engineering, pp. 452–466 (2011)

Fortnow, L.: CACM viewpoint: time for computer science to grow up. Commun. ACM **52**(8), 33–35 (2011)

Frank, U.: Evaluation of reference models. In Fettke, P., Loos, P. (eds.) Reference Modeling for Business Systems Analysis IGI. Idea Group, Hershey (2007)

Gane, C., Sarson, T.: Structured Systems Analysis: Tools and Techniques. Prentice Hall, Englewood Cliffs (1979)

Gruhn, V., Laue, R.: 2 Approaches for business process model complexity metrics. In: Abramowicz, Mayr, H.C. (eds.) Technologies for Business Information Systems. Springer, Netherlands, pp. 13–24 (2007a)

Gruhn, V., Laue. R.: Good and bad excuses for unstructured business process models. In 12th European conference on pattern languages of programs (EuroPLoP 2007). UVK—Universitaetsverlag, Konstanz (2007b)

Gruhn, V., Laue, R.: Detecting common errors in event-driven process chains by label analysis. Enterp. Model. Inf. Syst. Architect. **6**(1), 3–15 (2011)

Hella, L., Krogstie, J.: A structured evaluation to assess the reusability of models of user profiles. In: Proceeding of EMMSAD—Conference on Evaluating Modeling Methods in Systems Analysis and Design, Hammamet, Tunis (2010)

ISO 9000: Quality management systems—fundamentals and vocabulary. International Organization for Standardization, Switzerland (2005)

Kano, N.: Attractive quality and must-be quality. J. Japanese Soc. Qual. Control 14(2), 39–48 (1984)

Kindler, E.: On the semantics of EPCs: resolving the vicious circle. Data Knowl. Eng. 56(1), 23–40 (2006)

Koehler, J., Vanhatalo, J.: Process anti-patterns: how to avoid the common traps of business process modeling. In: Tech. Rep. Report RZ-3678. IBM Zurich Reseach Lab (2007)

Krogstie, J.: Supporting a decentralized organization using WWW: the ISDO'95 conference Invited talk at the IFIP 8.1. Conference on Information Systems Development for Decentralized Organizations. Trondheim, Norway (1995)

Krogstie, J.: Using quality function deployment in software requirements specification. Paper presented at the Fifth International Workshop on Requirements Engineering: Foundations for Software Quality (REFSQ'99), Heidelberg, Germany, June 14–15 (1999)

Krogstie, J.: A semiotic approach to quality in requirements specification. In: Proceedings of IFIP 8.1. Working Conference on Organizational Semiotics, Montreal, Canada, 23–25 July (2001)

Krogstie, J.: Evaluating UML using a generic quality framework. In: Liliana F. (ed.) UML and the Unified Process, pp. 1–22. IRM Press, USA (2003)

Krogstie, J.: Integrated Goal, Data and Process modeling: From TEMPORA to Model-Generated Work-Places. In Paul Johannesson & Eva Söderstrøm (Eds.), Information Systems Engineering From Data Analysis to Process Networks (pp. 43–65): IGI. (2008)

Krogstie, J.: Model-based Development and Evolution of Information Systems: A Quality Approach. Springer, Berlin (2012a)

Krogstie, J.: Quality of Business Process Models. Proceedings PoEM'2012, Lecture Notes in Business Information Processing, vol. 134, 76–90. (2012b)

Krogstie, J.: Quality of conceptual data models. In: Proceedings 14th ICISO, Stockholm Sweden, April (2013a)

Krogstie, J.: A Semiotic framework for data quality. In: Proceedings EMMSAD 2013, Valencia, Spain, June (2013b)

Krogstie, J.: Capturing Enterprise Data Integration Challenges Using a Semiotic Data Quality Framework Business & Information Systems Engineering February 2015, Vol. 57, Issue 1, pp. 27–36 (2015)

Krogstie, J., Jørgensen, H.D.: Quality of interactive models. In: First International Workshop on Conceptual Modelling Quality (IWCMQ'02). 11 Oct 2002. Tampere, Finland. Springer, Berlin (2002)

Krogstie, B.R., Krogstie, J., Maiden, N., Lockerbie, J., Wessel, D., Knipfer, K.: Collaborative Modelling of Reflection to Inform the Development and Evaluation of Work-Based Learning Technologies Proceedings of i-KNOW 2012. ACM Press, New York (2012)

Larsson L., Segerberg R.: An Approach for Quality Assurance in Enterprise Modelling, MSc thesis. Stockholm University, Sweden (2004)

Lassen, K.B., van der Aalst, W.M.P.: Complexity metrics for Workflow nets. Inf. Softw. Technol. 51(3), 610–626 (2009)

Laue, R., Mendling, J.: The impact of structuredness on error probability of process models. In: Kaschek, R., et al. (eds.) Information Systems and E-Business Technologies. Springer, Berlin, pp. 585–590 (2008)

Laue, R., Mendling, J.: Structuredness and its significance for correctness of process models. IseB 8(3), 287–307 (2010)

Lin, Y., Strasunskas, D., Hakkarainen, S., Krogstie, J., Sølvberg, A.: Semantic annotation framework to manage semantic heterogeneity of process models. Paper presented at the CAiSE'2006, Luxembourg (2006)

Lindgren, P. (ed): A framework for information systems concepts. Interrim report FRISCO (1990)

Lindland, O.I.: A Prototyping Approach to Validation of Conceptual Models in Information Systems Engineering. Unpublished doctoral dissertation, IDT, NTH (1993)

Lindland, O.I., Sindre, G., Sølvberg, A.: Understanding quality in conceptual modeling. IEEE Softw. **11**(2), 42–49 (1994)

Mendling, J.: Detection and Prediction of Errors in EPC Business Process Models, in Institute of Information Systems and New Media. Vienna University of Economics and Business Administration (WU Wien), Austria (2007)

Mendling, J., Neumann. G.: Error metrics for business process models. In International Conference on Advanced Information Systems Engineering (2007)

Mendling, J., Recker, J.: Towards systematic usage of labels and icons in business process models. In: Halpin, T., Proper, H.A., Krogstie, J. (eds.) 13th International Workshop on Exploring Modeling Methods in Systems Analysis and Design, CEUR Workshop Proceedings Series, Montpellier. See http://ceur-ws.org/ France (2008)

Mendling, J., Reijers., H.A.: The impact of activity labeling styles on process model quality. In European Symposium on Analysis, Design, Use and Societal Impact of Information Systems. Marburg, Germany (2008)

Mendling, J., Strembeck, M.: Influence factors of understanding business process models. In Abramowicz, W.F.D. (eds.) Business Information Systems. Springer, Innsbruck, Austria, pp. 142–153 (2008)

Mendling, J., Reijers, H. A., Cardoso, J.: What makes process models understandable? In: G., Dadam, P., Rosemann, M., (eds.) Business Process Management, Alonso. Springer, Berlin, pp. 48–63 (2007a)

Mendling, J., Neumann, G., van der Aalst, W.M.P.: Understanding the occurrence of errors in process models based on metrics. In: Meersman, R.T.Z., (ed.) On the Move to Meaningful Internet Systems, pp. 113–130 (2007b)

Mendling, J., et al.: Detection and prediction of errors in EPCs of the SAP reference model. Data Knowl. Eng. **64**(1), 312–329 (2008)

Mendling, J., Reijers, H.A., Recker, J.: Activity labeling in process modeling: Empirical insights and recommendations. Inf. Syst. **35**(4), 467–482 (2010a)

Mendling, J., Recker, J., Reijers, H.A.: On the usage of labels and icons in business process modeling. Int. J. Inf. Syst. Model. Des. **1**(2), 40–58 (2010b)

Mendling, J., Reijers, H.A., van der Aalst, W.M.P.: Seven process modeling guidelines (7PMG). Inf. Softw. Technol. **52**(2), 127–136 (2010c)

Mendling, J., et al.: Thresholds for error probability measures of business process models. J. Syst. Softw. **85**(5), 1188–1197 (2012)

Moody, D.L.: Metrics for evaluating the quality of entity relationship models. In: Proceedings of the Seventeenth International Conference on Conceptual Modelling (ER '98), Singapore, November 16–19. Elsevier Lecture Notes in Computer Science (1998)

Moody, D.L.: The method evaluation model: a theoretical model for validating information systems design methods. In: Proceedings of the 11th European Conference on Information Systems, ECIS 2003, Naples, 16–21 June (2003)

Moody, D.L., Shanks, G.G.: What makes a good data model? Evaluating the quality of entity relationship models. In Proceedings of the 13th International Conference on the Entity-Relationship Approach (ER'94), pp. 94–111. Manchester, England (1994)

Moody, D.L., Sindre, G., Brasethvik,T., Sølvberg, A.: Evaluating the Quality of Process Models: Empirical Testing of a Quality Framework. In: Spaccapietra, S., March, S.T., Kambayashi, Y. (eds.) Proceedings ER 2002, LNCS 2503, pp. 214–231 (2002)

Moreno-Montes de Oca, I., Snoeck, M.: Pragmatic Guidelines for Business Process Modeling. Technical report KU Leuven (2014)

Nelson, H.J., Poels, G., Genero M., Piattini, M.: A conceptual modeling quality framework. Softw. Qual. J. **20**(1), (2011)

Nossum, A., Krogstie, J.: Integrated Quality of Models and Quality of Maps. Proceedings EMMSAD. Springer, Berlin (2009)

Pohl, K.: The Three dimensions of requirements engineering. In: Proceedings of CAiSE'93, Springer, LNCS 685 (1993)

Price, R., Shanks, G.: A semiotic information quality framework. In: IFIP WG8.3 International Conference on Decision Support Systems (DSS 2004), Prato, Italy, 1–3, pp. 658–672 (2004)

Price, R., Shanks, G.: A semiotic information quality framework: Development and comparative analysis. J. Inf. Technol. **20**(2), 88–102 (2005)

Recker, J., Mendling, J.: On the translation between BPMN and BPEL: conceptual mismatch between process modeling languages. In: Latour, T., Petit, M. (eds.) Proceedings of the CAiSE Workshops at the 18th Conference on Advanced Information Systems Engineering (CAiSE 2006), Luxembourg, Luxembourg, pp. 521–532. Presses Universitaries de Namur, Belgique (2006)

Reggio, G., et al.: On business process modelling with the UML: a discipline and three styles. Dipartimento di Informatica e Scienze dell'Informazione (DISI). University of Genova, Italy (2011a)

Reggio, G., Leotta, M., Ricca, F.: Precise is better than light—a document analysis study about quality of business process models. In First International Workshop on Empirical Requirements Engineering (2011b)

Reijers, H., Mendling, J.: Modularity in Process Models: Review and Effects. In Dumas, M., Reichert, M., Shan, M.-C. (eds.) Business Process Management. Springer, Heidelberg, pp. 20–35 (2008)

Reijers, H.A., Mendling, J., Dijkman, R.M.: On the usefulness of subprocesses. In Business Process Models. BPM center report, Eindhoven, p. 32 (2010)

Reijers, H.A., Mendling, J.: A study into the factors that influence the understandability of business process models. IEEE Transac. Syst. Man Cybern. Part A **41**(3), 449–462 (2011)

Reijers, H.A., Mendling, J., Dijkman, R.M.: Human and automatic modularizations of process models to enhance their comprehension. Inf. Syst. **36**(5), 881–897 (2011a)

Reijers, H.A., et al.: Syntax highlighting in business process models. Decision Support Systems, **51**(3), 339–349 (2011b)

Reijers, H., Mendling, J., Recker, J.: Business Process quality management. In: vom Brocke, J., Rosemann, M. (eds.) Handbook on Business Process Management 2nd ed. Springer, Berlin (2015)

Rolón, E., et al.: An exploratory experiment to validate measures for business process models. In: International Conference on Research Challenges in Information Science. Ouarzazate, Morocco (2007)

Rolón, E., et al.: Prediction models for BPMN usability and maintainability. In 2009 IEEE Conference on Commerce and Enterprise Computing (2009a)

Rolón, E., et al.: Analysis and validation of control-flow complexity measures with bpmn process models. In: Halpin, T., et al. (eds.) Enterprise, Business-Process and Information Systems Modeling. Springer, Berlin, pp. 58–70 (2009b)

Rosemann, M., Recker, J.: Systemic Ideation: A playbook for creating innovative ideas more consciously. 360° Bus. Transform. J. 13 Jul (2015)

Rumbaugh, J., Blaha, M., Premerlani, W., Eddy, F., Lorensen, W.: Object-Oriented Modeling and Design. Prentice-Hall, Englewood Cliffs (1991)

Sánchez-González, L., et al.: Quality assessment of business process models based on thresholds. In: Meersman, R., Dillon, T., Herrero, P., (eds.) On the Move to Meaningful Internet Systems, p. 78–95. (2010)

Sánchez-González, L., et al.: Towards thresholds of control flow complexity measures for BPMN models. In ACM Symposium on Applied Computing. ACM (2011a)

Sánchez-González, L., et al.: Improving quality of business process models. In: Maciaszek, L.A., Zhang, K., (eds.) Evaluation of Novel Approaches to Software Engineering, ENASE 2011. Springer: Beijing, pp. 130–144. 8 (2011b)

Sánchez-González, L., et al.: Quality indicators for business process models from a gateway complexity perspective. Inf. Softw. Technol. **54**(11), 1159–1174 (2012)

Sandkuhl, K., Stirna, J., Persson, A.,Wiβotzki, M.: Enterprise Modelling—Tackling Business Challenges with the 4EM Method. Springer, Berlin (2014)

Schrepfer, M., et al.: The impact of secondary notation on process model understanding. In: The Practice of Enterprise Modeling, Working Conference. Stockholm, Sweden (2009)

Sedera, W., Rosemann, M., Doebeli, G.: A process modelling success model: insights from a case study. 11th European Conference on Information Systems, Naples, Italy (2003)

Sharp, A., McDermott, P.: Workflow Modeling: Tools for Process Improvement and Application Development, Artech House (2001)

Silver, B. Ten tips for effective process modeling. BPMS watch, (2008)

Silver, B., BPMN: Method and Style. Cody-Cassidy Press, Aptos (2012)

Snoeck, M., Moreno-Montes de Oca, I., Haegemans, T., Schedeman, B., Hoste, T.: Testing a Selection of BPMN Tools for Their Support of Modelling Guidelines. Proceedings PoEM (2015)

Tsichritzis, D., Klug, A.: The ANSI/X3/SPARC DBMS framework. Inf. Syst. 3, 173–191 (1978)

van der Aalst, W.M.P., ter Hofstede, A.H.M., Kiepuszewski, B., Barros, A.P.: Work flow patterns. Distrib. Parallel Databases 14(3), 5–51 (2003)

Vanderfeesten, I., et al.: On a quest for good process models: the cross-connectivity metric. In: Bellahsene, Z., Leonard, M., (eds.) Advanced Information Systems Engineering, pp. 480–494. (2008)

Vanhatalo, J., Volzer, H., Leymann, F.: Faster and more focused control-flow analysis for business process models through sese decomposition. In 5th International Conference on Service-Oriented Computing. Lecture Notes in Computer Science, Vienna, Austria (2007)

Wand, Y., Weber, R.: On the ontological expressiveness of information systems analysis and design grammars. J. Inform. Syst. 3(4), 217–237 (1993)

Wand, Y., Weber, R.: Research commentary: Information systems and conceptual modeling—a research agenda. Inf. Syst. Res. 13(4), 363–376 (2002)

Weber, B., et al.: Refactoring large process model repositories. Comput. Ind. 62(5), 467–486 (2011)

Willoch, B.E.: Business Process Reengineering—En praktisk innføring og veiledning. Fagbokforlaget Vigmostad og Bjorke AS, Bergen (1994)

Chapter 3
SEQUAL Specialized for Business Process Models

Our main contribution in this chapter is a specialization of SEQUAL for business process models. In addition to specializing the existing SEQUAL framework, we have also extended it, taking into account aspects of other frameworks described in Chap. 2. As illustrated in Fig. 3.1, there are a number of specializations of SEQUAL. As with GoM, we have a first level that is meant to be relevant for all node-edge-oriented models (SEQUAL-GEN). A second level views a particular type of model (in this book and in this chapter in particular focusing on business process models). Finally, one can have specific guidelines on an even more detailed level, e.g., for business process modeling using BPMN. In real-world modeling activities, we find that all quality levels are important, but the *weight* on the different levels is different based on the different goals of modeling, as will be exemplified and discussed in more detail in Chap. 4.

In presenting the specialization of SEQUAL here, we will include not only aspects inherited from the general SEQUAL framework briefly described in Sect. 2. 2.1, but also aspects specific to business process modeling, based on aspects noted in Sect. 2.3 in particular. For some areas, such as empirical and syntactic quality, we will also illustrate with aspects specific to process modeling language, using BPMN as the main example.

The other current specializations, explaining the abbreviations used in Fig. 3.1, are the following:

- SRS—software requirements specifications (Krogstie 2001)
- DM—data models (Krogstie 2013a; Krogstie 2015)
- DQ—data quality (Krogstie 2013b; Krogstie 2015)
- IM—interactive models (Krogstie and Jørgensen 2002)
- EM—enterprise models/modeling languages (Krogstie 2012a)
- BPM—business process models (Krogstie 2012b)

© Springer International Publishing Switzerland 2016
J. Krogstie, *Quality in Business Process Modeling*,
DOI 10.1007/978-3-319-42512-2_3

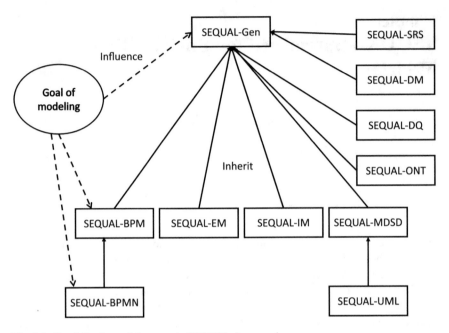

Fig. 3.1 Specializations of the generic SEQUAL framework

- ONT—ontologies (Hella and Krogstie 2010)
- MDSD—models used in model-driven software development
- UML—UML models (Krogstie 2003)
- MAPS—MAPQUAL (not in Fig. 3.1) (Nossum and Krogstie 2009)

The high-level SEQUAL framework has many similarities with Krogstie (2012a), but we have added reference models and reference languages/ontologies due to their importance in the business process modeling area when we present the updated SEQUAL framework below.

3.1 Sets in the Quality Framework

G, the Goals of the Modeling Task

What goals are meant to be fulfilled through the modeling? In simple cases, there is one well-defined goal, whereas oftentimes (views and versions of), the same model is used to achieve many, often partly contradictory goals. As discussed in Chap. 1, conceptual models are used for a number of different purposes, and as observed from practice, even within the same project, different stakeholders can have different goals, i.e., the process models can be multivalent. In Chap. 4, we will present more examples of this phenomenon linked to large case studies. The initial goals of modeling are normally defined before the modeling starts, but can often be changed and extended during a project, either in a planned or in an emergent fashion (Krogstie et al. 2006). Goals also include other organizational and economic issues, e.g., whether a requirements specification model will be constrained because one wants to produce a computerized information system based on the software requirements specifications under the given time and resource constraints.

A, the Audience

The audience is represented through the part of the model that they can access and indirectly through their explicit knowledge (K) and interpretation of the models (I). The audience is the union of the set of individual actors $A_1, \ldots, A_k$, the set of organizational actors (an organizational actor typically consists of a group of people with at least one shared goal) $A_{k+1}, \ldots, A_n$, and the set of technical actors $A_{n+1}, \ldots, A_m$ who need to relate to the model. The individuals who are members of the audience are called the *participants* of the modeling process. The participants P are a subset of the set of stakeholders S of the process of creating the model.

Those actively creating models (modelers) are a subset of the participants.

A technical actor is typically a computer program, e.g., a modeling tool, which must "understand" parts of the model at a certain level to automatically manipulate it to, e.g., perform code generation, model layout, or model analysis based on the models to which they have access.

The audience often changes during the process of developing and evolving the process model when people leave or enter the project or organization.

L, the Language Extension

The language extension is the set of all statements that are possible to make according to the vocabulary and syntax of the process modeling languages used. Several languages can be used in the same modeling effort, corresponding to the sets $L_1, \ldots, L_j$. One example is the different diagrams defined in BPMN. These languages can be interrelated (typically by sharing concepts across sublanguages). Sublanguages are related to the complete language by the limitations on the vocabulary, the set of allowed grammatical rules in the syntax of the overall language, or (typically) both. The statements in the language model of a formal or semiformal language L_i are denoted as $M(L_i)$. This model is often called the meta-model of the language, a term that is appropriate only in connection with work on repositories for process models. Another term that could be used for this is language model.

The languages used in a modeling effort are often predefined, but it is increasingly common that one creates specific modeling languages or extensions to existing languages, using a meta-modeling environment for the modeling effort, in which case the syntax and semantics of the languages must be intersubjectively agreed upon by the audience as part of the modeling. If one is using an existing language, the "correct" syntax and semantics of the language (to the extent that it is formally defined) can be regarded as predefined. One often chooses to apply only *parts* of the predefined process modeling languages for a given modeling effort and changes this subset during a project as appropriate (e.g., it is seldom that the whole of BPMN is used within one project (zur Mühlen and Recker 2008)), and as we will see in cases in the next chapter, companies often develop their own specific, reduced but also, in parts, extended versions of the standard process modeling languages.

M, the Externalized Model

This is the set of all statements in the explicitly represented model of part of the perceived reality expressed in a process modeling language. M_E is the set of explicit statements in a model, whereas M_I is the set of implicit statements, i.e., the statements not made but implied through the deduction rules of the modeling language. For example, in a process model, if activity A is before activity B and activity B is before activity C, then activity A is before activity C. A model written in language L_i is denoted as M_{L_i}. The meaning of M_{L_i} is established through the (intersubjectively) agreed-upon syntax and semantics of L_i. If the language has a formal operational or logical semantics, then the achievement of this agreement is easier to assure.

For each participant, the part of the externalized model that is considered relevant can be viewed as a projection of the total externalized model; hence, M can be divided into projections M^1, ..., M^k, corresponding to participants A_1, ..., A_k. Generally, these projections will not be disjoint, but the union of the projections should cover M. The actor should at least have access to what is relevant, as will be discussed as part of physical quality. M will clearly evolve during modeling as statements are inserted into and deleted from the model.

D, the Modeling Domain

The modeling domain is the set of all statements that can be made about the situation at hand. One can differentiate between domains along two orthogonal dimensions:

- Temporal: Is the model of a past, current (e.g., as-is), or future situation (e.g., to-be) as it is perceived by someone in the audience? The first two models are descriptive models, whereas the last type will typically be a prescriptive model, although it may also be of a future unwanted situation, as discussed in Chap. 1.
- Scope: Examples of different scopes are (a subset of) the physical world (a subset of) the social world, an organization, an information system, and a computerized information system (CIS).

The domains evolve during modeling, both through external changes outside the control of the modeling activity and through the deployment and activation of the model itself. Note that the precise delimitation of the scope often can be tricky. As discussed in Sect. 2.1.4, the scope might be blurred or hidden, and there might be disagreement among stakeholders for what is within scope. One can differentiate between the current domain D and a perceived optimal domain D^O (often represented by the ought-to-be model) that one attempts to achieve (e.g., through the information systems development).

K, the Relevant Explicit Knowledge of the Participants

The relevant explicit knowledge is the union of the set of statements, K_1, ..., K_k, one for each participant. K_i is all possible statements that would be correct and relevant for addressing the problem at hand according to the knowledge of the participant A_i. K_i is a subset of K^i, the explicit knowledge of the social actor A_i that can be externalized. M_i is an externalization of K_i and is a model made based on the knowledge of the individual or organizational actor. Even if the internal reality of each individual will always differ, the internal reality that can be made explicit (externalized) concerning a constrained area may be equal for all practical purposes, especially within well-defined groups of participants (Gjersvik 1993; Orlikowski and Gash 1994). Thus, it can be meaningful to also speak in terms of the explicit knowledge of an organizational actor. $M_i \backslash M^i = \varnothing$, whereas the opposite may not be true, i.e., more of the total externalized model than the part that is an externalization of parts of an actor's internal reality is potentially relevant for this actor. K will and is often expected to change during modeling to achieve both personal and organizational learning. At a given point, the knowledge of different members of the audience on the domain may be different and even inconsistent.

I, the Social Actor Interpretation

The social audience interpretation is the set of all statements that the social audience perceives that an externalized model consists of. Precisely similar to the externalized model itself, its interpretation can be projected into I_1, ..., I_n, denoting the statements in the externalized model that are perceived by each social actor.

T, the Technical Actor Interpretation

Similar to the above, I_{n+1}, ..., I_m denote the statements in the conceptual model as they are interpreted by each individual technical actor in the audience.

M (D^0) Reference models

As discussed earlier in Chap. 2, reference process models and reference process modeling languages (ontologies) have received a considerable interest in this field. Thus, in the description of the quality of business process modeling, we also include these in the main framework. A reference model can be viewed as a model of the same (or at least an overlapping) part of the domain that is of relevance in the modeling initiative. Contrary to the model, which is made to support a specific goal in an organizational setting, the reference model can be used to depict a generic solution in a certain area not being limited by the concrete situation in the organization.

O, Reference Modeling Languages—Ontologies

Similarly, we have reference modeling languages (often termed ontologies) that serve a similar role in the modeling language, where one often wants the language used to be compatible to this language, even if the organizational reality and goals often mandate the use of specialized modeling languages rather than the use of standard notations out of the box.

The overall framework is depicted in Fig. 3.2, with only some minor differences at this level from the general framework presented in Fig. 2.2. Throughout this

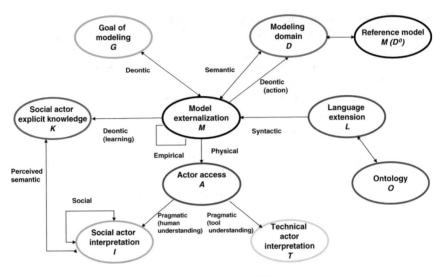

Fig. 3.2 SEQUAL specialized for business process modeling

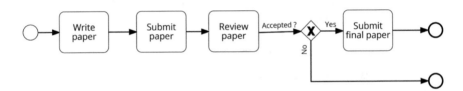

Fig. 3.3 Simple BPMN model from the conference organizing domain

chapter, we will use part of a BPMN model from the domain of conference organizing, as depicted in Fig. 3.3, to illustrate the different types of model quality. The modeling goal in this limited case is to support communication among authors, conference organizers, and reviewers with respect to the flow of a research paper review. This figure (also used in Chap. 1) states that, first, a paper is written. Then, it is submitted for review, is reviewed, and then is accepted or not. If the paper is accepted, then a final version of the paper must be written and submitted.

In the next 7 sections, we present each of the seven core quality levels illustrated by relationships between the model and the other sets in Fig. 3.2. For each quality level, there are one or more quality characteristics. We describe the different means that can be beneficially used to reach these goals. The means can be of different types:

- Model properties, which are the subcharacteristics of the high-level goal.
- Beneficial existing qualities, i.e., other quality levels that one would normally attempt to address before addressing the quality at the given level. This points to guidelines for a modeling methodology. Modeling methodology to achieve high-quality models is discussed more in Chap. 5.

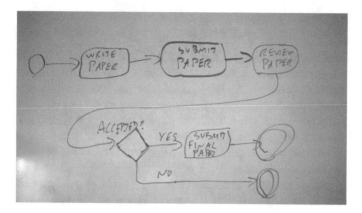

Fig. 3.4 Model with limited physical quality

- Language properties, which are the characteristics of the modeling language being used.
- Modeling methods and techniques.
- Modeling tool functionality (often in combination with a modeling technique, but some modeling techniques are not dependent on tool support).

Metrics for these quality characteristics and subcharacteristics are described. The structure follows the same structure as in the description of the generic SEQUAL framework in Krogstie (2012a), and here, we also include generic aspects. In addition, we specialize the treatment to focus on business process models (and, in some cases, specific modeling notations such as BPMN), including material described in Sect. 2.3.

3.2   The Physical Quality of Business Process Models

Although information systems models are not typical of the physical (three-dimensional, tactile) type, any model must be represented physically somehow, e.g., on disk, on paper, or on a blackboard. An early version of the model in Fig. 3.3 is depicted in Fig. 3.4.

It is also represented in a more formal form on paper as in Fig. 3.3 (and naturally in the electronic source of the book, albeit in a version that cannot be edited for anyone). Originally, this model was made in the Signavio modeling tool; thus, I have access to also update this model (and can make it available to other users of Signavio for comments and additional work if interesting). The basic quality features on the physical level are that the externalized model is persistent, current, and available, enabling the audience to make sense of it (and for modelers to change it when necessary). Making sense of the model is not the same as the participants actually internalizing the model; at the physical level, we only look at how it is made available for possible interpretation by different actors. Some aspects of this are as follows:

- Persistence: How persistent is the model and how protected is it against loss or damage? The method of storing the model should be efficient, i.e., not use more space than is necessary. A simple metric for persistence is the proportion of model statements that are electronically stored in a model repository. This aspect is particularly relevant when business process modeling is performed as part of enterprise modeling, where a large portion of the model statements are elicited through informal modeling techniques (e.g., participatory techniques using wall charts as discussed in more detail in Sect. 5.4), which needs to be transferred into the model repository at a later stage to be made generally available.
- Currency: How long ago was the model statements included in the model (assuming that the statements were current when entered). Depending on the type of model, the age of the model statements is of differing levels of importance. If the model is to be of a past situation, it needed only to be current at the time of modeling. For an as-is model, when the domain is changing rapidly (i.e., has high volatility), the currency of the stored model is of greater importance for the model to have appropriate timeliness. This aspect is particularly important in models on the instance level (for instance, event data in a process support environment).
  Metrics on currency can easily be devised and calculated if the model repository supports the time-stamping of the statements. This area will relate to semantic quality, not only in relation to the time a model statement was entered, but also in relation to the last time the model statement was validated.
- Availability: How available is the model to the audience? Clearly, this aspect is dependent on whether the model is externalized and made persistent in the first place. Availability also depends on distributability, especially when members of the audience are geographically dispersed. A model that is in an electronically distributable format will be more easily distributed than a model that must be printed on paper (or is only on paper in the first place). What exactly is distributed may also matter, e.g., the model in an editable form or merely in an output format or a format where one can add annotations but one cannot change the actual model. The entire model should be available to at least someone in the audience, i.e., $A = M$. Security aspects also come into play here, since not all statements should necessarily be available to anyone.

A metric for availability is the proportion of the model statements relevant for a member of the audience that is available for that audience member. In connection with currency and availability, the term "timeliness" is often used; i.e., the model is not only current but also available in time for events that correspond to its usage, which relates directly to the goal of modeling. Thus, timeliness is established as a deontic goal (see Sect. 3.8).

Many of the modeling techniques and tool functionalities in connection with physical quality are based on traditional database functionality, using a model repository solution for the internal representation of the model. In addition, it is regarded as necessary for advanced tools for business process modeling (Wesenberg 2011) to include functionalities such as version control and configuration management, in addition to advanced concurrency control mechanisms that are not normally found in conventional DBMSs.

A more detailed list of general modeling tool mechanisms, most of them concerning availability and support with regard to meta-model evolution, is presented in Krogstie (2012a). Although most of these are also relevant for business process model repositories, we have not included this here.

3.3 The Empirical Quality of Business Process Models

As described briefly in Chap. 1, empirical quality addresses the variety of elements distinguished, the error frequencies when being written or read, coding (including the shapes of boxes), and ergonomics for both documentation and models as presented in modeling tools. The term is based on that this layer collects the traits of visual or textual communication, which has empirically been shown (e.g., through work in cognitive psychology) to result in models that are easier to understand in general.

Changes to improve the empirical quality of a model do not change the statements that are included in the model; thus, we have no set-theoretic definition of this quality characteristic.

For longer descriptions of concepts and informal textual models, several means for text readability have been devised, such as the different types of readability indices. This issue is discussed generically in (Krogstie 2012a). A specific example of this issue is presented in Sect. 4.2 related to one of the case studies.

For computer output specifically, many of the principles and tools used for improving human–computer interfaces are relevant at the empirical level (see, e.g., Shneiderman et al. (2009)). For the visual presentation of process models, one can also base the guidelines on work, e.g., in cognitive psychology and cartography, based on the fact that the models are meant to be useful in connection with *communication* between people. Going back to Shannon and Weaver (1963), communication entails both encoding by the sender and decoding by the receiver. Encoding has been discussed in detail, e.g., in the work of Bertin (1983). According to Bertin (1983), there are 4 different effects of encoding:

1. Association: The marks can be perceived as similar.
2. Selection: The marks can be perceived as different.
3. Order: The marks can be perceived as ordered.
4. Quantity: The marks can be perceived as proportional.

Eight different variables for conveying one or more of these meanings in a model are as follows:

- Planar variables: the horizontal position and the vertical position.
- Retinal variables: shape (association and selection), size (selection, order, and quantity), color (association and selection), brightness (value) (selection and order), orientation (association), and texture (association, selection, and order).

Rules for color usage are also useful in connection with evaluating diagrammatical models (if different colors are used). Approximately 10 % of the male population and 1 % of the female population suffer from some form of color vision deficiency (Ware et al. 2000); thus, many modeling notations (e.g., UML) explicitly avoid the use of colors as a part of the notation for conveying meaning. However, many modeling tools may give the modeler freedom to assign any color to the background, symbols, and labels and to the icon/shape used to represent the concept. Color is an important differentiator in other visual representations that is meant to be widely used (e.g., maps, see Bertin (1983)). Shneiderman et al. (2009) has listed a number of guidelines for the usage of color in visual displays in general.

- Use color conservatively.
- Limit the number of colors used. Many design guidelines suggest limiting the number of colors in a display to four, with a maximum limit of seven colors. According to the opponent process theory (Ware et al. 2000), there are six elementary colors, and these colors are arranged perceptually as opponent pairs along three axes: black-white, red-green, and yellow-blue.
- Red attracts the eye more than other colors.
- Ensure that the use of colors supports the task, i.e., makes useful differentiations between different parts of the model.
- Have color coding appear with minimal user effort.
- Place the application of color coding under (guided) user control.
- Use color to help in formatting.
- Be consistent in color coding.
- Be aware of common expectations about color codes. This issue can be dependent on the local culture.
- Be aware of problems with color pairings. If saturated (pure) red and blue appear on a display simultaneously, it may be difficult for users to absorb the information. Similarly, other combinations will appear difficult, such as yellow on purple and magenta on green. Too little contrast is also a problem (yellow letters on a white background or brown letters on a black background). Note that this phenomenon may be different on different screens and projectors.
- Use color changes to indicate status changes.
- Use color in graphic displays to enable greater information density.
- When using color coding, take into account that the model may need to be presented or distributed in gray scale (e.g., when printed). Although there are techniques to also ensure differentiation when transferring to a black and white printout, normal printers do not necessarily use the best algorithms to do so (Alsam 2009).

Overall, it may be better to have the use of colors under the control of the modeling language design rather than allowing it to be up to the individual modeler. The same is partly the case for other usages of emphasis. The use of emphasis can also be in accordance with the relative importance of the statements in a given model. Factors that have an important impact on visual emphasis are as follows:

- Size (the big is more easily noticed than the small).
- Solidity (e.g., **bold** letters vs. ordinary letters, full lines vs. dotted lines, thick lines vs. thin lines, and filled boxes vs. non-filled boxes).
- Difference from the ordinary pattern (e.g., *slanted* letters will attract attention among a large number of ordinary letters).
- Foreground/background differences (if the background is white, things will be more easily noticed the darker they are).
- Change (blinking or moving symbols attract attention).
- Position (when looking at a diagram, people tend to start at its middle).
- Connectivity (objects that connect to many others (having a high degree) will attract more attention than objects with few connections).

For diagrammatical models (diagrams), layout modification is a meaning-preserving transformation that can improve the comprehensibility of a model. A layout modification is a spatially different arrangement of the elements in the diagrammatical representation of the model.

Graph aesthetics has a long tradition, and general lists of guidelines for graph aesthetics are presented in Battista et al. (1994), Tamassia et al. (1988). These guidelines, summarized below, can act as a starting point for automatic layout modification techniques and metrics to be calculated to support the manual improvement of the model layout. Note that a model that is optimal according to one of these aesthetics is not necessarily optimal for another.

- ANGLE: Angles between edges going out from the same node should not be too small.
- AREA: Minimize the area occupied by the drawing.
- BALAN: Balance the diagram with respect to the axis.
- BENDS: Minimize the number of bends along the edges.
- CONVEX: Maximize the number of faces drawn as convex polygons.
- CROSS: Minimize the number of crossings between the edges.
- DEGREE: Place nodes with high degree in the center of the drawing.
- DIM: Minimize differences among nodes' dimensions (given nodes of the same type).
- LENGTH: Minimize the global length of the edges.
- MAXCON: Minimize the length of the longest edge.
- SYMM: Have symmetry of sons in hierarchies.
- UNIDEN: Have a uniform density of the nodes in the drawing.
- VERT: Have verticality of hierarchical structures. The implication is that in a tree/hierarchy, nodes at the same level in the tree are placed along a horizontal line with a minimum distance between them.

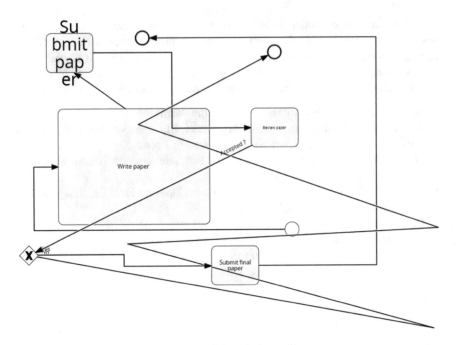

Fig. 3.5 Example of a model with poor model aesthetics

These guidelines overlap the guidelines for process model presentation described in Sect. 2.3.4. In addition, a few BPMN/process modeling-specific guidelines are included there:

- Consider the use of partitions, e.g., pools and swimlanes.
- Specify task types, especially user (human task) and service (automated task) tasks.

A number of metrics can be produced relatively easily based on these guidelines, e.g., the number of crossing edges divided by the total number of edges in a model or compared with the minimum possible number of crossings, provided that one does not duplicate symbols. Similar metrics can be devised for the other aesthetics and be used during modeling to assess the potential for improving empirical quality. Based on such metrics, one could easily assess that the quality of Fig. 3.5 can be argued to be less than that of Fig. 3.3, although it contains the same statements. In particular, we can observe a worsening of the aspects in relation to the ANGLE, AREA, BALAN, CROSS, DEGREE, DIM, LENGTH, MAXCON, SYMM, UNIDEN, and VERT guidelines.

However, we should remember that aesthetics is a subjective issue; thus, familiarity with a diagram is oftentimes just as important for comprehension. As noted by Petre (1995), one of the main advantages of diagrammatic modeling languages appears to be the possibility of using the so-called secondary notation, i.e., the use of layout and perceptual cues to improve the comprehension of the model. Thus, one

Table 3.1 A taxonomy of constraints for graph layouts

Aspects	Explanation
CENTRE	Placing a set of given nodes in the center of the drawing
DIMENSION	Assigning the dimensions of symbols
EXTERNAL	Placing specified nodes on the external boundary of the drawing
NEIGH	Placing a group of nodes close together
SHAPE	Drawing a subgraph of selected nodes with a predefined shape
STREAM	Placing a sequences of nodes along a straight line (a specialization of SHAPE)

oftentimes needs to constrain automatic layout modifications. Although it would be more accurate to place such constraints as a mean for pragmatic quality (see below), we include them here because they are used in techniques for automatic graph layout that it is natural to cover as part of empirical quality. A list of constraints used in connection with automatic graph layout is presented in Table 3.1. Additionally, manual diagram layout mechanisms should be available in a modeling tool to quickly make an existing model visually pleasing (including horizontal and vertical alignments, minimizing the number of alignment points, and equal spacing when selecting more than 2 nodes). Tool functionality to make the size and font size of selected elements in the model equal is also useful.

Clearly, it should be easy to retain the aesthetically pleasing diagram when we have to update the model at a later point in time. Doing so includes the possibility of selecting and moving a group of nodes as one, the moving of complete subtrees as one in a hierarchical model, rerouting connections when changing the relative position of two interconnected nodes, and tool functionality, such as snap to grid. In advanced modeling tools, one finds all of these mechanisms. In tools such as Troux Architect, one can also define layout strategies so that one automatically keeps, e.g., a collection of elements in a matrix format when adding new elements to the model.

Finally, there are structures that one has found beneficial in general (e.g., limiting the number of tasks on a decomposition level in a DFD).

A number of such guidelines were presented for BPMN models in Sect. 2.3.4, in relation to both the number of elements and the composition of the elements. Most of these are style guidelines (Silver 2012), whereas some of these point to potential violations of the syntax rules of BPMN and thus are more correctly positioned as part of syntactic quality. To provide a complete overview of the quality of business process models in this chapter, we thus repeat here those aspects relevant for process modeling.

Number of elements

1. The model contains a high number of elements (i.e., gateways, activities, and events) → Decompose models with more than 31 elements.

2. The model contains duplicate elements (e.g., identical start events, identical end events, and identical activities) or fragments, capturing the same control flow logic → Avoid duplicate elements and fragments in the process models.
3. Models contain unnecessary elements (e.g., one empty arc between an AND split and an AND join) → Avoid unnecessary elements.
4. A high number of events → Avoid models with more than 7 events.
5. The model contains multiple start/end events → Use no more than two start/end events in the top process level, use one start event in the subprocesses, and use two end events to distinguish success and fail states in subprocesses.
6. Do not omit start and end events → Have at least one start and one end event.
7. A high number of intermediate events → Avoid high numbers of intermediate events in the process model.
8. The model contains too many arcs → Avoid models with more than 34 arcs.
9. The model contains too many gateways → Avoid models with more than 12 gateways.
10. A high number of activities → Minimize the number of activities.
11. A high number of routing paths per gateway → Use no more than 3 routing paths per gateway.
12. Split/join gateways have more than one incoming and outgoing flows (i.e., two behaviors in the same gateway) → Do not combine multiple inputs and multiple outputs in the same gateway.
13. There are too many outgoing sequence flows from an event → Do not use more than 4 outgoing sequence flows from events.

Composition of components

1 The model has deeply nested structured blocks → Avoid deeply nested structured blocks.
2 The model contains multiple cycles → Avoid cycles in the process models if possible, especially unstructured cycles (i.e., cycles with multiple exit points).
3 Badly formed cycles: The backward connection of a loop construct does not begin in an XOR split or does not lead back to an XOR join → When modeling cycles, the backward connection should begin in an XOR split and lead back to an XOR join.
4 Multiple exit points per cycle → Avoid multiple exit points per cycle.
5 A high level of parallelism (the sum of the output degrees of AND and XOR gateways should be 8 at most) → Avoid a high level of parallelism in the process models.
6 Bad parallelism: Parallel paths do not reach end events or do not synchronize → Each parallel path must reach an end event or must be synchronized.
7 A high level of unstructuredness → Every split gateway should match a respective join gateway of the same type.
8 The model contains a long path from the start node to the end node → Keep the path from a start node to the end node as short as possible.

9 High gateway diversity → Minimize gateway diversity (i.e., avoid having a mix of "XOR," "OR," "AND," and complex gateways in the same model.
10 The existence of inclusive OR gateways in the process models → Avoid the use of inclusive OR gateways.
11 High complexity in the model → Select the less complex alternative when modeling.
12 The model lacks modularity → There should be no more than 31 nodes in a diagram (cf. guideline 1) and no less than 5 activities in a subprocess.

Techniques to keep the model in an adequate structure as the model develops are called model refactoring. In programming, refactoring is "the process of changing a software system in such a way that it does not alter the external behavior of the code yet improves the internal structure" (Fowler and Beck 1999). Similar information-preserving model transformations can be defined for process models. Refactoring techniques are oftentimes specific to a modeling perspective or modeling language (as the example with the number of tasks on a given decomposition level above for functional models).

Refactoring will often support expressive economy and, as a result, indirectly improve many of the graph layout metrics. Many of the above guidelines could act as a basis for suggestions for refactoring. A comprehensive overview of model refactoring strategies is found in Conesa et al. (2011).

3.4 Syntactic Quality of Business Process Models

Syntactic quality is the correspondence between the model M and the language extension L of the language in which the model is written. Referring to the discussion on meta-levels in Sect. 1.4.1, L is constrained by a model on a higher meta-level (the language model).

There is only one syntactic quality characteristic, **syntactical correctness**, which means that all of the statements in the model are according to the syntax and vocabulary of the language, i.e.,

$$M_E \backslash L = \varnothing,$$

which is illustrated in Fig. 3.6.

There are two types of syntax errors:

- **Syntactic invalidity**, in which words or graphemes that are not part of the language are used. An example of syntactic invalidity is given in Fig. 3.7, where an actor symbol (triangle with the label JK) that is not part of the chosen language (BPMN) is used.
- **Syntactic incompleteness**, in which the model lacks constructs or information to obey the language's grammar. An example of syntactic incompleteness is given in Fig. 3.8, where the graph is not connected.

Fig. 3.6 Illustration of a
model with syntactic errors

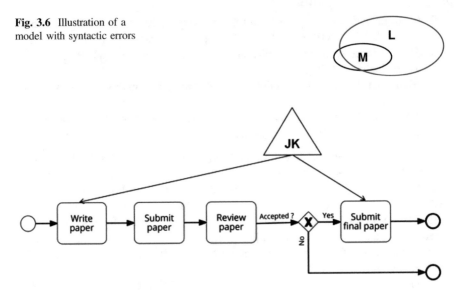

Fig. 3.7 Example of syntactic invalidity

Fig. 3.8 Example of syntactic incompleteness

The degree of syntactic quality can be measured as one minus the rate of erroneous statements, i.e.,

$$\text{Syntactic quality} = 1 - (\#M_E \backslash L + M_{\text{missing}})/\#M_E,$$

where M_{missing} is the number of statements that would be necessary to make the model syntactically complete (in Fig. 3.8 $M_{\text{missing}} = 2$).

To ensure the syntactic quality of the model, *syntax checks* should be provided as an integral part of the modeling support of a modeling tool, supported in either the modeling tools or the modeling techniques applied. The checks may be performed along two main directions:

- Error prevention: This type of check adapts the principles of *syntax-directed editors*. Thus, only the modeling constructs defined in the language's vocabulary are available through the modeling tool. This includes having modeling palettes (the concepts available to choose for modeling) that are limited to the allowed concepts of the language or sublanguage used in the given diagram or decomposition and limitations on the types of relationships that can be established between two or more concepts. Additionally, when a modeler violates a syntax rule of the language, the modeling session should be temporarily interrupted to restore a legal model. This type of check is controlled by the tool.

- Error detection: During a modeling session, some syntactical errors, particularly errors related to *syntactic incompleteness*, should be allowed on a temporary basis. For instance, although BPMN requires that all activities must eventually be linked to a sequence flow, it is difficult and/or inconvenient to draw an activity and a flow simultaneously. In this case, syntactical completeness must be checked at the user's request. One may also imagine cases where one wants to allow syntactic invalidity for a moment to be able to capture insights during a modeling session that are at odds with the chosen language. An example of this situation will be presented in the next chapter. Thus, in contrast to implicit checks, where the tool "forces" the user to follow the language syntax, explicit checks can only detect and report on existing errors. The user has to make the corrections.

By distinguishing between these types of syntax checks, *modeling freedom* can be encouraged. Throughout the modeling process, the tool will accept some syntactical errors, but these can be detected at the user's request. The developer is free to construct the model to achieve semantic and pragmatic quality, as discussed below, unless the syntax rules are directly violated. Although error-free models are the ultimate goal of model quality assurance, it can be advantageous to have some errors early in model development. Placing too much focus on syntactic quality at an early stage may hamper the creativity of the modeling process. This idea is summed up in what was originally termed "the Heisenberg Uncertainty Principle of CASE" (Hewett and Durham 1989): "High levels of inconsistency and incompleteness are permissible if they are confined to a small region of space and time."

A third syntactic means is error correction. Error correction, i.e., replacing a detected error with a correct statement, is more difficult to automate. When implemented, it typically works as a typical spell-checker found in a word processor, giving suggestions for the correct modeling structure or a term found in some controlled vocabulary or ontology as discussed, e.g., in Lin et al. (2006), but leaving it up to the modeler to perform the actual change.

All of the syntactic means are only meaningful to provide if the languages used have a well-defined syntax. There are several ways to describe the syntax of languages for conceptual modeling, as described, e.g., in Krogstie (2012a), and we refer to this for further details.

A model consists of both graphics and text. Although the diagrammatical aspects are most focused in connection with conceptual models, there are also relevant aspects linked to the textual parts of the models, which we will return to in one of the cases reported in Chap. 4. The text can be in the form of labels (naming the concepts) and longer descriptions. With respect to labels, for a long period of time, there have existed simple guidelines for the labeling of particular types of concepts.

For example, in process modeling (returning to the definition of DFDs (see Gane and Sarson (1979))), there is the guideline that one should name a process in an "active verb, noun" manner (i.e., "register participant"). One reason for doing so is, clearly, to ensure that the process is actually named as a process (and not as an organizational unit, for instance). As reported in Mendling and Recker (2008), this practice also has a positive effect on the comprehension of the model. In addition, Hawryszkiewycz (2001) provides more detailed guidelines for naming processes, data stores, and flows in DFDs. Detailed metrics for labeling are very much dependent on the type of modeling language used (e.g., process modeling) and, in certain cases, for concrete modeling languages (e.g., DFD or BPMN). A general metric that can be specialized is the proportion of concepts that are labeled in a manner that does not conform to the guidelines for the labeling of the concrete concept. Oftentimes, simple linguistic techniques can be utilized to determine these labels automatically, although it is normally not supported in standard modeling tools. Labeling guidelines for BPMN models are found in Sect. 2.3.4.2:

- Labels do not follow the verb–object style.
- Labels are too long.
- The pools label is different from the process name.
- Timer events are not labeled with the duration or date/time parameter.
- Gateways are not labeled.
- A black box pool is not labeled with the participant's name.
- There are constructions other than send/receive task types that are labeled as send or receive.

Figure 3.9 provides an example of poor labeling of our standard example model.
An example of more concrete syntax rules for a specific process model notation is found in Sect. 4.2.

3.5 Semantic and Perceived Semantic Quality of Business Process Models

Semantic quality was originally defined as the correspondence between the model and the modeling domain (Lindland et al. 1994).

The framework contains two primary semantic quality characteristics: validity and completeness.

- Validity means that all of the statements made in the model are regarded as correct and relevant for the problem, i.e.,

$$M \backslash D = \varnothing$$

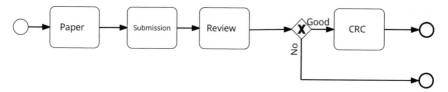

Fig. 3.9 Example of poor labeling

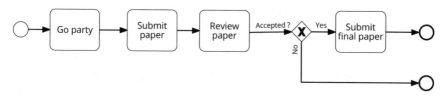

Fig. 3.10 Example of a model with semantic invalidity

A definition for the degree of validity could be:

$$\text{validity} = 1 - (\#(M_E \backslash D))/\#M_E$$

However, how useful such a metric may be can be called into question because it cannot typically be measured automatically due to the intractability of the domain. An example of invalidity is given in Fig. 3.10 because we believe that most persons would agree that the first task (Go party) is invalid (in the sense that it is not a relevant task to perform in connection with developing a scientific paper).

- Completeness means that the model contains all of the statements that would be correct and relevant about the domain, i.e.,

$$D \backslash M = \varnothing$$

Similarly, a definition for the degree of completeness could be:

$$\text{completeness} = 1 - (\#(D \backslash M))/\#D$$

Completeness would only be interesting in well-defined and limited domains, for instance temporarily deciding on a model of a new CIS. Then, one would like to view all of the statements in the model as also being part of the implemented CIS. However, *D* is not completely represented in the previous model in this case; thus, validity here is also more relevant. To summarize, a useful model will most likely still be a subset of the domain, as illustrated in Fig. 3.11. An important question, often answered by clarifying the goal of the modeling and the other modeling constraints as we discuss as part of deontic quality, asks what parts of the domain to leave out to avoid analysis paralysis. This issue is further discussed below under deontic quality.

Fig. 3.11 Illustration of the
validity of a model

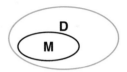

An example of incompleteness can be the original as shown in Fig. 3.3, which is missing, e.g., an indication of who is performing the different tasks.

The primary goal of semantic quality is a correspondence between the externalized model and the domain, but this correspondence can be neither established nor checked directly: To build the model, one must go through the participants' knowledge (**K**) regarding the domain, and to check the model, one must compare this knowledge with the participants' interpretation (**I**) of the externalized model. Hence, what we observe at quality control is not the objective semantic quality of the model but what we term *perceived semantic quality* based on comparisons of the current knowledge with the current interpretation of the model.

Perceived validity and completeness, related to the individual performing validation, can be expressed as follows:

- *Perceived validity* of the model externalization: $I_i \backslash K_i = \emptyset$
- *Perceived completeness* of the model externalization: $K_i \backslash I_i = \emptyset$

These error classes are illustrated in Fig. 3.12. The metrics for the degree of perceived validity and completeness can be defined by means of the cardinalities in the same way as for semantic quality. Thus, we can define perceived validity in the following manner:

$$\text{Perceived validity} = 1 - (\#(I_i \backslash K_i))/\#I_i$$

That is, it is the number of invalid statements interpreted, divided by the total number of statements interpreted by the actor A_i, and similarly, one can establish a sum over all of the participants to obtain an overall number. An example of a model with a perceived invalid statement is the example in Fig. 3.10, where I (the author of this book playing the role of the actor A_i), in the subjective role of an end user, may claim that the "Go party" task is not part of the paper-writing process.

Perceived completeness can be defined in the following manner:

$$\text{Perceived completeness} = 1 - (\#(K_i \backslash I_i))/\#K_i$$

That is, it is the number of statements regarded to be relevant but not seen in the model divided by the total number of relevant knowledge statements known by the actor A_i, and similarly, a sum over all of the participants can be established to obtain an overall number. As in semantic quality, I (in the subjective role of an end user of a conference system) miss a number of tasks (such as "write paper" in Fig. 3.10).

Atomic modeling activities for establishing higher semantic quality are statement insertion and deletion. Conceptually, an update can be viewed as a deletion

Fig. 3.12 Illustration of the
concepts of perceived validity
and perceived completeness

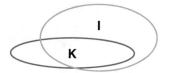

followed by an insertion. Statement insertions and deletions can also clearly result in lower semantic quality. Statement insertion and deletion can generally be viewed as meaning-updating transformations, which can be performed either manually or automatically.

Of specific importance is *model reuse* (which is a specific type of statement insertion), particularly the reuse of reference models (see Sect. 2.3.5). Either it can be the reuse of a previous model of a similar domain (e.g., a reference process model of the domain), or it may be a translation of a previous baseline model.

Consistency checking is another activity on the semantic level. Note that consistency can be argued to be subsumed by the combination of validity and completeness because an inconsistency must be caused by at least one invalid statement or the lack of a statement to sort out the inconsistency. To be able to perform consistency checking, the model must be made in a formal, preferably logical, language, and to enable and assess the impact of updates, the model should be modifiable. Properties such as structure, the locality of changes, and control over redundancy are included. Consistency checking can be viewed as one of the several types of model testing that are beneficial at this level. For process models, in particular, to ensure the possibility of consistency checking, two of the guidelines in 7PMG described in Sect. 2.3.3 are specifically important

- G3: Use one start event and one end event.
- G5: Avoid OR routing elements.

We noted that these were given low priority in the 7PMG report. However, if consistency and formal analysis (or the simulation vs. analysis of throughput (Kuntz et al. 1998)) are important, then one may want to prioritize these higher. There are two main approaches for formal specifications as the basis for consistency verification:

1. The algebraic specification approach specifies a system as a set of abstract data types (ADTs). The theory of an ADT consists of a set of symbols (sorts and operators, the signature) and a collection of formulae (the axioms of the theory); the interpretation of the theory is a multisorted algebra. The specification is a set of theories and the relationships among them.
2. On the other hand, the logical theory approach treats the complete model (including both structural and behavioral parts) as a logical theory.

Of particular interest in models with decomposition possibilities as is found in most process modeling languages is testing for constructivity. The notion of constructivity was introduced into the field of information systems by Langefors

(1973). It entails that one can derive the properties of a system based on the properties of the subsystem and check whether the derived properties are the same as those previously specified for the system (if any). Thus, constructivity is necessary when we want to check the consistency of a hierarchical model, i.e., to check whether decompositions are correct. Krogstie and Sølvberg (2003) provide an in-depth description of techniques for constructivity checking, which, incidentally, also depend on G5 (avoiding OR gates).

A wide range of conceptual modeling techniques begin by verbalizing cases. The verbalizations resulting from this step are then used for the development of the first version of the model. A technique for the further elaboration of the model is the use of driving questions based on the already existing model as used, e.g., in Tempora (Wangler et al. 1993) and 4EM (Sandkuhl et al. 2014). Driving questions can be both intralanguage and interlanguage. A simple example of an interlanguage driving question is ensuring that what is depicted in a store in a dataflow diagram is also found in the accompanying data model. More concrete guidelines for this type of technique will be linked to particular modeling languages and the combination of modeling languages.

In the area of semantic quality, general automated tools are difficult to develop for the simple reason that the domain and audience are beyond automatic manipulation as discussed above. The means of achieving a high perceived validity and completeness are similar to those for traditional validity and completeness, with the addition of participant training (in the modeling language and the domain). As we understand it, the actual checking of perceived semantic quality involves the view of the participants and cannot be totally automated, which is also why we place semantic quality into the social and not the technical realm in the discussion in Sect. 1.4.

By using a formal language, one can in a sense translate some semantic problems into syntactic problems, but doing so sets additional requirements to the domain appropriateness of the language used. In many cases, the modeling language chosen is not appropriate for representing the knowledge on the domain, thus making it very difficult to achieve semantic completeness. One important activity for addressing this issue is the adaptation of the meta-model of the modeling language used to suit the domain, not only by adding concepts but also by removing concepts (temporarily) from the language if they are not relevant for the modeling of the particular domain. This activity is treated in more detail in the case studies presented in Chap. 4. Not only domain appropriateness, modeler appropriateness, participant appropriateness, and organizational appropriateness are relevant dimensions in connection with this type of language development, but also comprehensibility appropriateness, tool appropriateness, and ontological appropriateness come into play as we will see in the cases.

When working on process improvements, one compares to an improved domain; thus, in relation to the validity of the model, one can devise a number of guidelines, as described in Sect. 2.3.1. We will not repeat all of these here but note only that the different guidelines/heuristics focus on improving some of the characteristics of the process outcome. Which characteristic(s) to optimize is something that is treated at the level of deontic quality, underlining the important ways in which deontic quality (the goals of modeling) directly influences the semantic quality measures.

3.6   Pragmatic Quality of Business Process Models

As we define it, pragmatic quality concerns the comprehension of the model by participants. Two aspects can be distinguished:

- The interpretation of the model by human stakeholders is correct in relation to what is meant to be expressed in the model. Note that a model can be said to formally mean anything only if the syntax and semantics of the language used are intersubjectively agreed upon and are at least semiformal, but preferably formal (with an operational semantics); thus, one can trace or execute the model and experience the dynamic behavior of the process model. In addition, it will often be useful to have different metadata of the process models represented (e.g., who has made the model and when it was made). In particular, it can be useful to have the *intention* of making the model explicitly represented (because a model created to achieve one goal oftentimes may have little value in achieving a different goal). This issue is also important to take into account model reuse (e.g., of reference models), as described briefly in Sect. 3.5 on semantic quality.
- The tool interpretation is correct in relation to what is meant to be expressed in the model, making it possible to manipulate the model with tools, e.g., for code generation or process simulation.

Starting with the human comprehension component, pragmatic quality on this level is the correspondence between the process model and the audience's interpretation of it. Not even the most comprehensive model would be of any use if no one was able to understand it. Moreover, not only that the process model has been understood but also *who* has understood (the relevant parts of) it are important.

Individual comprehension is defined to mean that the individual actor A_i understands the part of the model available to that actor, i.e., $I_i = A^i$.

The corresponding error class is *erroneous comprehension*, meaning that the above formula does not hold. As illustrated in Fig. 3.13, it actually covers two aspects:

- Part of the model is not understood.
- The model is interpreted to contain statements that are not there.

It is important to observe that the pragmatic goal is stated as *comprehension*, i.e., that the model has been understood, not as *comprehensibility*, i.e., the model's ability to be understood (which is what we treat under empirical quality in Sect. 3.3). There are several reasons for doing so. First, the ultimate goal is that the

Fig. 3.13 Illustration of the
issues in pragmatic quality

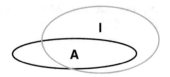

process model is understood, not that it is understandable per se, although this characteristic can be an important *means* of achieving comprehension. Moreover, comprehension is very dependent on the process by which the process model is developed, the manner by which the participants communicate with each other and the various types of tool support.

From the technical actors' perspective, that a model is understood means that all of the statements that are relevant to the technical actors to be able to perform, e.g., code generation or simulation, are comprehended by the relevant technical actors (modeling or development tools). In this sense, formality can be viewed as being a pragmatic means, and the formal syntax and formal (operational) semantics of the modeling language are the means of achieving pragmatic quality. This aspect illustrates that pragmatic quality is dependent on the different actors involved. This issue also applies to social actors. Whereas some individuals are familiar with formal languages from the outset and a formal model will also be best for them for comprehension, other people will find a mix of formal and informal statements to be more comprehensive, even if the set of statements in the complete model is redundant. Another important aspect is that familiarity with the domain will make a model of the domain easier to understand even if it is less complete than what is needed for a novice in the domain.

A process model can be difficult to comprehend due to the formality or unfamiliarity of the modeling language used, the complexity or size of the model, or the effort needed to deduce its important properties. A process modeling environment may make use of certain techniques to enhance user comprehension. Examining the linguistic aspects of process modeling, we can describe such strategies along the following four dimensions:

- *Language perception* concerns the user's ability to understand the concepts of the process modeling language.
- *Content relevance* indicates the possibilities of distinguishing between irrelevant and relevant model properties so that at any point in time, one is able to focus on only the relevant parts based on previous domain knowledge.
- *Structured analysis* depends on the environment's abilities to analyze and reveal the structural properties of the model.
- *Behavior experience* is related to the process model execution facilities offered.

Some of the activities to achieve pragmatic quality are as follows:

- Participant training: One should educate the audience in the syntax and semantics of the modeling languages used or on relevant aspects of the domain when needed.

- Model inspection and walk-throughs: One should manually read a model, go through it in an orderly manner, and potentially explain it to others. Having stakeholders who have not developed the model themselves but who need to understand the model go through it and explain what it represents aloud is often a very good method of testing the current comprehension of the model. Other techniques from code inspections have been adapted to (requirements) model inspection (van Lamsweerde 2009). Useful support for this in a modeling tool supports navigation and the browsing of the model. This support also includes the possibility of scrolling through the model, either incrementally (pan) or one page at a time (page), and zooming.
- Model transformations. Generally, these are performed to transform a model into another model in the same language. This activity can generally be expressed as follows:

$$T : M1_{L_i} \rightarrow M2_{L_i}$$

The need to transform models arises for several reasons. First, models may be transformed to improve efficiency. In several approaches, an initial operational specification gradually evolves into the final implementation by a continuous replacement of real-world modeling constructs with more efficient constructs from the programming world. Second, models or programs may achieve improved readability through the use of transformations. This issue is discussed under layout modifications in Sect. 3.3 on empirical quality. As a final example, models may need to be changed if the modeling language evolves.

- Model rephrasing is a meaning-preserving transformation where some of the implicit statements of the model are made explicit. It is related to model refactoring, discussed under empirical quality above.
- Model filtering is a meaning-removing transformation that concentrates on and illuminates specific parts of a model. Filtering has been defined in Seltveit (1993) based on the notion of a *views V*, which is a model that contains a subset of the statements of another model in the same language, i.e., *V* is a subset of *M*, as illustrated in Fig. 3.14.

Another method of specifying a filter is to say that it is a set of not necessarily syntactically complete deletes of statements. Filters can be classified into two groups:

- Language/meta-model filters: Suppress details with respect to graphemes and symbols in the modeling language. An example is illustrated in Fig. 3.15, where we show only activities and the sequence flow between them (including also collapsing the gateway).
- Model/specification filters: Suppress details with respect to a particular model. An example is given in Fig. 3.16, where only the nodes that can be reached from the gateway are included.

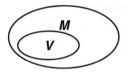

Fig. 3.14 An illustration showing that a view is a subset of a model

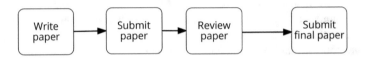

Fig. 3.15 Example of the use of a language filter

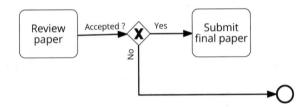

Fig. 3.16 Example of the use of a model filter, based on anythings being linked by one edge to a selected node (here, the gateway)

Fig. 3.17 Example of a user-selected filter—the happy path

One could also imagine specifically selected parts of the model. In process modeling, it may often be needed, for instance, to pick out the preferred sequence, the so-called happy path (see Fig. 3.17).

Other relevant aspects of filters include the following:

- Inclusiveness/exclusiveness: A filter can be defined by specifying the components to be included in the view or by specifying the components to be excluded in the view. These are referred to as the inclusiveness and exclusiveness properties of the viewspecs, respectively.
- Query: A filter can be defined as a query after elements that have certain attributes or attribute values.
- Determinism/non-determinism: A filter is deterministic if the resulting views of performing the filter on a model M are the same each time, given that it operates on M each time. If the result is not predictable, the filter is non-deterministic.

- Global/local effects: We distinguish between two cases: (1) The scope of the effects is local if there is no effect of the filter beyond the model upon which it operates and (2) it is global if the scope of the effects goes beyond the model upon which it operates. How to propagate changes to affected models is a challenging problem for filters with global effects.

Tools for addressing large models (e.g., enterprise architecture models) such as Troux Architect have good facilities for creating views of models, with different types of filters, where it is also possible to update the views, propagating changed values back to the main model.

- Model translation: A translation can generally be described as a mapping from a model in one language to a model containing all or some of the same statements in another language:

$$T : M_{L_i} \rightarrow M_{L_j}, \ i \neq j$$

In *paraphrasing*,, both L_i and L_j are textual languages. Often, this term is used more generally. In *visualization*, L_i is a textual language, whereas L_j is a diagrammatical language.

Translations between different diagrammatical languages can also be useful for comprehension in case different persons are fluent in different related languages. For example, for those who are familiar with UML activity diagrams, it may be easier to relate to a process model in this language than in a semantically equal BPMN model.

Finally, one may want to translate a diagrammatical model into a textual language, for instance to translate a BPMN model into BPEL so that the resulting model can be executed, or into a natural language for linearizing the model for improved comprehensibility. In this case, L_i is diagrammatical, and L_j is textual.

Although most translations and transformations will be easier and faster to perform when there is tool support, they can also be performed manually. Manual translations and transformations can also be used as part of participant training. However, participant training may also be enhanced by using tool support. Several specific applications of translations and transformations and combinations of these exist. Some examples are the following:

- Model execution: Translating or transforming the model into a model in an executable language, e.g., in a workflow environment. When manually performing this translation, we speak in terms of *prototyping* in the traditional sense.
- Animation: Making system dynamics explicit by using moving pictures. This may take the form of icons, such as a telephone ringing or a customer arriving at a registration desk, or it may apply the symbols of the modeling language. Recently, techniques applying virtual reality environments for enacting process models have been illustrated as a validation technique (Brown 2010).
- Explanation generation (Gulla 1996): This practice can be manual or tool-supported. An explanation generator can answer questions about a process model and its behavior.

- Simulation: Using statistical assumptions about the domain, such as the arrival rate of customers and the distributions of processing times, to anticipate how a system built according to the model would behave if implemented. It is not practical without tool support for large models. Simulation can be combined with execution, animation, and explanation.

The properties that a model and the languages it is made in must have to support these techniques include those for syntactic and semantic quality, in addition to executability (i.e., the execution of the model has to be efficient). The 7MPG Guideline G3 (only one start node and one end node) may also be relevant, making it possible to execute the process model. Other beneficial characteristics are expressive economy and aesthetics (empirical quality), as noted above.

3.7   Social Quality of Business Process Models

The goal defined for social quality is *agreement*. Six types of agreement can be identified according to the following dimensions:

- Agreement in knowledge versus agreement in model interpretation. In the case where two models are made based on the view of two different actors, we can also talk in terms of agreement in model.
- Relative agreement versus absolute agreement.

Relative agreement means that the various sets to be compared are consistent; hence, there may be many statements in the model of one actor that are not present in that of another, provided that they do not contradict each other. Absolute agreement, on the other hand, means that all of the models are the same.

Agreement in model interpretation will typically be a more limited demand than agreement in knowledge because the former means that the actors agree on what is stated in the model, whereas there may still be much they disagree on that is not stated in the model so far, even if it may be regarded as relevant by one or both participants for the current modeling task. The agreement of models will be easier to check in practice, especially if the languages have formal syntax or semantics, although this is limited to the situation described above. Hence, we can define the following:

- Relative agreement in interpretation: All I_i are consistent.
- Absolute agreement in interpretation: All I_i are equal.
- Relative agreement in knowledge: All K_i are consistent.
- Absolute agreement in knowledge: All K_i are equal.
- Relative agreement in the model: All M_i are consistent.
- Absolute agreement in the model: All M_i are equal.

Metrics can be defined for the degree of agreement based on the number of inconsistent statements divided by the total number of statements perceived or by the number of non-corresponding statements divided by the total number of statements perceived.

Because different participants will have their expertise in different fields, relative agreement is regarded as being more useful than absolute agreement. In process modeling, one typically wants to link the different areas of the organization, where the different stakeholders primarily have expertise on a limited number of activities. However, the different actors must have the *possibility* to agree and disagree on something, i.e., the parts of the model that are relevant to them should overlap to some extent. This would in a process model at least amount to the interfaces between tasks, i.e., what is produced in one task that is to be consumed in another. Since process improvements often span the whole process, achieving a good overall process often necessitates that the different persons get an understanding of and agree to the whole process, not only their own parts.

The pragmatic goal of comprehension is viewed as a means of achieving social quality. The reason is that agreement without comprehension is not very useful, at least not when democratic ideals are held. The area of *model monopoly* (Bråten 1973) discussed in Chap. 1 is related to this aspect; thus, one should be aware of the dangers of particular modelers consciously or (more likely) unconsciously misleading other participants.

Tool support related to social quality is most easy to establish based on achieving agreement in models created according to the internal reality of the participants who are to agree. Figure 3.18 provides an example of model merging, where one merges the paper process viewed from the perspective of both the author and the organizer. Accordingly, the main activities for investigating and hopefully achieving agreement are the use of model integration techniques, with a specific emphasis on the conflict resolution of the integrated models.

The general model integration process has many similarities with view integration, which has been a topic of much research in the database community over the last 20+ years. The process can be considered to consist of four subprocesses (Francalanci and Pernici 1993).

- Preintegration: When more than two models are used as inputs in the process, one must decide on how many models should be considered at a time. A number of strategies have been developed, such as binary ladder integration, N-ary integration, balanced binary strategy, and mixed strategies. The strategy chosen will often depend on the organizational setting for the modeling project. For instance, in the case of participatory modeling in modeling conferences described in Chap. 5 (Gjersvik et al. 2004), one first integrates the 2 or 3 individual models in the first 4 workshops and then integrates all of the resulting 4 models into the final model.
- Viewpoint comparison: This includes identifying correspondences and detecting conflicts among the viewpoints. Some types of conflict that may be detected are as follows:

  - Naming conflicts: Problems based on the use of synonyms and homonyms. When using different labeling styles, problems of detecting equal concepts are even larger, which is another reason to standardize on one style (e.g., "active verb and noun").

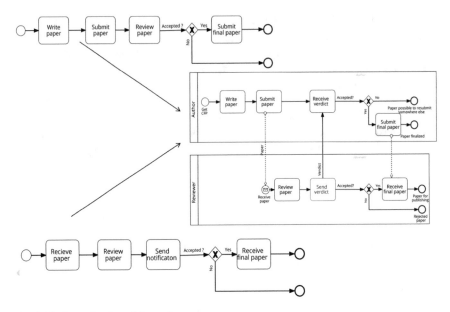

Fig. 3.18 Example of model merging

- Type conflicts: That the same statements are represented by different concepts in different models.
- Value conflicts: An attribute has different domains in two models.
- Constraint conflicts: Two models represent different constraints on the same
  phenomena.

- Viewpoint conforming: This aims at solving the previously detected conflicts.
  Representations of statements in two different models can be classified as follows: identical, equivalent, compatible, and inconsistent. To address such
  conflicts, either traditional approaches are mostly based on transformational
  equivalence, or they trust the skills of the participants by only providing
  examples that are valid for the particular model. According to Francalanci and
  Pernici (1993), few of the early approaches addressed inconsistent statements.
  An exception is Leite and Freeman (1991).

In this regard, other useful techniques are goal modeling, particularly where
one can explicitly represent conflicting goals, such as in EEML (Krogstie 2008),
and the use of argumentation systems (Conklin and Begeman 1988; Conklin
2005; Hahn et al. 1990) for supporting the argumentation process. These systems
use the issue-based information system (IBIS) approach originally proposed by
Rittel (1972) or extensions thereof. IBIS focuses on the articulation of the key
issues in the problem area. Each issue may have many *positions*, which are
statements or assertions that resolve the issue. Each of the issue's positions in turn

may have one or more *arguments* that either support or oppose the position. Going from one node type to another is done through the so-called rhetorical moves.

- Merging and restructuring: The different models are merged into a joint model and then restructured. The latter involves checking the resulting model against criteria for empirical, (perceived) semantic, pragmatic, and social quality. It is taken for granted that syntactic quality issues are taken care of automatically in the process.

Generally, it is not to be expected that apart from syntactic matching, matching can be performed in a manner that is fully automatic, although several modeling tools have this type of functionality. Matching business process models are discussed in Dijkman et al. (2010), Rittgen (2011). Three aspects of model similarity are discussed: node matching, structural similarity, and behavioral similarity. *Node matching* attempts to map the nodes from one model to the nodes of the other model by comparing the labels, attributes, and types of nodes. Node matching can be affected with semantic or syntactic measures. The latter is based on the string-edit distance, i.e., the number of letters that need to be added, replaced, or deleted to transform the label of an activity in one model to that of an activity in the other model. This is clearly easier when all models use the same labeling style. Semantic matching is based on a database of synonyms or an ontology (Lin et al. 2006). Based on the node matching, the two models can be compared with the help of structural similarity or behavioral similarity. The former uses only structural information on the model, i.e., the manner in which activities are connected with "arrows," but does not examine their meaning in terms of the control flow. Behavioral similarly examines the actual execution of the processes described by the models. Here, two models are considered equivalent if, at any time during process execution, an activity that can be performed in one process can also be performed in the other and vice versa. A weakness with these types of similarity measures is that they typically do not focus on which areas of the model where similarity is the most important.

One should also be able to address inconsistencies and variants, in the sense that not all need to follow the same process in all areas. If two models are inconsistent, it would be useful to generate some type of information on the differences. Are the parts that do not match important parts of the model? How difficult is it to change parts to make them consistent? Are the inconsistent parts automated or manual processes? After the analysis, the tool could suggest which processes or process parts to change. Model merging can be supported in several ways, having computerized support for manual integration, possibly with the use of CSCW techniques. This issue is discussed in more detail for models in general in (Krogstie 2012a), techniques that can be applied also for business process models.

3.8 Deontic Quality of Business Process Models

Modeling is (normally) not performed for the fun of it but to achieve some goal (termed the goals of modeling, G) that is typically linked to some business and organizational goals. This linkage introduces the need to examine both the costs and benefits of modeling. Here, the means are related to the modeling of these goals and checking their fulfillment (i.e., that all goals are achieved and that there are no goals that are not achieved).

For everything apart from extremely simple and highly intersubjectively agreed-upon domains, total validity, completeness, comprehension, and agreement, as described above, cannot be achieved. Hence, for the goals in these areas to be realistic, they must be somewhat relaxed by introducing the idea of *feasibility*. Attempts to reach a state of total validity, completeness, comprehension, and agreement will potentially lead to an unlimited use of time and money in the modeling activity. The time to terminate a modeling activity is thus not when the model is "perfect" (which will never occur) but when it has reached a state where further modeling is regarded as being less beneficial than applying the model in its current state. This resonates well with the concept of "just enough method" found in agile methods. Accordingly, a relaxed type of these human-related goals can be defined, which we term feasible validity, feasible completeness, feasible comprehension, and feasible agreement.

- Feasible validity : $M \backslash D = R, R \neq \varnothing$, but there are no statements $r \in R$ such that the benefit of performing a syntactically valid delete of r from M exceeds the drawback from eliminating the invalidity r. (A syntactically valid delete is the deletion of statements from the model in a manner that does not introduce syntactic errors in the model.)
- Feasible perceived validity : $I \backslash K = R, R \neq \varnothing$, but there are no statements $r \in R$ such that the benefit of performing a syntactically valid delete of r from M exceeds the drawback from eliminating the invalidity r.
- Feasible completeness : $D \backslash M = S, S \neq \varnothing$, but there is no statement $s \in S$ such that the benefit of inserting s in M in a syntactically complete manner exceeds the drawback from adding the statement s.
- Feasible perceived completeness : $K \backslash I = S, S \neq \varnothing$, but there is no statement $s \in S$ such that the benefit of inserting s in M in a syntactically complete manner exceeds the drawback from adding the statement s.
- *Feasible comprehension* means that although the model may not have been correctly understood by all audience members, there is no statement in the model such that the benefit of rooting out the misunderstanding related to a statement here exceeds the drawback from making that effort.
- *Feasible agreement* is achieved if feasible perceived semantic quality and feasible comprehension are achieved and inconsistencies are resolved by choosing one of the alternatives when the benefits of doing so are greater than the drawbacks from working out an agreement.

Thus, feasibility introduces a trade-off between the *value* and the *drawbacks* of achieving a given model quality. We have used the term "drawback" here instead of the more usual "cost" to indicate that the discussion is not necessarily restricted to purely economic issues. Judging completeness with respect to some intersubjectively agreed-upon standard, as suggested by Pohl (1993), is one approach to feasibility. Additionally, reference models can be used in this manner. We see also from Sect. 2.3.5 that similar value/drawback deliberations must be done on the use of reference models.

By making the standard a part of the language, one can also transform this inherently semantic problem into a syntactic problem to enable automatic checks for conformance to the standard. Note that this is only workable if the use of the standard is appropriate for achieving the goals of modeling in the first place. Another relevant issue on this level is how to decide the timeliness of model updates, as discussed in Sect. 3.2.

As we can observe from the variety of goals of modeling discussed in Sect. 1.5.1 , in addition to changing the models, these may also be meant to change other aspects, including the following:

- The participants learn as a result of the modeling (i.e., K is increased).
- If the modeling is intended to bring about change (e.g., a process improvement), then the domain D is changed, preferably in a positive direction in relation to the goal of modeling.

3.9 Summary

In this chapter, we have described the main parts of a specialization of SEQUAL for process model quality. Inspired by earlier discussions on the quality of conceptual models and requirements specifications, combined with semiotic theory, process model quality has been divided into seven areas:

- Physical quality: The persistence, currency, and availability of the process model.
- Empirical quality: The relationship between the process model and another process model that contains the same statements, which are somehow regarded as better through a different arrangement or layout.
- Syntactic quality: The relationship between the process model and the process modeling language. Is the modeling language used correctly?
- Semantic quality: The relationship between the process model and the domain of the modeling. Perceived semantic quality is the parallel relationship between the knowledge of the participants and their interpretation of the process model. Is the process model complete (containing all valid statements) and valid (not containing invalid statements)?

- Pragmatic quality: The relationship between the process model and the stakeholder's interpretation of the model. Does the audience understand the implications of the part of the process model relevant to it? Do process modeling tools, e.g., for model execution "understand" the model?
- Social quality: The relationship between different process model interpretations. Do the different participants of the modeling agree on the semantic quality of the process model?
- Deontic quality: How do the process models contribute to fulfilling the overall goals of modeling?

Although the same levels developed for the quality of models in general are also relevant for the quality of business process models and they share many of the same means for improving model quality, we have also identified a number of specific aspects that are related to the use of process modeling languages, the use of reference models, and process improvement.

References

Alsam, A.: Contrast enhancing colour to grey. In: SCIA '09 Proceedings of the 16th Scandinavian Conference on Image Analysis, Oslo (2009)

Battista, G., Eades, P., Tamassia, R., Tollis, I.G.: Algorithms for drawing graphs: an annotated bibliography. Technical report, Brown University (1994)

Bertin, J.: Semiology of Graphics: Diagrams, Networks, Maps. University of Wisconsin, Madison (1983)

Bråten, S.: Model monopoly and communications: systems theoretical notes on democratization. Acta Sociol. J. Scand. Social. Assoc. 16(2), 98–107 (1973)

Brown, R.A.: Conceptual modelling in 3D virtual worlds for process communication. In: Proceedings of the 7th Asia-Pacific Conference on Conceptual Modelling (APCCM 2010), Brisbane (2010)

Conesa, J., Olive, A., Caballé, S.: Semantic web personalization and context awareness information science reference. In: Refactoring and Its Application to Ontologies, pp. 107–136 (2011)

Conklin, J.: Dialogue Mapping: Building Shared Understanding of Wicked Problems. Wiley, New York (2005)

Conklin, J., Begeman, M.J.: gIBIS: a hypertext tool for exploratory policy discussion. ACM Trans. Inf. Syst. 6(4), 303–331 (1988)

Dijkman, R., Dumas, M., van Dongen, B., Käärik, R., Mendling, J.: Similarity of business process models: metrics and evaluation. Inf. Syst. 36, 498–516 (2010)

Fowler, M., Beck, K.: Refactoring: Improving the Design of Existing Code. Addison-Wesley Professional, Reading (1999)

Francalanci, C., Pernici, B.: View integration: a survey of current developments. Technical Report 93–053, Politecnico de Milano, Milan (1993)

Gane, C., Sarson, T.: Structured Systems Analysis: Tools and Techniques. Prentice Hall, Englewood Cliffs (1979)

Gjersvik, R.: The construction of information systems in organizations. Unpublished PhD thesis, Norwegian University of Science and Technology, Trondheim (1993)

Gjersvik, R., Krogstie, J., Følstad, A.: Participatory development of enterprise process models. In: Krogstie, J., Siau, K., Halpin, T. (eds.) Information Modelling Methods and Methodologies. Idea Group Publishers, Hershey (2004)

Gulla, J.A.: A general explanation component for conceptual modeling in CASE environments. ACM Trans. Inf. Syst. **14**(3), 297–329 (1996)

Hahn, U., Jarke, M., Rose, T.: Group work in software projects: integrated conceptual models and collaboration tools. In: Gibbs, S., Verrijn-Stuart, A.A. (eds.) Multi-user Interfaces and Applications: Proceedings of the IFIP WG 8.4 Conference on Multi-user Interfaces and Applications, pp. 83–102. North-Holland, Amsterdam (1990)

Hawryszkiewycz, I.: Introduction to Systems Analysis and Design. Prentice Hall, Upper Saddle River (2001)

Hella, L., Krogstie, J.: A structured evaluation to assess the reusability of models of user profiles. In: Proceeding of EMMSAD—Conference on Evaluating Modeling Methods in Systems Analysis and Design, Hammamet, Tunis (2010)

Hewett, J., Durham, T.: CASE: The Next Steps. Technical report, OVUM (1989)

Krogstie, J.: A semiotic approach to quality in requirements specification. In: Proceedings of IFIP 8.1. Working Conference on Organizational Semiotics, Montreal, Canada, (2001)

Krogstie, J.: Evaluating UML using a generic quality framework. In: Favre, L. (ed.) UML and the Unified Process, pp. 1–22. IRM Press (2003)

Krogstie, J.: Integrated goal, data and process modeling: from TEMPORA to model-generated work-places. In: Johannesson, P., Søderstrøm, E. (eds.) Information Systems Engineering From Data Analysis to Process Networks, pp. 43–65. IGI (2008)

Krogstie, J.: Model-based Development and Evolution of Information Systems: A Quality Approach. Springer, Berlin (2012a)

Krogstie, J.: Quality of business process models. In: Proceedings of PoEM'2012, Lecture Notes in Business Information Processing, vol. 134, pp. 76–90 (2012b)

Krogstie, J.: Quality of conceptual data models. In: Proceedings of 14th ICISO, Stockholm Sweden, (2013a)

Krogstie, J.: A semiotic framework for data quality. In: Proceedings of EMMSAD 2013, Valencia, Spain (2013b)

Krogstie, J.: Capturing Enterprise Data Integration Challenges Using a Semiotic Data Quality Framework Business and Information Systems Engineering Feb 2015, vol. 57, issue 1, pp. 27–36 (2015)

Krogstie, J., Jørgensen, H.D.: Quality of interactive models. In: First International Workshop on Conceptual Modelling Quality (IWCMQ'02), 11 Oct 2002, Tampere, Finland. Springer, Berlin (2002)

Krogstie, J., Sølvberg, A.: Information Systems Engineering: Conceptual Modeling in a Quality Perspective. Kompendiumforlaget, Trondheim (2003)

Krogstie, J., Dalberg, V., Jensen, S.M.: Increasing the value of process modelling. Paper presented at the 8th International Conference on Enterprise Information Systems ICEIS 2006, Cyprus (2006)

Kuntz, J.C., Christiansen, T.R., Cohen, G.P., Jin, Y., Levitt, R.E.: The virtual design team: a computational simulation model of project organizations. Commun. ACM 41(11) (1998)

Langefors, B.: Theoretical Analysis of Information Systems, 1st edn. Studentliteratur, Auerbach (1973)

Leite, J.C.S.P., Freeman, P.A.: Requirements validation through viewpoint resolution. IEEE Trans. Softw. Eng. **17**(12), 1253–1269 (1991)

Lin, Y., Strasunskas, D., Hakkarainen, S., Krogstie, J., Sølvberg, A.: Semantic annotation framework to manage semantic heterogeneity of process models. Paper presented at the CAiSE'2006, Luxembourg (2006)

Lindland, O.I., Sindre, G., Sølvberg, A.: Understanding quality in conceptual modeling. IEEE Softw. **11**(2), 42–49 (1994)

Mendling, J., Recker, J.: Towards systematic usage of labels and icons in business process models. In: Halpin, T., Proper, H.A., Krogstie, J. (eds.) 13th International Workshop on Exploring Modeling Methods in Systems Analysis and Design, CEUR Workshop Proceedings Series, Montpellier. See http://ceur-ws.org/ France (2008)

zur Mühlen, M., Recker, J.C.: How much language is enough? Theoretical and practical use of the business process modeling notation. In: Proceedings CAiSE'08. Springer-Verlag, Montpellier, France (2008)

Nossum, A., Krogstie, J.: Integrated quality of models and quality of maps. In: Proceedings of EMMSAD 2009. Springer, Berlin (2009)

Orlikowski, J.W., Gash, D.C.: Technological frames: making sense of information technology in organizations. ACM Trans. Inf. Syst. **12**(2), 174–207 (1994)

Petre, M.: Why looking isn't always seeing. Readership skills and graphical programming. Commun. ACM **38**(6), 33–44 (1995)

Pohl, K.: The three dimensions of requirements engineering. In: Proceedings of CAiSE'93, Springer, LNCS 685 (1993)

Rittel, H.: On the planning crisis: systems analysis of the first and second generations. Bedriftsøkonomen **34**(8) (1972)

Rittgen, P.: Business process model similarity as a proxy for group consensus. In: Johannesson, P., Krogstie, J., Opdahl, A.L. (eds.) PoEM 2011. LNBIP, vol. 92, pp. 12–24. Springer, Heidelberg (2011)

Sandkuhl, K., Stirna, J., Persson, A., Wißotzki, M.: Enterprise Modelling—Tackling Business Challenges with the 4EM Method. Springer, Berlin (2014)

Seltveit, A.H.: An abstraction-based rule approach to large-scale information systems development. In: Proceedings of the 5th International Conference on Advanced Information Systems Engineering (CAiSE'93), Paris, France, 8–11 June 1993, pp. 328–351. Springer, Berlin (1993)

Shannon, C.E., Weaver, W.: The Mathematical Theory of Communication. University of Illinois Press, Champaign (1963)

Shneiderman, B., Plaisant, C., Cohen, M.S., Jacobs. S.M.: Designing the User Interface: Strategies for Effective Human—Computer Interaction, 5th edn. Addison Wesley, Reading (2009)

Silver, B.: BPMN: Method and Style. Cody-Cassidy Press (2012)

Tamassia, R., Di Battista, G., Batini, C.: Automatic graph drawing and readability of diagrams. IEEE Trans. Syst. Man Cybern. **18**(1), 61–79 (1988)

van Lamsweerde, A.: Requirements Engineering: From System Goals to UML Models to Software Specifications. Wiley, Chichester (2009)

Wangler, B., Wohed, R., Ohlund, S.-E.: Business modelling and rule capture in a CASE environment. In: Proceedings of the Fourth Workshop on the Next Generation of CASE Tools, Twente (1993)

Ware, C.: Information Visualization. Morgan Kaufmann, Burlington (2000)

Wesenberg, H.: Enterprise modeling in an agile world PoEM 2011. In: Proceedings of the 4th conference on Practice of Enterprise Modeling, Oslo, Norway (2011)

Chapter 4
Business Process Modeling in Practice

4.1 Business Process Modeling in International Projects

Process modeling is often used in connection with the introduction of standardized information systems. Existing work on the success measures of process modeling has summarized important issues in the context of that setting.

In this section, we present an investigation of process modeling success in connection with harmonizing work across units in an international company that traditionally has been largely autonomous. We present the case of a global service-providing enterprise, from which we have attempted to extract the value of process modeling in a networked organization, comparing our case to existing frameworks of process modeling success.

The case organization was established 150 years ago as a maritime classification organization. Over the years, new offices were established around the world. Business rules and work procedures were established centrally at the organization's head office and applied locally in its other offices, with local adaptation when necessary. Approximately 20 years ago, small, independent initiatives to provide certification services began in some of the organization's international offices. Certification activity within the various units soon increased, and the business area of "certification" was established on an international level. In contrast to the organization's maritime classification business, the certification business was not initiated from the main office. Instead, each certification unit was developed based on local needs and procedures. Each certification unit developed its own systems and work procedures for back-office and support activities, such as marketing, sales, planning, and issuing certificates. Some units also developed their own software applications. At first, common software applications were locally implemented in some units. Over the years, each unit personalized this tool to serve local needs.

© Springer International Publishing Switzerland 2016
J. Krogstie, *Quality in Business Process Modeling*,
DOI 10.1007/978-3-319-42512-2_4

After 10 years, the certification department made a decision centrally to focus on improved efficiency and chose to begin harmonizing its work processes, which were required to be standardized processes capable of local adaptation. In this way, the certification department intended to implement centrally based processes in a business that was accustomed to working pursuant to local procedures. A new software application to support the harmonized work was to be implemented throughout the organization.

The project actively used process modeling both in developing the harmonized processes and in communicating those processes to various types of audiences. The main activities of the overall project are depicted in Fig. 4.1. The project has reused both knowledge and models from earlier process model activities within the business area, and the harmonized work process models are also being used in other, later-initiated projects within the organization.

The work processes within the business area were first modeled at a high level in the mid-1990s as part of an official document describing the business. Although these models were created in a spreadsheet (Excel, see Fig. 4.2), they were later modeled using IDEF0 process modeling (Krogstie et al. 2004).

Later, the organization decided to investigate possible changes in the business area's work processes, how those processes were developed and locally adapted, and what aspects of the processes could be improved. A preproject was put through several workshops involving partners from various offices within the network, in which domain experts from all of the business area's worldwide locations defined a list of areas in which the work processes could be improved. The preproject concluded that the proper approach to starting an efficiency and harmonizing project would be to first develop an ideal process and then—because it was obvious that full standardization was unfeasible—to develop a harmonized process. The preproject also investigated the possibility of information systems support.

First, the "ideal" work process was described. When defining the harmonized process, technical, cultural, and economic constraints have influenced the models.

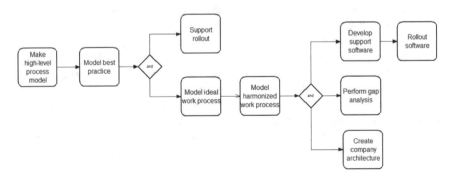

Fig. 4.1 Modeling projects in the case study

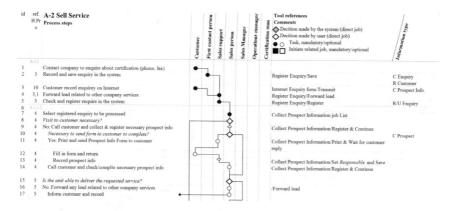

Fig. 4.2 Example on process modeling in Excel

This modeling was performed by the process developer, and the target audience for validation of the models was that of certification domain experts. The results of this process included both textual descriptions and high-level models of the harmonized processes.

An information systems development project was then established. The process models were initially used by the process developer to communicate with the software engineers. The process developer later modeled the work processes at a detailed level using swimlanes (a variant of role-activity diagrams (Ould 1995)).

To implement the harmonized processes worldwide, key personnel from the business area's management traveled to the various local units and performed a gap analysis of those units' local work processes in relation to the harmonized processes. The units were required to refrain from implementing the new information system until the gaps were closed. The IDEF0 models of the harmonized processes were actively used during the analysis process. The top-level processes are depicted in Fig. 4.3 as laid out in a reverse Z-pattern that turned out to function like an icon for the project.

We will below discuss the effect of modeling in each of the areas mentioned by Sedera et al. (2003) (cf. Sect. 2.3.6).

4.1.1 Model Use

Models can be used for numerous purposes, as discussed in Chap. 1. This case follows the evolution of a set of models over a longer time period, as depicted in Fig. 4.1, with a gradual extension of the usage areas for the model (which we call "goal creep") because many of the goals were not originally intended.

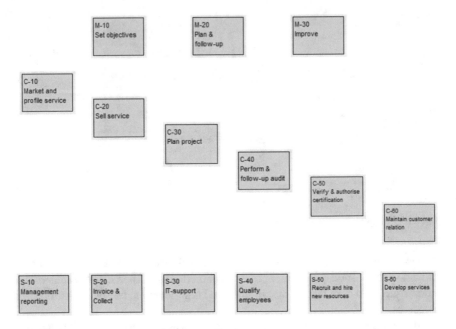

Fig. 4.3 Top-level process model in the certification case

The IDEF0 models in our case study were first used for various types of communication within the business area (usage area 2 in Fig. 1.8). Examples include the use of the models as a communication artifact between domain experts to improve work processes or their use as an input to the requirements specification of the information systems development project.

Although the swimlane models were used for the software developers during IS development (versus usage area 6) and to understand the domain, they needed significant adaptation to be useful for this purpose. The IDEF0 models were used to develop the user interfaces of the information system. The work process models were reflected through the menu structure in the information system, and in this way, there is a direct link between the models and the information system.

The IDEF0 models were also used as a tool to perform the initial gap analyses in the units. For rollout purposes, the modified swimlanes were used both to reveal the gaps and to train the users. The process models were also used when communicating with units that were reluctant to change their existing processes.

During the project, the IDEF0 models, which provided an overview of the new work processes, were satisfactorily used for high-level discussions; however, they were insufficient in situations that required details and specific information. This was especially evident in the initial gap analysis of the various units.

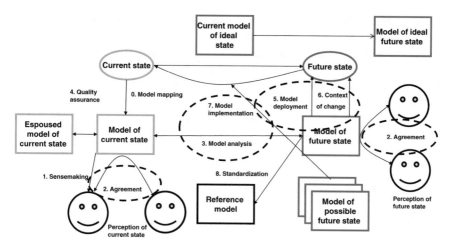

Fig. 4.4 Goals of modeling addressed in the case

In Fig. 4.4, the stippled lines overlaid on Fig. 1.9 indicate the various goals of modeling in the case. As we can observe, numerous goals for modeling were identified throughout the project:

- Communication to achieve agreement around models of the current state

  - The models developed should help share best practices among various organizational units.
  - The models developed should be helpful in refining the processes.

- Communication and agreement around models of the future state

  - The models should document the new work process.
  - The models developed should help harmonize the current work processes across various parts of the organization.
  - The models developed should be used to teach the software developers about the domain.

- Computer-assisted analysis

  - The models developed should help analyze existing work processes for bottlenecks and improvement possibilities.

- Model deployment

  - The models developed should be used as a procedural tool in everyday work.
  - The models developed should support the use of the software application developed for process support.

- Context of change

  - The models developed should define the scope of the software application.

A summary of the usage areas of different versions of the process model is found in Table 4.1, including the concrete modeling tasks and various stakeholder groups present at each step. Modeling activities to support the project's main goals were identified. This summary, which is related to the taxonomy of the modeling areas presented in the introduction, provides the following overview. (Here, we have further differentiated between the model developers and the model interpreters (those only reading/commenting on the model) because they have very different functionality needs.) The tasks that were prioritized in the project are highlighted in boldface.

Table 4.1 Modeling tasks with different objectives in the case

Modeling task		Model developers	Model interpreter
2 Visualize processes for communication			
	2.1 Model harmonized process	Process modeler Process owner	Worker Tool user Tool superuser Process owner Software designer
	2.2 Model local process for comparison	Process owner Process developer Local worker	Process owner Local user
3 Analyze processes for improvements		Corporate process owner Local operating manager	Process owner
5. Manual activation of model			
	5.1 Learning the job		"Doers" Worker trainers
	5.2 Assisting job performance		Doers (a) workers (b) managers (c) planners (d) administrators
	5.3 Learning to use the tool	Tool superuser	Tool superuser Tool user
	5.4 Assistance in the use of the tool		
6. Use model as basis for tool development		Process modeler	Software designer
7. Implementation		Process modeler	Process owners

4.1.2   User Satisfaction

There are several categories of model users. There might also be unidentified users. Examples of types of users and stakeholders include domain experts; workers; end users; superusers; and management, including the project sponsor, process modeler (external, e.g., a consultant, or internal), process owner, and CIS developer.

These user categories are complicated further by the aspects related to the distribution of users across numerous partly autonomous units that organize their work quite differently based on cultural and other issues, such as unit size.

The users of the IDEF0 models were divided based on their level of satisfaction of the models, depending on their needs. The domain experts using them in discussions of the harmonized process seemed satisfied with the models and what they could offer in their setting. The CIS developers did not find these models satisfactory because the models did not teach them about the domain and were not detailed enough to specify the requirements of the information system to be developed. Although the swimlanes were to provide a great deal of help during the development, they were not entirely satisfactory because it was difficult to consistently update models from several modeling tools and with varying levels of detail.

The overall impression of the process developer was that end users have reacted positively to the visual presentation of their new work processes in the form of models. Overall, project management also seems satisfied with the model. On the other hand, more work could have been done to enable the more active involvement of the various users up front by using a more user-centered process modeling approach.

4.1.3   Process Impact

Several different processes can be impacted, e.g.,

- The process of developing the harmonized process;
- The model's effect on creating the harmonized process;
- The previous work processes in each local unit;
- The harmonized work process;
- The new work processes in each local unit;
- The process of creating the application; and
- The process of implementing the application and through this the harmonized process in the organization.

The consequence of implementing the harmonized processes is that all units must change their work processes somewhat, supported by a new information system. Some aspects related to this consequence are discussed below under the rubric of deontic quality.

Issues that do not fit into the model that is used as a communication artifact are left out of the conversation, one of the process modelers claimed. To avoid influencing the units' explanation of their work processes, the models were only used as a checklist by the rollout manager. In the following meeting, he used the swimlanes in training and discussions with the units, focusing on the areas that did not fit with the harmonized process. In this way, the models have changed the rollout process within the project because they were found to have an overly strong effect on the participants, hindering the identification of gaps.

4.1.4 Process Model Quality in the Case

The focus on the quality of the process models varied from user group to user group in a manner that was related to their different modeling goals. The IDEF0 harmonized process models were initially created to act as a communication artifact among domain experts, whose needs were fulfilled by representing the models on a level that was high, but detailed enough to permit discussion of an agreement on the new processes. The IDEF0 harmonized process models did not satisfy either the needs of the software developers or the needs later identified by a gap analysis performed at the individual units.

Physical quality: As noted above, the amount of detail necessary varied by usage area. For software development, the amount of detail in the original model was too small, and it was impossible to easily add to the existing models because of both the availability of resources and the limitation of the chosen modeling tool. The models were not updated for some time and became outdated.

Empirical quality: This aspect was important in connection with the task of creating a common overall picture that could be adapted across all of the units. The high-level model view depicted in Fig. 4.3 was successful for this purpose. In addition, the swimlane view of the detailed processes was useful in connection with matching the harmonized model with local processes.

Syntactic quality: Several syntactic errors are found in all of the models. Thus far, these errors have not been regarded as important for the main uses of the models.

Semantic quality: Because of resource and tool limitations, it has been difficult to keep the models updated and internally consistent. This problem has spawned the need for improved tool support. Many areas within the organization had not been modeled in detail. One specific aspect in a case like this is the need to develop a harmonized and not standardized model, i.e., a model that can be locally adapted to heterogeneous IS infrastructures, different quality control procedures, and local culture. Thus, the model is neither right nor wrong, but instead either more or less appropriate for the various units. However, to act as an integrating artifact, e.g., to support communication and learning across organizational units and national borders, it is important to be able to define a common core in the process model.

Perceived semantic quality: For certain tasks, the model has been perceived as better than it actually is. One example is the gap analysis, in which the gaps were not discovered early enough.

Pragmatic quality: Comprehension of the high-level model appeared to be good, partly because people were able to ascribe their own meaning to it. The more detailed the models were, the more difficult it became to understand for people other than those working with the models on a daily basis. Thus far, technical pragmatic quality has been missing.

Social quality: High social quality is the most important at high levels, and indeed, the high-level model has high social quality. The process and model developer explained that because of the models' low level of detail during the gap analysis, everybody could agree on the new processes, which created a loyalty to the processes and solidarity within the overall certification business area. One informant claimed that the project was truly dependent upon this quality, which has greatly facilitated the process of implementing the new harmonized processes. The harmonization approach also made it easier to deal with social quality issues, since not the whole model had to be agreed upon by everyone, but one could get by with local variants in different offices and countries.

Deontic quality:

- Change in domain D: The IDEF0 models in our case study have been used for communication for various purposes within the business area. Examples include the use of the models as a communication artifact between domain experts to improve work processes. The consequence of implementing the harmonized processes is that all units must change their work processes somewhat, supported by a new information system. One informant claimed that it was not the models, but the process of doing the modeling, which changed the unit's work processes. The models acted as a very important artifact around which to focus the discussions. The representative of the IT department claimed that the process models had created "a fantastic foundation for the participants in the project" and that it was important to be able to change the work processes in the business area by establishing a common understanding across the various units.
- Change in knowledge K: The swimlane models were used to enable the software developers to understand the domain. The IDEF0 models were also used as a tool to perform the initial gap analysis in the units. For rollout purposes, the modified swimlanes were used both to reveal the gaps and to train the users. The IDEF0 models were also used as a basis for developing the information system's user interfaces. The work process models were reflected through the information system's menu structure.

It is interesting to note how the use of the models for different goals and modeling tasks shifts the emphasis on model quality. To create a common vision across the partly autonomous units (the high-level harmonized process models), it is very important that the model is empirically good ("looks nice") and agreed upon (high social quality), whereas syntactic correctness and semantic completeness are usually only of minor importance at this level. However, for use by CIS developers, semantic completeness was an important issue. In connection with gap analysis, it was actually important that the models were not shown at first, because they had very high perceived semantic quality in the sense that they were apparently accepted at face value, without being questioned. This is an interesting example of the model monopoly problem (Bråten 1973). It also highlights a major weakness of Sedera et al.'s original framework. Those authors' dimensions are not orthogonal. Model use and types of users influence both how to view a process model's quality and which quality aspects to emphasize.

4.1.5 Developing Specialized Process Modeling Language

A consequence of the work with process modeling in this case was the identification of a need for an improved method of representing enterprise process knowledge. The chosen enterprise modeling language was seen as too comprehensive and complex for the organization's needs, covering much more than needed and not covering some issues important to the project and organization. At this point, we participated in an activity that created a specially adapted modeling language; implemented this language in the chosen modeling tool; and remodeled the existing IDEF0 models, Excel swimlanes, supplemented with the word-text descriptions in the tool, using the tailored language. Our goal was both to make the resulting language more user-friendly and to satisfy the organization's needs. To establish the requirements for the new language, workshops with the project's modelers were convened; in addition, we studied the existing documentation and models and followed the thinking behind SEQUAL, identifying the relevant sets to be involved in the modeling. Parts of an existing modeling language were removed, and some new features were added. When the new language's requirements were implemented in the chosen modeling tool, we remodeled the old models, swimlanes, and text descriptions in the new tool, using the new, specially adapted and extended process modeling language.

This work's basic hypothesis was that "It is necessary to adapt existing standard enterprise modeling languages to support the diverse modeling needs of the project and the organization in an optimal way." The work started by examining the sets defined in SEQUAL. First, we identified the goals of the projects, and based on that, we identified the goals of modeling within the project, developing a goal hierarchy. The overall approach can be described relative to Fig. 4.5, which is a screenshot of the model's top-level containers. Looking back at Fig. 2.1, we see that the top-level containers (including different submodels) largely correspond to the sets in SEQUAL:

- Goals of modeling correspond to G;
- The model developers have the knowledge K;
- The model interpreters perform model interpretation I;

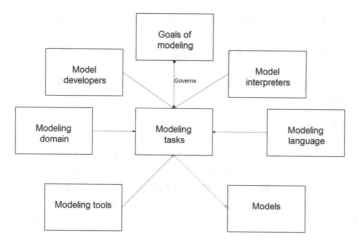

Fig. 4.5 Overall structuring of language RE approach

- A modeling task is performed to fulfill the modeling goals using modeling language that enables the required language extension (**L**) and that models a modeling domain (**D**) creating models and documentation (**M**); and
- Modeling tools are used in connection with this approach, also interpreting the model as needed based on the goals of modeling (**T**).

The goals of the overall project are structured and linked to the goals of modeling to support the fulfillment of these goals. The goals of modeling are then linked to relevant modeling tasks, taking into account the modeling domain. Roles and specific people to occupy them are identified for each modeling task relative to both model developers and model interpreters. Representatives of these roles were then involved in a more detailed specification of both the necessary modeling tasks and an appropriate modeling language for representing relevant knowledge in a comprehensible way. In addition, requirements for a modeling tool were elicited and linked to the identified modeling tasks. Based on the implementation of the language in a tool, models were made to elicit further requirements for what needed to be represented.

As described above, numerous modeling goals were identified. The process of developing the language is described further below.

Identifying Requirements for the Modeling Language
The work related to defining the new modeling language included workshops and interviews with people in the different relevant roles (as identified in the Table 4.1) in connection with the development, use, and evolution of the existing models, in addition to remodeling the existing harmonized models using ITM (a generic modeling language used in IT management and enterprise architecture). ITM has later (2015) been renamed Troux Semantics in the current version of the tool earlier known as METIS (now Troux Architect). Troux Architect was a leading candidate

to act as the basis of a new modeling approach because other parts of the organization were using the tool.

First, we identified numerous concepts and relationships in various modeling domains based on the existing models. These concepts and relationships were then matched to existing domains in ITM. Any necessary changes and additions were then described.

Process modeling

The model was primarily structured around work processes. In connection with process modeling, it was recognized that two views of the model were important to support: the functional IPO view (ala IDEF0) and the role-oriented RAD view (ala BPMN with pools and lanes). These views express different concepts in different ways. Only models on the type level were regarded as obligatory.

Using ITM as a basis, one could address this issue by taking a subset of ITM's process logic domain (a sublanguage within ITM that is an implementation of IDEF0) and add properties to the main modeling types as illustrated in the middle of Fig. 4.6. As in IDEF0, processes can be decomposed, and it is possible to indicate

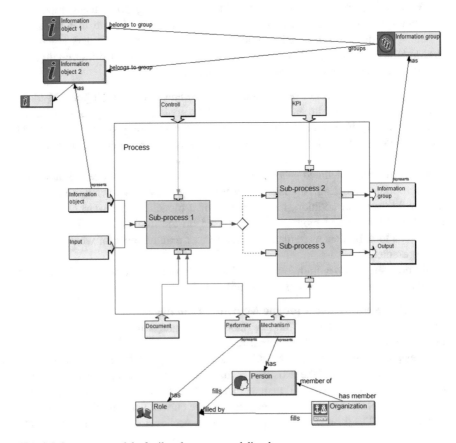

Fig. 4.6 Language model of tailored process modeling language

input, output, control (e.g., KPIs (key performance indicators)), and resources. Input and output can be linked to information objects or information groups (see below); examples of mechanisms include a process's performer (possible to link to a role) and documents and information objects linked to a process.

Information modeling

Although more traditional data modeling (e.g., using UML class diagrams) was perceived as useful in the future, for the first version, the choice was made to use simple information modeling, as illustrated at the top of Fig. 4.6, which shows how information objects can be decomposed and grouped into information groups. Information attributes can be specified for information objects. In addition, relationships to processes and other parts of the language were included, as indicated above.

People and organization

There was also a need for organizational modeling showing relationships from the organizational model to the process models. The main parts of the language for organizational modeling are found in the bottom of Fig. 4.6. Here, we see the possibility of representing an organizational structure and linking roles to organizational units. Persons can be members of organizations and can fill roles in those organizations. The persons and roles could be linked to the process models as mechanisms (e.g., indicating who was performing each task).

The full ITM language contains 26 domains (sublanguages) compared to the three domains described above as a basis for the language, of which only some parts from each domain were necessary. Thus, a special sublanguage of ITM needed to be provided and extended. These extensions were not too complicated to create in the chosen tool (Troux Architect), at least not for a meta-modeling expert. This specialized modeling language was used and further adapted according to needs revealed through practical use.

In Fig. 4.7, we illustrate the overall model architecture, with the process model in the middle. Figure 4.8 illustrates the top-level view of the process model. (Figure 4.3 is a view of model in Fig. 4.8 in which all of the edges are removed.) In Fig. 4.9, we see the model when exploding both the process model and the information model, illustrating some of the overall complexity of such models (and indicating the need to have good tools for navigating and creating views from such models). (It is not intended that you should be able to read the legends in this model.)

We evaluate the language as developed using the modeling language quality aspects of SEQUAL described in Sect. 2.2.1.

1. *Domain appropriateness.* The language has been developed to cater to the users' domain and to exclude concepts not in that domain. The domain appropriateness was validated by remodeling information found in the existing models and further developing the models based on current needs in the organization. Extensions to the language are possible to create in the tool if new needs arise in the future. This functionality requires the organization to

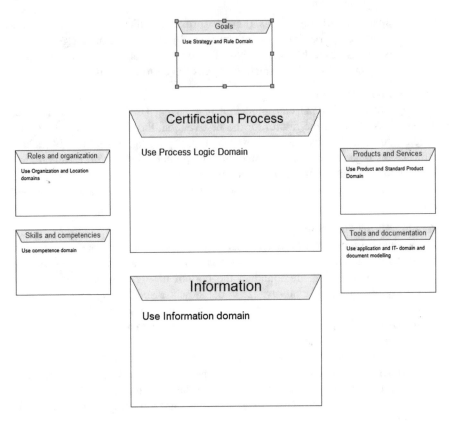

Fig. 4.7 High-level model architecture

understand the need to have a person who is responsible for meta-model management and to invest in the necessary knowledge and tools to do so.

2. *Comprehensibility appropriateness.* The language has been made with quite few modeling concepts. More expressiveness has been put into relationship classes and object properties. Using traditional complexity metrics such as Rossi and Brinkkemper (1994), the inclusion of expressiveness in relationships and properties does not necessarily result in a less complex language. Conversely, because of specific functionalities of the modeling tool that could enforce the permissible relationships between two concepts (not only to prevent errors but also to provide assistance in correct language use, because recognition of a limited set of possibilities is easier than recall), the complexity of having many relationship classes is easier to manage than is complexity induced by many object classes. Note that this will result in less visual emphasis on these aspects, cf. Chap. 1's discussion on modeling perspectives. Therefore, there is a trade-off with respect to how much to represent as nodes and attributes and how much as edges (designating the most central concepts as nodes).

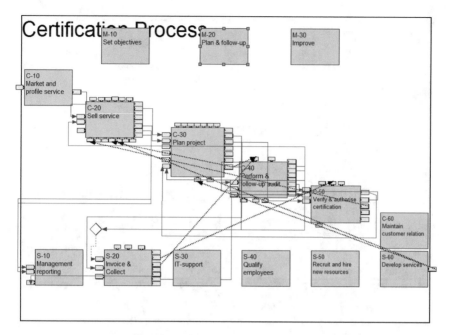

Fig. 4.8 Top-level process model

3. *Participant appropriateness.* The language was based on concepts already in use in the organization and therefore should be easy to learn. In practice, it turned out that although some people in the organization were accustomed to work being supported by the models, there was a learning curve for others who were not originally involved in modeling.
4. *Modeler appropriateness.* As indicated above, the language was created using familiar concepts for the modelers. In addition, some of the graphical notations were made to specifically fit the current organization.
5. *Tool appropriateness.* The language that we developed had a formally defined syntax, and syntax checks could thus be provided by the modeling tool. Because the need for automated model analysis and model activation was not a focus in the first version of the language, no formal semantics were provided.
6. *Organizational appropriateness.* The language is a further development of a language used in other parts of the organization. The language's extensions are created in such a way that it is possible for others in the organization to use the models written in this language using standard ITM.
7. *Ontological appropriateness.* This was not a particular concern in the work, although we notice that the underlying IPO structure is found in a number of process modeling notations.

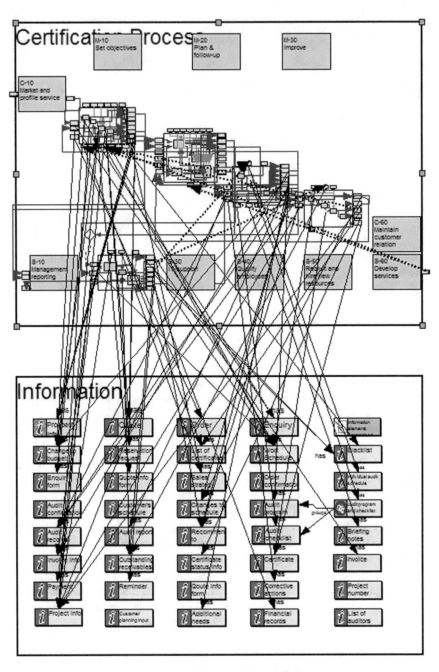

Fig. 4.9 Connections between process and data models exploded

Tool requirements

In addition to have appropriate modeling languages, as illustrated in Chap. 3, it is beneficial to be able to support a variety of techniques to achieve high-quality models with tools. Below, we summarize the needs identified by the project for modeling tool support, indicating the extent to which the modeling tool could address the requirements. The structure of the presentation is based on the quality levels of SEQUAL presented in Chaps. 2 and 3.

Physical quality

- Support a model repository with versioning: The Troux toolset includes this, but the repository solution was not bought by the organization, and thus, the models were only stored as files.
- Possible to see differences between versions of models: Only indirectly supported in the Troux toolset as used at the time.
- Models available for annotation by many: Possible using an annotator.
- Models available for browsing on the Web by all users: Possible using a model browser, or alternatively by creating Web reports based on the models.
- The English single-language interface to the models was regarded as sufficient, because English is the organization's official work language.
- There were no requirements for import/export of models to other tools.

Empirical quality

- Possible to differentiate different types of relationships (with text, color, etc.): Troux Architect can provide different colors, text, etc., for the relationships. This was not exploited in the language developed.
- Role (swimlane view) available on process model: Included in Troux Architect and adopted for the language developed, although not in the same way as the project had used previously (Excel spreadsheets).

Syntactic quality

- Support syntax check of the model: Troux Architect enables both the possibility of syntax error prevention and syntax error detection.

Semantic quality

- As the requirements for the modeling language illustrate above, it is necessary for the tool to provide meta-modeling facilities, not only for the ability to choose only limited parts of a language to prevent the modeling of things that are not included in the domain, but also for the ability to add object types, relationship types, and properties to enable modeling of what actually is in the domain.
- Support consistency checking when making changes to models: Troux Architect has some possibilities for supporting validation, although limited possibilities for defining new rules of consistency.

- Support constructivity (e.g., to be able to model a detailed process and then obtain the outer properties of a collection of detailed processes automatically derived). Minimally, to be able to check for constructivity in the decomposition structures: Partly supported in the IDEF0 implementation.
- No specific support for process improvement analysis.

Pragmatic quality

- Support views according to user group

    - Model views: Troux Architect supports this well, and model views can be made persistent. The main model and the views can be updated in a coordinated manner. However, normal users experienced great difficulty in using this functionality.
    - Language view: This related to have different parts of the language available for different user types and purposes. Troux Architect can support this using the concept of viewstyles. This was not exploited in the language that we developed.

- Scenario views: Because the models are on a type level (and not on the instance level), it is difficult to support scenario views with the current modeling language. Very large changes must be made to also support models on an instance level, but this would be possible to implement. For example, in EEML (Krogstie 2008), one operates with a task concept that can be used on both type and instance levels, supported by viewstyles that show the instance-level properties only when you are in a certain mode.
- It should be possible to view the model at different levels of abstraction: Troux Architect supports this ability through different types of hierarchical modeling constructs. In the language developed, this is witnessed both in process decomposition mechanisms and in the organizational breakdown structure.

Social quality

- Support differentiating between harmonized and local processes: Troux Architect can support this, e.g., by having specific properties indicating whether a process is global or local. This ability was not implemented in the language developed.
- Support the explicit modeling of exceptions: Troux Architect can support this function, but the chosen modeling language then must be further extended.
- Support an argumentation process relating to obtaining agreement for new versions of the harmonized process. Not specifically supported in Troux Architect, although the annotation mechanism in Troux Architect can support this type of process.

Deontic quality

- The tool should be aligned with company standards: Troux Architect had been tested in other parts of the organization and partly adopted for use.

- Cost/benefit of tool should be favorable: Troux Architect is a fairly expensive tool, and thus, this was an issue from the beginning because it is often difficult to quantify the value of introducing a new technique or tool.
- Need available training for users to be able to learn the system locally: Troux Architect is delivered with both "canned" and human-taught courses at different levels of detail, although human-taught courses were experienced as very expensive.
- The tool should be available for the next five years: Troux Architect has a substantial user base and has existed (in different versions) for 20 years.

4.2   Business Process Modeling Across the Organization

The next case involves a large organization in the oil and gas sector. The company has used process modeling and other type of modeling for many years. It has more than 23,000 employees and approximately the same number of external contractors. Permanent employees are divided between organizational units of varying size, with DPN and TDP being the largest. The company operates worldwide, and particularly over the last decade, it has used process modeling to structure its vast amount of organizational knowledge. This section builds upon material from Heggset et al. (2014, 2015a, b).

4.2.1   History of Modeling in the Company

As an advanced technology company, the organization has a long tradition of adopting new approaches to IT and organizational development. In the 1980s, the organization experimented with the use of process and data modeling in connection with the application of what were then called CASE tools (Solum and Østerud 1989). In the 1990s, modeling was used for a broader set of tasks. As summarized in Christensen et al. (1995), the use of process and enterprise models was divided into three purpose-based categories:

1. Construction of reality: Modeling as a technique for creating a common understanding among people whose cognitive models do not necessarily coincide.
2. Analysis and simulation: Making changes to simulated enterprise models and monitoring the consequences to decide whether a change should be implemented.
3. Model deployment and activation: The use of an enterprise model for controlling and performing work. The enterprise operates through and in the enterprise model.

Detailed case studies, particularly in the first usage area, were performed and reported in Totland (1997), which analyzes four case studies in detail:

1. VPT—Creation of value across organizational and disciplinary borders. Enterprise modeling of the value chain related to the Norwegian continental shelf, arguing for new and improved ways of working across existing boundaries.
2. PA30—Process Plant 30+: Enterprise modeling as an activity in a large restructuring project at a gas-processing plant operated by the company, conducted to provide an overall view of business processes before changing them.
3. Gazz—Gas logistics—Development of an enterprise modeling software tool to be used for holistic and strategic thinking concerning the company's gas business.
4. TEK-s Technology strategy: Enterprise modeling as an aid in both the development and the dissemination of a corporate technology strategy.

Although the notations used in the different cases differed and partly covered a larger part of the enterprise than did the business processes, a standardized process modeling notation appeared in the company. In 2001, this notation was evaluated and compared with other notations (Krogstie and Flon Arnesen 2005) using the current version of SEQUAL, but at that stage, the home brew notation was kept, albeit with some changes. Some years later, when BPMN arose as a standard, the company chose and adapted it (in 2001, BPMN was not yet available). In 2004, the company decided to use enterprise process models as part of its corporate management system (CMS). The introduction of models is experienced as having a positive effect on operations. The models contribute to risk reduction from an operational, environmental, and safety perspective (Wesenberg 2011). Drawing the line to the introduction of Chap. 1, the number of serious incidents per million work hours has been reduced from 6 to approximately 0.8 since the introduction of enterprise models (known as the SIF index). Whereas other aspects certainly have contributed to this reduction, enterprise modeling has played a prominent role in changing the company's way of working during the last decade.

4.2.2 Description of Current Modeling Structure and Tool

The current enterprise process model is realized through the company management system. This system is described as "the set of principles, policies, processes, and requirements which support the organization in fulfilling the tasks required to achieve our goals." It defines how work is done within the company, and all employees are required to act according to its relevant governing documentation.

The management system consists of three main parts:

- Process models using a restricted subset of BPMN represented in the ARIS tool, the modeling solution from which all governing documentation (GD) is

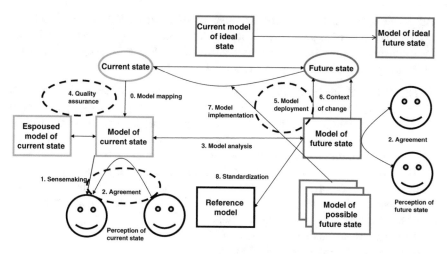

Fig. 4.10 Overview of goal of modeling in the petroleum case

accessed by the end users. The models are as-is models that are manually activated, i.e., representing how people are to work at the company (Fig. 4.10).

- Docmap, used for handling and publishing textual GD.
- Disp, a tool that supports the process of handling applications for deviation permits in cases in which compliance with a requirement is difficult or impossible to achieve.

The three main objectives of the management system are as follows:

1. Contributing to safe, reliable, and efficient operations and enabling compliance with external and internal requirements.
2. Helping the company incorporate its values, people, and leadership principles into everything it does.
3. Supporting business performance through high-quality decision making, fast and precise execution, and continuous learning.

GD describes what is to be achieved and how to execute tasks; in addition, it ensures standardization. Each process area has GD in the form of documents and/or process models accessible from the ARIS start page.

The management system's organizational function is responsible for creating and improving the management system based on business needs, ensuring that the GD is understood and used, and monitoring compliance with work requirements. The work of the function follows a five-step cycle: (1) assess and plan; (2) design; (3) implement; (4) use; and (5) monitor and control. This cycle is carried out in close collaboration with line management and the owners of the GD.

The enterprise process model is created according to a set of rules for structuring and using notation, and it can be used for a variety of purposes, including compliance management, competence management, portfolio management, decision making, and performance analysis. There are three levels of abstraction in the enterprise model—the contextual level, the conceptual level, and the logical level—including the following interrelated diagrams, as illustrated in Fig. 4.11. Examples of each diagram type are found in Figs. 4.11, 4.12, 4.13, 4.14, 4.15, 4.16, and 4.17.

- The top-level diagram (Fig. 4.12) is a mandatory navigation diagram that visualizes core value chain processes, management processes, and support processes, capturing what the company terms the contextual level. This is similar to what is known as a process map (Malinova et al. 2014), depicting core, support, and management processes at the highest level.
- The navigation diagram(s) (Fig. 4.13) are optional diagrams that support more tailored access to the processes than provided by the top-level diagram.
- The model diagram (Fig. 4.14) is a mandatory diagram that visualizes the model of one process area in the organization.
- The process navigation diagram (Fig. 4.15) is an optional model for navigational support on the conceptual level.
- The workflow diagram (Fig. 4.16) contains BPMN models (Aagesen and Krogstie 2010; Silver 2012) on the descriptive level. The quality system contains approximately 2000 BPMN models at this level, qualifying the case to be an example of BPMN in the large (Houy et al. 2011).

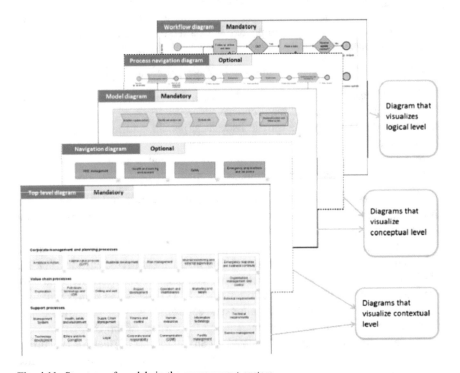

Fig. 4.11 Structure of models in the management system

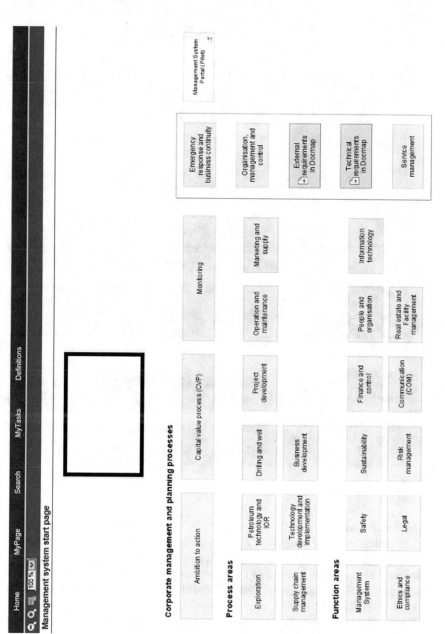

Fig. 4.12 Top-level diagram, aka company process map

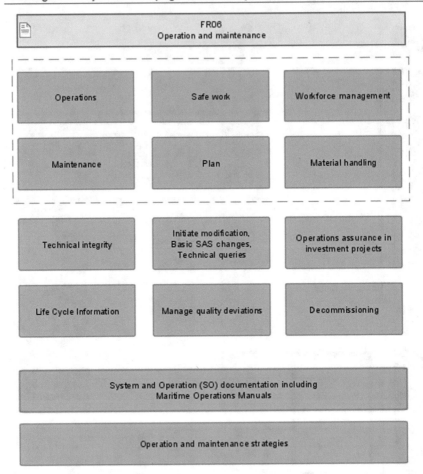

Fig. 4.13 Navigation diagram

Below, we will describe the various parts of the model structure in more detail.

The contextual level consists of a top-level diagram and navigation diagrams; in addition, it gives a high-level overview of the enterprise. The top-level diagram is mandatory and contains a model of the enterprise in terms of both process areas and function areas. The management system's start page, which is shown in Fig. 4.12, is a top-level diagram.

The navigation diagrams are optional, and the purpose of these diagrams is to help the user navigate to the correct model by structuring and detailing the content within a process area. The navigation diagram can contain symbols representing closed content groups, document model groups, and document models. A stippled

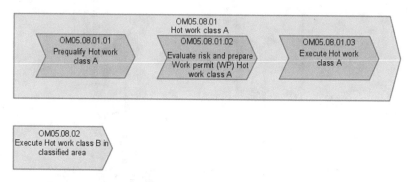

Fig. 4.14 Example of model diagram

rectangle can be used to group a set of closed content groups. An example of a navigation diagram is given in Fig. 4.13.

The conceptual level gives a conceptual view of the enterprise as model diagrams and process navigation diagrams; its primary purpose is to show relationships between or within models.

The model diagram, as shown in Fig. 4.14, is a mandatory diagram that shows the content of a closed content group or a process area. It may contain collapsed workflow models, process models, and document models. A rectangle can be used to group a set of collapsed process models. For quicker navigation, collapsed work flow diagrams can be placed inside a collapsed process model symbol.

The process navigation diagram (Fig. 4.15) is optional. It is used to show how workflow models are related to each other and uses collapsed workflow models, start events, end events, and intermediate events. A sequence flow in the form of an arrow visualizes the order in which the workflow models shall be executed.

The logical level shows the breakdown of the enterprise model into generic elements. The only diagram visualizing the logical level of the enterprise model is the workflow diagram. The workflow diagram is a mandatory diagram that is modeled using an adapted subset of BPMN 2.01, which has several activities and possibly decision gateways arranged in a sequence within lanes that represent the process role responsible for those activities. The activities are carried out by an actor representing the process role. An overview of a workflow model's possible symbols is provided in Appendix A. An activity is represented by a task symbol and can be either mandatory or optional. A task symbol with a stippled line is used to represent a collaboration activity including more than one role. The diagram can also either contain collapsed subprocesses that lead to another workflow diagram detailing the subprocess or call task symbols representing a reference to a workflow model in a different process model. The workflow diagram also contains start and end events and various types of gateways. An example of a small workflow diagram

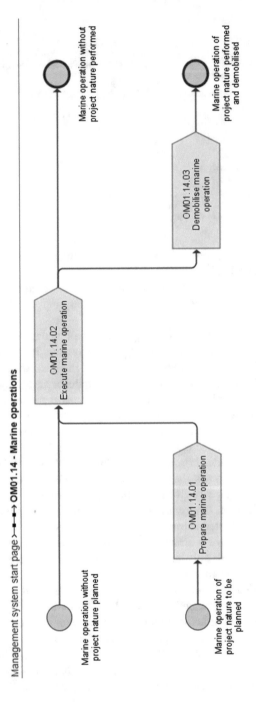

Fig. 4.15 Optional process navigation diagram

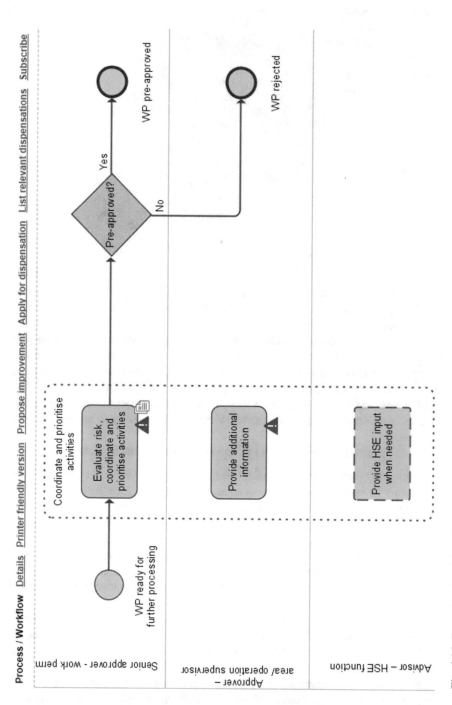

Fig. 4.16 Example of workflow diagram

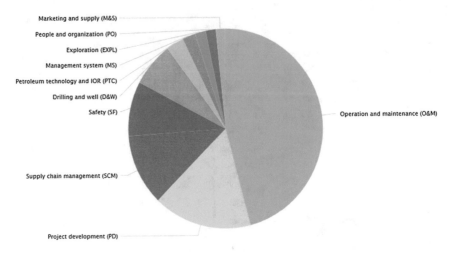

Fig. 4.17 Most frequently used process areas

is given in Fig. 4.16. It shows the interaction between three roles (as swimlanes) relative to a coordination activity involving risk assessment and activity approval. The approver and senior approver are mandatory participants in the task, whereas the advisor is an optional participant. When the coordination activity is done, the task ends successfully if preapproval has been made. Note that this example follows the specific version of BPMN made by the company, which differs somewhat from the official BPMN definition (e.g., including special semantics in the grouping mechanism) and links to extra requirements and guiding documentation from the models. Additional examples of workflow models from the case are provided in Appendix A.

There are several ways for users to access governing documentation:

- Navigating through process areas: When accessing the ARIS start page, the user obtains an overview of all process areas. He/she can click on a process area for an overview of the content belonging to this process area. From there, work processes, documents, workflow models, and other relevant information can be accessed.
- Using the navigation history: The user has the opportunity to access his or her navigation history from anywhere in ARIS using the drop-down menu in the upper right-hand corner. This menu displays previously visited pages in the management system.
- Using "breadcrumbs": From all levels in the hierarchy except for the top level, users can navigate to the higher levels using "breadcrumbs" located at the top of the page. The breadcrumbs also help users keep track of where they are in the process hierarchy.
- Searching: ARIS search is a simple search interface in which the user can input search words in a text field and use a drop-down menu to choose the type of

governing documentation that they seek. The results appear as a list of full or partial hits that is dynamically updated as the user types.

- Using "MyPage": Each user has a personal space called "MyPage," which is accessible from the menu at the top left of each page. Beginning from a workflow model page, the user can click the "Subscribe" tab and confirm that she wants to subscribe to that particular model. Within a short time, a direct link to the model will be available in the "Subscriptions" section of the user's "MyPage."

4.2.3   Use of Models in the Organization

In recent years, the company has been using the Splunk Enterprise tool to monitor the use of its management system. Splunk Enterprise is a platform for collecting and indexing machine-generated data. The data collected by Splunk are indexed as events and can be searched using the search processing language (SPL), a query language developed by Splunk. The search results provide information about how employees use the enterprise model, e.g., how often a certain page or model is accessed and how users navigate through the enterprise process model. According to a user survey, Operation and Maintenance is the most frequently used management system process area. This is confirmed by the results collected from Splunk, visualized in Fig. 4.17, which shows that this process area is by far the most used. The number of navigational elements and levels in ARIS varies greatly by process area. Thus, if all clicks were to be included in the search, the process areas with many navigational pages would seem to have very high usage. Because of this, only clicks on workflow models at the bottom level were included in the search. The search also excludes events that lack the process area field, which means that the calculated percentage for each process area is the percentage of the total number of events that do contain the field.

Table 4.2 lists the ten most frequently used workflow models. Twelve of the 20 most used models represent safety-critical processes; i.e., they are either classified as Safe work (a subcategory of Operation and Maintenance) or belong to the Safety process area. The high number of distinct users gives an indication of the high level of use of the models, which is partly because their use is mandatory in many operational areas to be compliant to the regulations in the area.

Figure 4.18 visualizes how workflow model hits are divided between the top ten organizational units. The search only includes clicks on "Workflow" models (bottom-level models), not all clicks in the management system. It also excludes all events that do not contain an "org" field, but those events are in minority. Table 4.3 lists the total number of clicks for each organizational unit, along with the average number of clicks per user (this value was only calculated for organizational units with more than a thousand total clicks). As shown in the table, DPN is the organizational unit responsible for the largest number of workflow hits. However, DPN

Table 4.2 Ten most used process models

Workflow model	Click count	Distinct users	Hits per user
Prepare isolation plan	34,580	4054	8.5
Apply for and evaluate work permit	24,471	4145	5.9
Initiate modification	22,975	2342	9.8
Perform work at night	20,041	3953	5.1
Commission and handover systems	18,285	2308	7.9
Checklist for safe work	16,349	3572	4.6
Safety incident	15,649	1628	9.6
Prepare for activity that weakens safety system	15,340	3438	4.5
Execute mechanical completion	13,560	1993	4.5
Perform bolt tightening	13,013	2076	6.3

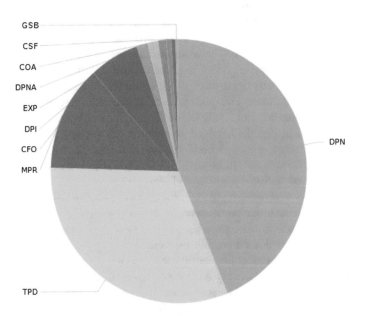

Fig. 4.18 Ten organizational units that use the process models the most

does not have the highest number of average hits per employee: Both COA and CSS have much higher numbers, i.e., 186.8 and 138, respectively. This is easily explained because one of the COA's primary responsibilities is to evaluate and improve the effectiveness of the management system. For CSS, this unit contains a subunit CSS CMS, which is responsible for the corporate function, related to the management system. Thus, although employees in these units work directly with the management system, they do not really represent its end users.

Table 4.3 Workflow model hits per organizational unit

Organization unit	Workflow hits	Percentage of hits	Workers in total	Hits per worker
Development and Production (DPN)	653,791	44.8	8954	73
Technology, Projects and Drilling (TPD)	471,055	32.27	6778	69.5
Marketing, Processing and Renewable Energy (MPR)	193,160	13.23	3526	54.6
Chief Financial Officer (CFO)	93,552	6.41	2124	44
Development and Production International (DPI)	20,500	1.40	736	27.9
Exploration (EXP)	19,778	1.36	969	20.4
Development and Production North America (DPNA)	15,577	1.07	757	20.6
Corporate Audit (COA)	9152	0.63	49	186.8
Corporate Security and Safety (CSS)	8227	0.57	60	138
Global Strategy and Business (GSB) development	4668	0.32	262	17.8

Although used in different manners and at different levels, we see that the models are visited and searched for quite extensively. As described in the previous section, one can use various methods to access the workflow model of interest. The use of clickstream analysis enables a more detailed study of this phenomenon.

A path analysis emerges for the most frequently used workflow model, and "Prepare isolation plan" shows that the most common path corresponds to navigating from the start page and directly down through all of the layers above the model page. This indicates that 38.8 % of users know exactly what they are looking for and where to find it. The fact that so many users go directly to the model via the navigational pages is unsurprising, considering that this model is the most used workflow model. Most of the users probably use it frequently and have learned where it is located. Despite the fact that they use it often, they do not use "MyPage" or bookmarks to access it directly. However, 15.1 % either do that or access the model through the search function, because the second most popular path contains only one click—to the model itself. The fifth most common path found is the only one in the top five that implies that the user looks for the model in different places before locating it. Another example process that we investigated was "Chemical management." Whereas 11,753 sessions were found that ended with a view of "Prepare isolation plan," only 2096 ended with "Chemical management." However, as many as 42.4 % of users go directly to "Chemical management," whereas only 15.1 % access "Prepare isolation plan" in that way. In general, the amount of sessions in which the workflow model is accessed directly varies widely by model. There are many possible explanations for this result. One likely explanation is that awareness of "MyPage" functionality might be higher in some parts of the organization than in others. The intuitiveness of the model's placement in the hierarchy is another possible explanation. Users probably use the search function in cases in which they feel that it is difficult to locate the model using their intuition and knowledge about the process area.

When designing diagrams in the enterprise process model, specific company requirements must be met. In the next sections, we provide an overview of the company modeling requirements structured according to the quality levels of SEQUAL. More specifically, in the following section, we will examine models' current empirical and syntactic quality issues (including a lack of compliance with labeling guidelines).

4.2.4 Guidelines of Modeling Relative to SEQUAL

As indicated in Sect. 4.2.1, the company has used modeling for a number of years. During this period, the requirements that modeling achieve a balance of syntactic, semantic, and pragmatic quality has evolved based on the company's concrete needs, as identified through the quality cycle described above. Thus, although we examine the company's current requirements, we also review the development of those requirements, particularly relative to the first version of those requirements, which was made available on February 12, 2009. Although the levels of syntactic, semantic, and pragmatic quality are emphasized, the existing requirements are not structured according to those levels. As we will see later, other levels of SEQUAL are also relevant, partly because the original SEQUAL categories have been divided into subareas in the later versions of the framework (e.g., splitting pragmatic quality into empirical quality and pragmatic quality as described in Chap. 3). The detailed guidelines overlap the generic guidelines on each level as described in Chap. 3, but since a specific version of BPMN is used, some specific more detailed guidelines have been developed in the company that is not found in Chap. 3. Looking first at the sets of SEQUAL in the context of the case of this management system, we have the following:

- **M**: The specific models that we examine here involve the workflow model part of the overall model framework. Relative to the description of the purpose of modeling set forth in Chap. 1, the models are meant to be as-is models, to support communication about the current process, manual activation (i.e., supporting human action in the organization according to the models), and checking compliance (area 4: quality assurance).
- **G**: Whereas the general requirements for the quality system were described in Sect. 4.2.2, five more concrete usage areas of importance are as follows:
  1. Compliance management: Monitor and control how working complies with the standards set for how to work. This enables the production of predictable output from work.

2. Competence management: Document the competency profiles needed to perform tasks, compare required competency profiles with competence represented in the organization, and manage the competency gap.
3. Portfolio management: Gain an overview of the current portfolio of, e.g., processes, information systems, and technologies. This provides opportunities to analyze whether the existing portfolio will meet future needs and to plan the road map to move from the current to the future portfolio.
4. Analysis and decision making: The model and its subsets enable an analysis of the relationships among various objects in the models and how changes to one object (e.g., a process) will impact other objects (e.g., the information systems used by that process or relations among various work processes).
5. Performance analysis: Monitor results to obtain experience and data related to quality. This information can be used to analyze whether the method of working produces the best possible result.

Even if several possible purposes are listed, one model always has one primary purpose and potentially (a set of) secondary purposes. The current primary purpose of the enterprise process model is compliance management. Therefore, priority is given to achieving the right quality of governing documentation models, with corresponding governing elements, roles, and responsibilities. We notice that two of the above five goals were not included in version 1 of the requirements (competency management and performance analysis). This change is not an example of "goal creep" (i.e., the use of models over time for purposes that were not originally envisioned (Krogstie et al. 2008)); instead, it results from the requirement that the models be current as-is (because of the focus on compliance). Recently, the underlying infrastructure to support the areas of competency management and performance analysis has been put into production at the company.

- D: Domain: The work processes in the company.
- L: The language for workflow modeling is a subset of BPMN2.0. In the original version of the requirements, the language was a similar subset of BPMN 1. The subset is depicted in Appendix A.
- A: The target audience is the entire company. Therefore, it is necessary to perform a stakeholder analyses to ensure that models have the appropriate abstraction level, complexity, and terminology for the target audience.
- K: The relevant explicit knowledge of the actors (A).
- T: The tool currently used is ARIS.
- I: Relates to how easy it is for the various participants to interpret the models as presented in ARIS.

Physical quality: Relates to whether the model has the following characteristics:

- Available to the right people in a physical form (through the ARIS tool) when needed for interpretation.
- People are able to find the right model (e.g., through navigation and search), knowing whether all relevant parts of the model have been found.

- Both the current and the previous versions of the process model are available.
- Able to store relevant metadata, e.g., on purpose and validity (for which part of the organization the model is valid).
- Only available to authorized users to the extent that there are security aspects.

Each governing documentation model and governing element shall have only one documented, published, and valid version that is properly numbered. However, old versions must remain available. There are two types of updates of governing documentation models and other governing elements: regular and minor.

Some guidelines for how to use ARIS are described (the usage of the various aspects is described under other quality levels as appropriate). In ARIS, one must select the relevant increase option before publishing. Only a regular update triggers the publication workflow mechanism. Once the update has been approved, the system automatically increases the value and publishes the model or an element with the new version number.

In ARIS, information about the deviation handling process is to be given in the field "*Deviation Permit.*" The following options are available:

- Level 1: Process owner acceptance and line manager approval required.
- Level 2: Only line manager approval required.

The descriptive field "*Validity*" is used to provide information about *to whom* the model applies, using a validity register. The validity register is used to store and maintain a list of locations and organizational entities.

The purpose of the governing documentation model shall be represented by the "*Purpose*" attribute in the work process model and basic document model.

Empirical quality: Here, we focus on the language conventions described in the requirements. Labeling conventions are treated as part of syntactic quality. Few concrete guidelines for graph layout are provided in the company requirements. For documents with additional information, there are also language guidelines. Whereas one in the standard SEQUAL framework (Krogstie 2012) primarily mentions the use of readability indexes as a technique, the requirements mention a broader set of guidelines, including the following:

- Address the reader in the text: write "When you submit…" instead of "When someone submits…"
- Use words and phrases that are familiar to all users: e.g., "present" instead of "prevailing."
- Ensure that content is sufficiently explained.
- Mindfully use the word "focus": instead of writing "The purpose of this information is to focus on safety," write "The purpose of this information is to highlight safety."
- Apply negative confirmation: When the reader expects to find content in the text but no content exists, apply negative confirmation by using "not applicable" or "none."

- Use active sentences: write "The process owner representatives handle improvement suggestions" instead of "Improvement suggestions are handled in the Process Owner dimension."
- Use verbs (do not use heavy nouns): Write "When the role actor complied with the specific requirement..." instead of "When there has not been a deviation from the specific requirement by the role actor..."
- Organize your message content: Extract information using verbs and pronouns. Divide information into suitably sized pieces and use periods wherever possible (cf., readability index deliberations). Postpone restrictions and additions to the next sentence.
- Use lists where possible.

Syntactic quality: Diagrams shall be designed in accordance with the requirements and symbols table available in the requirements. A subset of BPMN is used, primarily following the BPMN visual notation. This is similar to the analytical subset of BPMN (Silver 2012), although it does not support intermediate events (which were supported in earlier versions of the language requirements). In addition, we see that the current version of the requirements supports the use of the various concepts with more detailed guidelines. In addition, some extensions to standard BPMN are included, and numerous specific requirements are introduced.

- Task: A task symbol represents what actors do as "individuals" in their process roles and therefore shall be limited to a specific lane. Tasks can be optional (dotted border). You shall not connect any governing elements classified as a requirement to an optional task. A task can be collapsed; i.e., decomposition as a separate workflow diagram can exist with the same title as the collapsed task. One should not introduce new roles into decomposition. The sequence flow inputs to and outputs from the collapsed subprocess workflow diagram shall match start events and end events of the subprocess workflow diagram.
- The call task, i.e., the ability to reuse subtasks between different process models, can be defined using a special border.
- A collaborative activity is a group of activities executed across lanes. These activities should not be sequenced in time or have other dependencies. Note that this is an extension specific to BPMN, which is arguably poor at depicting (multiparty) collaborations (Aagesen and Krogstie 2010). The name of the collaboration activity symbol shall be unique, and you shall not name the collaboration activity with names that have been used in the tasks framed by the collaboration activity symbol. Each of the tasks framed by a collaboration activity symbol must have a unique title clarifying various types of activities performed by different roles. You shall not place an optional task, a call task, or a subprocess within a collaboration activity.
- Start event: Describe the state of the asset that triggers work. You shall not connect any governing elements to an event because no assigned person will be accountable for complying with those elements. An event shall be placed inside a lane.

- An end event describes the state when terminating the workflow.
- Parallel gateway. Visualize parallel divergence and convergence. This can split the flow into two or more parallel flows. "Event," "exclusive gateway," or an activity-related symbol can be used as preceding or resulting symbols of the parallel gateway symbol. It is not permitted to leave split parallel flows that are not remerged into the same work process.
- Diverging exclusive gateway. Indicate a choice of path in the workflow. An event, any type of gateway, or an activity-related symbol can be used before resulting in symbols of the exclusive gateway symbol. Each exclusive flow may have different end events.
- Converging exclusive gateway. Match a diverging exclusive gateway with a converging gateway.
- Sequence flow: Sequence flows to and from collaboration activities are connected to and from the same task within that collaboration activity. The flow is connected to and from the task performed by the role that is responsible for the output of the collaboration activity. You shall not use more than one sequence flow arrow from an activity. You shall not connect sequence flows to an optional task.
- Data: Used to describe a physical collection of information. Data association: To link data to the rest of the model.
- Association: To link text annotations to other symbols.
- Lane: Represents a process role.
- Presence of requirement: A company-specific symbol is a triangle with an exclamation mark; that symbol indicates the presence of one or more governing elements classified as requirements. Symbols representing the presence of requirements or information shall be placed at the lower right-hand corner of an activity-related symbol. Any activity symbol or gateway symbol except for a collapsed activity can have requirements linked to it.
- Presence of information: Used to show the presence of one or more governing elements classified as information.

For developing more structured evaluations of syntactic quality, the guidelines are divided into the following groups:

- N: Naming conventions
- T: Task
- OT: Optional task
- G: Gateways
- SP: Collapsed subprocess
- CA: Collaboration activity
- SF: Sequence flow
- W: Wrongly used concept.

For calculating metrics, the size of the model is equal to the total number of nodes (symbols) and edges (arrows).

- N1: Names on symbols and expressions shall be formulated in the singular form.
- N2: Avoid names with more than four words if possible.
- N3: A name shall not be a detailed description.
- N4: The first letter of a symbol name shall be in upper case. All other letters should be lower case.
- N5: Proper names shall start with upper case letters.
- N6: The official name of a concept within the company shall be used when alternatives exist.
- N7: Abbreviations should be avoided.
- T1: The title of a task shall be a verb imperative (reflecting the activity performed to add value), followed by a noun (reflecting the asset).
- OT1: The title of an optional task shall be a verb imperative (reflecting the activity performed to add value), followed by a noun (reflecting the asset).
- OT2: The use of an optional task is only allowed within a collaboration activity.
- OT3: It is not permitted to connect sequence flows to the optional task symbol.
- SP1: The title of a collapsed subprocess shall be a verb imperative (reflecting the activity performed to add value), followed by a noun (reflecting the asset).
- SP2: The collapsed subprocess symbol is drawn using a standard activity shape with a "+" attached.
- CA1: The tasks grouped by a collaboration activity symbol shall not be sequenced in time or contain dependencies.
- CA2: The title of a collaboration activity shall be a verb imperative (reflecting the activity performed to add value), followed by a noun (reflecting the asset).
- CA3: The name of a collaboration activity shall be unique, and you shall not name the collaboration activity with names that have been used in the tasks that have been framed by the collaboration activity symbol.
- CA4: Each of the tasks framed by the collaboration activity symbol must have a unique title, clarifying different type of activities performed by different roles.
- E1: You shall define the title of a start or end event as a noun (reflecting the asset) followed by a verb past participle (reflecting the activity performed to add value to the asset).
- G1: You shall not name parallel gateways.
- G2: The title of a diverging exclusive gateway shall consist of the term control (can be replaced with check, verify, evaluate, or clarify) followed by a noun (reflecting the object submitted to control).
- G3: The exclusive flow shall be described through an adjective or a phrase describing the alternative flows. You shall not use the words "yes" or "no" when designing exclusive gateways.
- SF1: A sequence flow shall have only one source and one target.
- SF2: You should not use more than one sequence flow from an activity.
- W: Using the wrong symbol (or similar errors).

Semantic quality: The content of a governing element shall explain its scope, adhere to its purpose, and be described with the necessary level of detail. Special rules apply for describing the content of a key control. This description shall include the following information:

- Control activity;
- Actions in case of deviations;
- Audit trail; and
- Key control characteristics.

Process roles represent a method of grouping of activities and decision gates according to responsibility and competence within a work process. The purpose of a process role is as follows:

- To secure the necessary segregation of duties; and
- To achieve efficient recognition and allocation of the competence in the work process.

It is important that the end users easily recognize the process role names. Process role is organization and location independent and helps different process users to better relate to their work processes. Moreover, it indicates which activities are performed by the roles themselves. The process roles have been categorized to secure the necessary segregation of duties. Categorization is based on the Responsible-Accountable-Consulted-Informed (RACI) principle.

Pragmatic quality: A number of the guidelines listed under empirical and syntactic quality above are made to support the development of understandable models. In addition, it is important to understand the model's intention. As a minimum, each governing documentation model shall have a defined purpose that includes the following:

- Risk—a description of the risk that the model mitigates;
- Objective—a description of the intended result (output); and
- Target group—the main end users of the process and the main users of the result.

Social quality: Each governing documentation model and governing element shall have what the company calls documented validity (i.e., organizational area in which it applies, not to be confused with validity as part of semantic quality). There are 2 validity dimensions: location and organization. Location validity is based on geography. Organizational validity is based on business area. The following rules apply when defining validity:

- If validity is set for a specific organizational entity, then location validity is by default unspecified (covers all locations); and
- If validity is set for specific location, then organizational validity by default remains unspecified (covers all organizational entities).

Note that validity indicates who the model applies to and thus who needs to agree on the model. The deviation attribute is used to document the deviation approval method of the governing documentation model and its workflows or governing element categorized as requirements.

Each governing documentation model and governing element shall have documented one single owner and a minimum of one owner representative. The ownership attribute is used not only to identify who is responsible for the quality of a model or element's attributes, references, and links, but also to enable deviations and improvement proposals for the handling process and therefore to identify who makes the final decision when not everybody agrees on the model.

Deontic quality: As discussed above, the main goal of the models was to fulfill the goals of the quality systems, which are as follows:

1. Contributing to safe, reliable, and efficient operations and enabling compliance with external and internal requirements;
2. Helping the company incorporate its values, people, and leadership principles into everything that it does; and
3. Supporting business performance through high-quality decision making, rapid and precise execution, and continuous learning.

A straightforward relation among the various goals of modeling, various quality aspects, and the goals of the quality systems above is not explicitly written in the requirements, nor are the necessary cost/benefit trade-offs between effort used and sufficient quality achieved. For quality trade-off, it is clearly stated in Wesenberg (2011) that pragmatic quality is the most important, whereas syntactic quality and semantic quality are primarily a means to achieve pragmatic quality. How syntactic quality might influence the pragmatic quality is discussed in the next section.

4.2.5   Influence of Syntactic Quality on Pragmatic Quality

Surveys among users of quality systems have found, among several other challenges, issues related to understanding some of the models (pragmatic quality). Although a large proportion of users feel that governing documentation is easy to understand, others report issues of vagueness and ambiguity. For instance, many of the survey respondents do not understand all of the abbreviations used in texts and models, although the official requirements mention that abbreviations should not be used.

As we understand from the above, one of the main purposes of requirements for process models is to ensure the models' high syntactic quality.

In the following evaluation, the degree of syntactical correctness was first measured on seven workflow models. In the user survey, respondents were asked to give examples of processes that were interpreted differently within their department/unit. This list of processes was used as a basis for selecting models to evaluate. Because of the high number of models listed, not all could be evaluated. The following criteria were applied when selecting models:

Table 4.4 Syntactic quality measurements

Model	Size	Breaches	SYN	AVG
Apply for and evaluate work permit	21	7xN2, 2xG2, 2xG3, 2xN2, CA3	0.55	0.87
Prepare isolation plan	23	CA3, G2, N2	0.89	0.89
Project control	24	12xN4, N2, E1, CA2, CA4, G2, G3, SF1	0.48	0.82
Execute mechanical completion	30	2xN4, 4xN7, 4xE1, 3xW, 4x N2, 2xSF1, G2, G3	0.37	0.80
Set, verify, and approve isolation	30	2xN2, 2xSF1, CA4	0.87	0.80
Safety incident (SF103)	39	E1, 7xN2, 3xN2, 3xG2, 2xG3, SP2, 4xW	0.58	0.78
Commission and handover systems	46	2xE1, SP1, SP2, 2xSF1, 16xN4, 2xN2, 5xG2, 5xG3, 3xT1	0.39	0.78

1. The process is directly mentioned by respondents in the user survey as a cause of misunderstandings and different interpretations and implicitly mentioned at least twice.
2. The total number of nodes and edges in the model is higher than 20.
3. The model is one of the 100 most used workflow models.

Implicit mentions either could refer to a process chain of which the workflow is a part or could describe a process (or parts of a process) in a sentence without naming the process or its identifier.

After measuring the syntactic quality (SYN) of these seven selected workflow models, they were compared to other models of a similar size. The criteria used when choosing models for comparison were the same as the criteria listed above, except for criteria 1, which was inverted—only models without direct mentions were found appropriate. For each of the "troublesome" models, the three models closest in size from the top 100 list that also fit the set criteria were evaluated. The results are summarized in Table 4.4, indicating errors in the types found in the bullet list in the previous section.

Experiment design and results

In the experiment, two workflow models were selected and changes were made to these models to increase their syntactic quality according to the guidelines developed in the organization, as described above. Participants were asked to answer a range of questions related to the models to measure their understanding and, therefore the models' pragmatic quality.

The original intention was to use only company employees from different departments and locations as participants, but because it proved to be difficult to find enough company volunteers, a parallel student experiment was conducted. Overall, 18 students and 9 company employees participated in the study. To avoid participants answering based on personal knowledge of the process instead of consulting the models, the company participants did not have firsthand experience with the modeled processes. The models selected for the experiment had below-average syntactic quality and were found to be easily improvable by correcting mistakes in a manner consistent with the rules listed above. Improvements were made to several models before selecting the two workflow models chosen here.

- SF103—Safety incident
- OM05.07.01.03—Reset isolation and pressurize.

Key numbers for these workflow models are given in Table 4.5. SF103 was also part of the syntactic quality evaluation reported in Table 4.4 because it was highlighted in the user survey as a model subject to misinterpretation. OM05.07.01.03 was not directly mentioned, but has as many as 9 implicit mentions, mostly by listing the "parent" process.

Syntactic quality was measured on the Norwegian versions of the models, because the experiment was conducted in Norwegian. This was done to avoid language-related misunderstandings, because all of the respondents were native Norwegian speakers. With the conventions and metric used, there might be slight differences in measured quality between versions in different languages, because some of the rules are related to naming. The Norwegian version of SF103 had a low original syntactic quality of 0.56, whereas OM05.07.01.03 had a moderate syntactic quality of 0.72. When creating the new versions, the models were adjusted to make the syntactic quality as close to 1 as possible. Major changes were made to SF103, because many of its errors were large; e.g., the wrong symbol was used in several cases. With OM05.07.01.03, the changes made were mostly corrections in naming symbols and splitting arrows. (The identified errors were 4xN2, 2xG2, G3, and 2xE1, i.e., mostly involving naming and gateways.)

The participants were each given two models to interpret: one original and one modified. The participants were split into four groups, each of which was given a different combination of models following a Latin square design, as outlined in Table 4.6. As shown in the table, two groups were given the new SF103 and the old OM05.07.01.03. The other two were given the new OM05.07.01.03 and the old SF103. The order of presentation was reversed for half of the groups to avoid order affecting the results. In addition, the groups were given an overview of the language notation. The actual models are found in Appendix A.

Table 4.5 Characteristics of workflow models used in the experiment

Model	Hits	Size	Syntactic quality
SF103	16,752	39	0.56
OM05.07.01.03	6662	29	0.72

Table 4.6 Latin square experimental design

Group	First model	Second model
Group 1	SF103 (new)	OM05.07.01.03 (old)
Group 2	OM05.07.01.03 (old)	SF103 (new)
Group 3	SF103 (old)	OM05.07.01.03 (new)
Group 4	OM05.07.01.03 (new)	SF103 (old)

The participants were each given 15 questions connected to SF103 and 10 questions connected to OM05.07.01.03. When summarizing the results, each wrongly answered question was given −1 point, unanswered questions were given 0, and correct answers were given a score of 1. The total number of available points for each model is the result of (number of participants x number of questions), e.g., $9 \times 15 = 135$ for questions to the old SF103 in the student experiment. Results from the experiment with company employees should be emphasized in the analysis.

SF103—Safety incident

The overall results for SF103 are summarized in Table 4.7. As shown, the modified version of SF103 scored much higher than the original version both in the company experiment and in the student experiment. Some specific questions are worth examining more closely because they give insight into certain problem areas and normal misunderstandings. Question 2 stands out, because all of the company participants answered incorrectly when looking at the old version of the model, and half of those did so when looking at the new:

2. True or false: The process always starts with a safety incident occurring

Looking at the student respondents, the change is even bigger: As many as 7 out of 8 who received the original version answered the question incorrectly, whereas only two who received the new version made the same mistake. The question is related to events. In the process model, there are two possible triggers for the process. In the original version, many event-related symbols are used incorrectly; e.g., there are two cases of "end event" symbols with sequence flows pointing out from them, and event symbols are used instead of task symbols even though the process does not start or end at these points. It is therefore unsurprising that the respondents have trouble distinguishing the actual process triggers.

The next critical question is number 6 (the question had three alternatives):

6. What is special about the activity "categorize, classify, and decide causes"?

Two of the 4 employee groups answered incorrectly when looking at the old model, whereas everyone answered correctly when looking at the new version. This might be because the subprocess symbol used in the original model does not correspond exactly to the one defined in the standard notation overview, because it lacks the "+" that a collapsed subprocess is expected to have attached to it, according to the text. (This detail is not depicted in the legend overview in Appendix A.) However, this mismatch is not reflected in the students' responses: All of them answered the question correctly.

Table 4.7 SF103 results

Experiment	Old version	New version
Company	33/60 p (55 %)	52/60 p (87 %)
Students	93/135 p (69 %)	122/135 p (90 %)

Question 9 also drew two wrong answers with the original version and none with the new version:

9. The process ends when an accident investigation is carried out

Here, some of the students were also confused: The old version led to three wrong answers and one unsure response (i.e., the question was unanswered), whereas the new version led only to correct answers. This question is also event-related, so the reasoning is the same as for question 2.

OM05.07.01.03—Reset isolation and pressurize

The results for OM05.07.01.03 are shown in Table 4.8. The syntactic quality of the original model was higher than that of the model discussed above. In this case, the new version actually received a lower score, but the difference is not very large. Among company employees, the difference is also evenly spread among the questions: None of the questions differ by more than two points (corresponding to a minimum of one mistake less) between the two model versions.

The question with the lowest score for both versions was question 3:

3. Yes or no: Should the area technician always contribute to approving the execution?

A similar result can be seen among both groups. The question is connected to an optional task. Although it is specified in the legend that a task symbol with a stippled line is optional, many are unable to distinguish this from a regular task.

Question 6 also gave some interesting results:

6. What should be investigated when arriving at the symbol "Safety valve?" (old version)/"Check safety valve" (new version)?

All of the company employees answered the question correctly for both versions, except for one who was "unsure" (old version), whereas in the student experiment, four of the respondents looking at the old version skipped the question and one answered incorrectly. Everyone answered correctly when looking at the new version. The question pertains to a gateway symbol which in the old version is labeled merely "Safety valve?" ("Sikkerhetsventil?" in Norwegian), with exits labeled "yes" and "no." The text is not very descriptive, so without any domain knowledge, it could be very difficult to determine the meaning of this gateway symbol. This might explain why the company employees answered this one correctly, whereas many students were unsure: Even though the company respondents did not have firsthand knowledge of this particular process, they have probably picked up some knowledge about the domain over their years working in the petroleum industry.

Table 4.8 OM05.07.01.03 results

Experiment	Old version	New version
Company	31/40 p (78 %)	27/40 p (68 %)
Students	64/90 p (70 %)	59/90 p (66 %)

4.2.6   Evaluation of the Quality System Models

At the end of 2013 and the beginning of 2014, a large-scale user survey was conducted in the company to better understand users' experiences and opinions related to the management system and governing documentation. In addition to the issues related to syntactic and pragmatic quality as discussed above, several other aspects were identified. A similar survey was also conducted in 2012. The survey was answered by 4828 employee participants, which represented approximately half of those invited to respond. Many challenges were identified from the survey that were related to the management system itself, learning processes, and work practice, all of which contribute in some way to the management system's goals of safety, reliability, and efficiency (relative to objective 1 for the models). The survey is seen as very useful because of both the large amount of quantitative data and the amount of detailed feedback provided by the participants. The company is using the survey results as a basis for planning and implementing changes to the management system and will use a similar survey at later stages in the hopes of finding a measurable improvement. Many of the issues discovered can be connected to model quality, and the most important findings are summarized below using the SEQUAL quality levels.

Physical quality issues
The survey showed that many of the employees have trouble finding what they need when they look for governing documentation. Moreover, when they do find the relevant documentation, more than half of the respondents are unsure that they have found all of it. Some describe ARIS as a "maze" in which it is difficult to keep track of where the displayed page is situated in the hierarchy. According to the respondents, the search function often does not produce the desired result. As described earlier, each user has a personal space called "MyPage," which is accessible from the menu at the top left-hand corner of each page. From a workflow model page, users can click the "Subscribe" tab and confirm that they want to subscribe to that particular model. Familiarity with this functionality is unfortunately low among many respondents.

Many are not satisfied with how changes to GD affecting their work are communicated, which makes it difficult to know whether their information is current. Employees are not aware of the possibility of receiving updates on changes, and when they do, their experience is that the reasoning underlying those changes is not clearly communicated. Fourteen percent of the respondents report using paper copies to access GD. One reason for this is the limited access to IT systems out on the platform; therefore, unless employees are clearly notified of changes, they might continue to use old versions.

Empirical quality issues
Users feel that governing documentation suffers from a lack of clarity, and 42 % of the survey respondents often do not understand abbreviations used in the text and models. Note that the guidelines for modeling explicitly discourage the use of

abbreviation. Therefore, here it seems that it is not necessarily the guidelines that are the problem, but the lack of adherence to those guidelines.

Syntactic quality issues
Although there are many guidelines on this level, there are many examples of those guidelines being only partly obeyed, as discussed above. Although this was not explicitly mentioned as an issue, as we saw above, when a large number of syntactic errors are found in the models, comprehension can be affected.

Semantic quality issues
The ability for users with hands-on experience with the process to add improvement suggestions could improve the semantic quality of the workflow models, because it could impose an improved correspondence between model and domain. However, the process of handling improvement proposals appears too slow and inconsistent, as many users experience long waits for feedback on their suggestions and that the reasoning behind the outcome is often unclear. Almost half of the respondents have experienced receiving no feedback at all on their proposals. This could lead to a lack of motivation for posting suggestions in the first place, even though such suggestions might be useful. In addition, even though 68 % feel that the governing documentation has the right amount of detail, it is by many seen as too rigid or general to account for local needs and variations, leading to many requests for deviations because the models are not experienced as properly fitting the domain. Seventeen percent of survey respondents report often seeing gaps between what is described in the GD and what is done in practice.

Pragmatic and social quality issues
The survey uncovered challenges regarding the understanding and use of process models. Approximately half of the respondents feel that governing documentation is easy to understand. For others, governing documentation is perceived as vague and ambiguous, especially with respect to authorities and responsibilities. This ambiguity often causes different users to make different interpretations. One in five of the respondents often or always experiences this situation within their department or unit. A good support system for learning could improve users' understanding of the models and the system in general, but only 44 % report being satisfied with the support they are given. Approximately half of the respondents have participated in organized training related to the use of GD. These respondents have a higher score for confidence in, use of, and compliance with the GD than the respondents who have not participated in a training program. The survey showed that good leadership support has a strong positive effect on use, but in general, leaders do not sufficiently encourage better use of GD and often are unable to answer their employees' questions about the management system.

Deontic quality issues
Considering how GD contributes to the management system's goals, the results from the survey indicate that it makes a substantial contribution to a high level of safety (as confirmed by 75 % of the respondents) and moderate-to-high reliability,

but not to high efficiency (37 %). One in five of the respondents feels that safety and efficiency are not properly balanced. Reasons for this imbalance include the following:

- The GD is too focused on safety, and this results in longer task-execution times;
- Requirements are too rigid, and complying with them is time consuming;
- Low user-friendliness of the supporting tools: The relevant GD can be difficult to find;
- Differing interpretations lead to time-consuming discussions;
- Local best practice is not always reflected in GD;
- Lack of cost awareness; and
- Competitiveness is not addressed: Emphasis is put on meeting formal requirements to assure compliance.

We recognize in the list several of the issues meant to be handled by lean approaches as discussed in Sect. 1.2.2.

The quality system is developed especially to support compliance with requirements to reduce risk, an area in which large improvements have been observed over the last decade. Still, there are challenges related to, among other things, the comprehension of some of the models, as set forth above. Whereas the requirements are very detailed and structured, providing guidelines for most quality levels of SEQUAL, the detailed requirements primarily focus on empirical and syntactic quality. Although quality on these levels is also important for pragmatic quality, the guidelines are not always followed, resulting in potential problems for comprehension.

Through the user survey, interviews and conversations have provided valuable insights into how users experience the management system. The use of SEQUAL to structure this discussion points to issues on higher levels (semantic, pragmatic, social, and deontic), where compliance with concrete, objective guidelines for model quality of models is insufficient. Some measures can be taken to achieve higher model quality. Some users feel that the governing documentation is difficult to understand. Increased understanding is a necessity if 100 % compliance is the goal. Measures that can contribute to increased understanding include strictly applying the language guidelines and naming conventions and tailoring model complexity to the needs of the target audience. Processes for including employees' knowledge more directly in the loop, as in, e.g., the AKM approach (Lillehagen and Krogstie 2008), and for clearer model governance are also viewed as important. Interestingly, it can be noted that changing the organization's emphasis (i.e., to focus more on efficiency, not only safety and compliance) seems to influence the perception of quality. As described in Sect. 4.2.1, the use of modeling within the company has evolved over the years, and models and modeling practices that were regarded favorably at an earlier stage might come to be seen as insufficient. Therefore, the serious use of models must be consciously followed up over time.

4.3 Summary

We have in this chapter presented experiences from the use of business process modeling in two large international organizations over a longer period of time. Although covering many of the usage areas of business process modeling, the emphasis of these cases (and this book) is on sense-making, quality assurance, and manual activation of models. We have also seen how the specialization of SEQUAL for business process models is applicable for analyzing the use of process modeling in such cases. In the next chapter, we draw on the SEQUAL framework and the experiences from these and other cases for a better understanding of what it takes to get long-time value from business process modeling.

References

Aagesen, G., Krogstie, J.: Analysis and design of business processes using BPMN. In: vom Brocke, J., Rosemann, M. (eds.) Handbook on Business Process Management. Springer, Berlin (2010)

Bråten, S.: Model monopoly and communications: systems theoretical notes on democratization. Acta Sociol. J. Scand. Social. Assoc. **16**(2), 98–107 (1973)

Christensen, L.C., Johansen, B.W., Midjo, N., Onarheim, J., Syvertsen, T., Totland, T.: Enterprise modeling-practices and perspectives. Comput. Eng., 1071–1084 (1995)

Heggset, M., Krogstie, J., Wesenberg, H.: Ensuring quality of large scale industrial process collections: experiences from a case study. In: The Practice of Enterprise Modeling, pp. 11–25. Springer, Berlin (2014)

Heggset, M., Krogstie, J., Wesenberg, H.: Understanding model quality concerns when using process models in an industrial company. In Proceedings from EMMSAD 2015. Springer, Berlin (2015a)

Heggset, M., Krogstie, J., Wesenberg, H.: The Influence of Syntactic Quality of Enterprise Process Models on Model Comprehension. CAiSE Forum, Stockholm CEUR (2015b)

Houy, C., Fettke, P., Loos, P., van der Aalst, W.M.P., Krogstie, J.: Business process management in the large. Bus. Inf. Syst. Eng. **3**(6), 385–388 (2011)

Krogstie, J.: Integrated goal, data and process modeling: from TEMPORA to model-generated work-places. In: Johannesson, P., Söderstrøm, E. (eds.) Information Systems Engineering From Data Analysis to Process Networks, pp. 43–65. IGI, Hershey (2008)

Krogstie, J.: Model-Based Development and Evolution of Information Systems: A Quality Approach. Springer, London (2012)

Krogstie, J., Dalberg, V., Jensen, S.M. Harmonising business processes of collaborative networked organisations using process modelling. In: PROVE'04. Toulouse, France (2004)

Krogstie, J., Dalberg, V., Jensen, S.M.: Process modeling value framework. In: Manolopoulos, Y., Filipe, J., Constantopoulos, P., Cordeiro, J. (eds.) Selected Papers from 8th International Conference, ICEIS 2006, vol. LNBIP 3, pp. 309–321. Springer, Paphos, Cyprus (2008)

Krogstie, J., de Flon Arnesen, S.: Assessing enterprise modeling languages using a generic quality framework. Inf. Model. Methods Methodol. **1537–9299**, 63–79 (2005)

Lillehagen, F., Krogstie, J.: Active Knowledge Modeling of Enterprises. Springer, Berlin (2008)

Malinova, M., Leopold, H., Mendling, J.: A Meta-Model for Process Map Design. In: CAiSE Forum 2014, June 16–20, Thessaloniki, Greece (2014)

Ould, M.A.: Business Processes—Modeling and Analysis for Re-engineering and Improvement. Wiley, Beverly Hills (1995)

Rossi, M., Brinkkemper, S.: Complexity metrics for system development methods and techniques. Inf. Syst. **21**(2), 209–227 (1994)

Sedera, W., Rosemann, M., Doebeli, G.: A process modelling success model: insights from a case study. In: 11th European Conference on Information Systems, Naples, Italy (2003)

Silver, B.: BPMN Method and Style. Cody-Cassidy Press, Aptos (2012)

Solum, P.E., Østerud, M.: Integreret CASE-verktøy. Kartlegging av teknologien og problemer i forhold til tradisjonell systemutvikling. Master Thesis NTNU, Trondheim Norway (1989)

Totland, T.: Enterprise modeling as a means to support human sense-making and communication in organizations. PhD Thesis, NTNU Trondheim, Norway (1997)

Wesenberg, H.: Enterprise modeling in an agile world PoEM 2011. In: Proceedings of the 4th Conference on Practice of Enterprise Modeling, Oslo, Norway, 2–3 Nov 2011

Chapter 5
Organizational Value of Business Process Modeling

Figure 5.1 illustrates important aspects of achieving value from business process models.

- As discussed in Chap. 1 and further illustrated in Chap. 4, process modeling is done for a set of different goals. Sensible decision and common understanding of the goals to be achieved are necessary prerequisites for achieving value.
- Value is achieved through existing and new process models, and how models evolve and mature is important to follow-up as discussed in Sect. 5.1
- As should be clear from the cases in Chap. 4, having the appropriate modeling language does matter, and we discuss this in more detail in Sect. 5.3.
- Also, the modeling method is of major importance, and we touch aspects of this in Sect. 5.4.
- The long-term management of models depends on appropriate tools as also was illustrated in the cases in Chap. 4. We do not include a detailed exposition of tool aspect in this book though.

The framework was originally developed as it was applied relative to the practice and experience of process modeling across four business areas and across a number of projects and initiatives in a large, international company. The original framework was a further development of material originally presented in Krogstie et al. (2008). The framework was later extended through several additional cases. The original objective was to identify possible improvements and facilitate potential sharing of relevant resources developed as part of performing enterprise process modeling, aiming toward an optimization of the long-term value obtained from modeling and models, that is, not only focusing on the immediate value through individual projects.

© Springer International Publishing Switzerland 2016
J. Krogstie, *Quality in Business Process Modeling*,
DOI 10.1007/978-3-319-42512-2_5

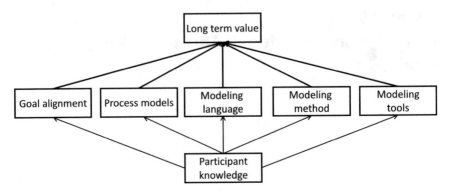

Fig. 5.1 Aspects relevant for achieving long-term value of business process models

Three important observations were made in the original work:

- Even within individual projects, a variety of model objectives can be found, spanning the categories presented in Sect. 1.5.1 and also illustrated in the case in Sect. 4.1. A corresponding variety was found in terms of tools, methods, and attitudes to the potential value of modeling.
- In some initiatives, there were significant differences in the expectations of the modeling results and value—between different stakeholders and also over time.
- Communication and the sharing of resources among projects will mainly be achieved through more or less ad hoc reuse of personnel and models known by project workers in advance if not explicitly planned and managed.

From this, we made three assumptions:

- Single project value and stakeholder satisfaction could be increased by, to a larger degree, focusing on, communicating, and prioritizing between diverging expectations and objectives.
- This would require a common platform for communication about modeling initiative expectations, objectives, and other attributes.
- Such a platform could also facilitate reuse of relevant knowledge, tools, models, methods, and processes between units and projects.

In Wesenberg (2011), Wesenberg describes the following characteristics of enterprise process models:

- Enterprise process models apply to communication through time or space. An enterprise model exists over a longer period of time and is distributed widely throughout the enterprise. The model is often found in a corporate repository of sorts and is accessed through Web portals or similar means.
- The use of the correct abstraction is central. Such abstractions often cover an enormous amount of complex enterprise knowledge that cannot be easily

transferred to a model. If the incorrect abstraction is chosen, a model will never become an enterprise model and will instead gather dust in a drawer somewhere.

- Enterprise models must be managed, and enterprise process models are (or at least should be) managed properly. They are often subject to strict versioning routines, configuration management practices, and release plans. In many ways, enterprise models are similar to source code and should be subject to the same professional practices. If the models are not managed properly, they will not be trusted, and they will subsequently fail to achieve their full potential as enterprise models.
- Enterprise process models must have the correct quality.

These assumptions lead to the development of a framework concerning best practices for increasing the value of process modeling and models over time. This proposal consists of a taxonomy, a recommended model of activities for process modeling value-increasing initiatives, and links to relevant knowledge and best practices for each step of the process.

The remainder of this chapter starts with an overview of the framework of best practices for increasing the value of process modeling and models and discusses its applicability with regard to challenges identified in earlier projects. Specific aspects relative to appropriate process modeling notations (Sect. 5.3) and methods (Sect. 5.4) are briefly discussed toward the end of the chapter.

5.1 A Framework for Increasing the Value of Process Modeling

This best practice framework attempts to increase the value of modeling and models through enhanced awareness about current and future stakeholders, any (potential) conflicts of interest, stakeholder expectations, and potential value to be gained, as well as any negative effects increasing total costs. Based on this knowledge, decisions regarding resource allocation, choice of modeling methods and tools, delegation of responsibilities, etc., can be made to optimize the value of a modeling activity and its resulting models on a project level as well as on a long-term organizational level. The basic elements of the framework are a recommended main process and some basic concepts, elaborated upon in the description of each step in the main process. The value framework process is broken down into four subprocesses:

1. Identify context: Context is the surroundings of an initiative that might influence decisions as for reuse of models, modeling languages, modeling methods, and modeling tools.
2. Identify potential value: Value is identified in relation to the identified context but also to potential value outside the initial project scope.

3. Choose practice: The practice focuses on the strategies and practice around the modeling and the models. Note that methods for the actual modeling, as discussed in earlier chapters, are not a central point here but are obviously related.
4. Managing modeling capabilities is the work performed at an organizational level to ensure the long-term capability of the organization of obtaining value from models, including assurance of the right knowledge and skills in the organization on goals of modeling, process models, modeling languages, modeling methods, and modeling tools.

The recommended process is initiated when a need for modeling has been identified. The three main steps related to the individual projects are detailed below.

5.1.1   Identifying Context

Identifying context is primarily about expressing the circumstances of the identified need for modeling as a basis for further communication, prioritization, and planning. This identification will usually coincide with the writing of an application for project funding, development of a project mandate, and/or a project plan. At this step, one should remain within the scope of the initial need, usually expressed in traditional project documentation with formal obligations. The main issues to be clarified include the following:

- Identification of the organization's installed base, including existing reusable models or descriptions, current usage and standards for the use of modeling languages, methods and tools in the organization, and other relevant tacit or explicit constraints.
- Identification of relevant reference models and constraints on their use.
- Identification of the context of the modeling or model activity/initiative, including users and other stakeholders, model uses, and objectives (cf. Sect. 1.5.1).

There are always different actors, holding one or more roles, related to a modeling initiative and a model. Users are using the models or participating personally in the modeling to achieve one or more objectives. Other stakeholders may not be directly using the models but do extract value from planned objectives. Techniques, e.g., from user-centered design, are useful at this stage during the identification of stakeholder types. Use includes how the modeling and models are going to be used to achieve the objectives. Objectives are the goals and purposes of the modeling and models. Installed base includes tacit and explicit assets already controlled by the organization that will have influence on the modeling and model context. Constraints include issues, such as personal and organizational knowledge, and may be tacit or explicitly expressed constraints, organizational guidelines or instructions (explicit constraints), existing tools, modeling languages, etc. Reusable models are models or other documentations that were created for other purposes either within the organization or outside the organization (reference models), but that could be reused in a new project.

5.1.2   Identifying Potential Value

In step 1, we identified the context in which the modeling and the models were meant to play a role. In step 2, "identify potential value," the objective is to capture any (potential) extra and positive benefits of the modeling and models, thus exceeding the primary objectives captured in step 1. Value may be connected to the resulting models or to the modeling activity in of itself.

The objectives identified in step 1 will often relate to the concrete modeling project, while any potential value to the remainder of the organization will typically be ignored in the formal project documentation developed at this stage—due to a lack of awareness or to avoid complicating responsibilities and bindings. This highlights an important challenge concerning obtaining value from modeling on a long term basis in an organizational setting (a similar challenge that confronts all initiatives for organizational change involving ICT). The primary objective is typically related to delivering value in the individual project; when push comes to shove, the top priorities of the current project are often all that matter when prioritizing resources. Because most organizations have lived with business processes being supported by an IT application portfolio for some time, the importance of also maintaining a long-term perspective has most likely larger understanding than in the past.

Value can be explicit and easy to grasp; however, often, more tacit value might also occur. Tacit value, e.g., the improved understanding of a work process for a modeler originally producing models for others, is often not explicitly captured in traditional project documentation, but may still affect decisions before or during a project, the perceived value of the project in retrospect, or value in future projects in a similar problem domain. Future reuse of the models can represent an added value provided by current modeling and models, especially if this potential is considered at an early stage.

5.1.3   Choosing Practice

The choice of a suitable practice should be based on the identified contexts of the modeling and models, as well as the identified expected value. Here, practice includes both modeling and management practice. Modeling practice includes reuse strategy, methods, languages, and tools, whereas managing practice defines how to manage the modeling, the models, and the work processes. SEQUAL is especially helpful here concerning modeling practice related to methods, languages, and tools, having the stakeholders of the models and the goals of modeling already defined in the previous steps. When goals or stakeholder types are changed during a modeling project, one needs to reassess these aspects and potentially select a new or updated modeling language, method, or tool, therein applying SEQUAL in one or more of the manners exemplified in Chap. 4.

The choice of modeling practice includes deciding what methods, languages, and tools are to be used for the development and evolution of the models. The need of formality may differ based on the context and on the expected value identified. The modeling of a model to be included in an enterprise architecture requires greater formality in terms of methods, tools, and languages compared to modeling for sense-making and informal communication, where the model might serve as a short-term artifact. Generally, the choice of practice is very much dependent on the process knowledge maturity in or across the organization.

Whereas knowledge often arises in collaborative sense-making tasks on the individual and small-group levels and for iterative shifts between user collaboration and automated design processes, it is in many cases also relevant to spread the knowledge established at this level to a higher organizational level. To examine this in greater detail, we base the discussion on the work on knowledge maturing from the MATURE project. The following is based on Kump et al. (2011) and Krogstie et al. (2013).

The knowledge maturing model outlines the following phases (see Fig. 5.2), which we will illustrate referring back to the case presented in Sect. 4.1:

- Ia. Exploration: New ideas are developed by individuals either through informal discussions or by "browsing" the knowledge available within the organization and beyond. Extensive search and retrieval activities potentially result in huge amounts of materials facilitating idea generation. At some stage, someone in one of the offices of the company got the idea for them providing certification services in addition to classification services.

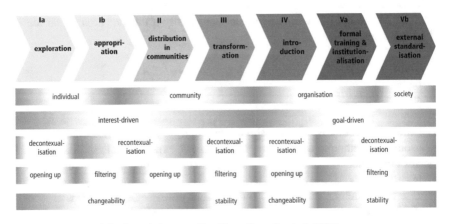

Fig. 5.2 Framework for knowledge maturing (from Krogstie et al. 2013)

- Ib. Appropriating ideas (individuation): New ideas that have been enriched, refined, or otherwise contextualized with respect to their use are now appropriated by the individual. Knowledge sources and new knowledge are "bookmarked" so that an individual can benefit from its future (re)use. Some can use process modeling and other type of modeling to support the internal structuring of material for individual sense-making. As for the certification case, a lot of material is available from ISO and others as for how certification could be done.
- II. Distributing in communities (community interaction): This phase is driven by social motives such as belonging to a preferred social group or the expectation of reciprocal knowledge exchange within the community or project. A common terminology for individual contributions is developed and shared among community members, and simple (process) models of the situation might be made for supporting communication within the community. Individual offices in this case took on provided certification services relative to limited set of given standards, based on local skill and market needs.
- III. Transformation (into information): Artifacts created in the preceding phases are often unstructured and restricted to a limited local context. They are only comprehensible to people in this community because shared knowledge remains needed for interpretation. In Phase III, more structured documents and models are created in which knowledge is made more transferable, and context is made explicit with the purpose of easing the transfer of knowledge to people other than those in the originating community or project. Some standard process modeling notation using standard tools might be used to support knowledge transfer. In the certification phase, transformation is related to creating common company-wide standards as for how to provide these types of services, first by modeling best practice in existing offices and then by developing the harmonized process.

From Phase IV on, there are two alternative paths of knowledge maturing:

- IV_1. Ad hoc training (instruction): Activities related to creating training materials out of documents and models that are typically not suited as learning material because they have not been developed with didactical considerations in mind. Topics are refined to ease teaching, consumption, or reuse. Tests help assess the knowledge level and select learning objects or paths. The material can be used for formal training in Phase V ($V1_a$ formal training (instruction)). The subject area becomes teachable to novices. A curriculum integrates learning content into a sequence using didactical concepts to guide learners in their learning process. Learning modules and courses can be combined into programs used to, for example, prepare for taking on a new role as part of contributing to a business process.
- IV_2. Piloting (implementation): Experiences are deliberately collected with a test case stressing pragmatic action and trying a solution before a larger rollout of a product or service to an external community or new rules, procedures, or processes to an internal target community such as project teams or other organizational units.

Know-how can be institutionalized at the beginning of Phase V. This was the approach done in the certification case. When the harmonized model was created, one piloted the implementation of this at selected offices, investigated the acceptance issues and estimated the implementation effort.

- $V2_a$. Institutionalizing (introduction): Within an organization, formalized models and documents that have been learned by knowledge workers are implemented into the organizational infrastructure in the form of business rules, business processes, or standard operating procedures. In the organization-external case, products or services are launched on the market as standard offerings. The institutionalization in the certification case was through the implementation of the models in a work support tool.
- V_b. Standardizing (incorporation): This phase covers standardization or certification, promoting the process model as a reference model for adaptation and reuse by others. Certificates confirm that participants of formal training activities achieved a certain degree of proficiency or justify compliance with a set of rules that the organizations have agreed to fulfill. Standards also assist in connecting products or services or showing that they fulfill laws or recommendations before being offered on a certain market. One did not get to this stage in the case presented in Sect. 4.1.

In the knowledge maturing process, models developed for other purposes can act as guidance, being more or less fully reused and adapted to the case at hand. Note that the learning and experiences will often need to be more restricted, the more widely one wants to share the knowledge.

Another dimension is the formality of the knowledge captured in models or in other forms, which is very much related to the level of knowledge maturity one wants to achieve. The formality can be as follows:

1. Informal annotations.
2. Relations (e.g., as open-linked data) to or between existing knowledge sources can be added.
3. Annotations linked to the context (thus potentially linking process labels to concepts in the common ontology (Lin et al. 2006)).
4. Codified knowledge (e.g., as part of a new formal business process in a limited area).
5. Structured to act as basis for ad hoc or organizational training.
6. Structured to act as a tool, product, or process to be reused across the organization (e.g., the quality system model described in Sect. 4.2).
7. Structured to act as input to external standards or reference process.

The availability and formality of the captured data might also be temporally restrained; e.g., all new knowledge is kept within a project until the end of the project. Then, one can first share information more widely, e.g., through reflection sessions shared either at the instance level (e.g., as examples of good or bad practices) or at the type level (e.g., updating some organizational methodology). In all cases, it is important to clarify the level of knowledge maturity that you have

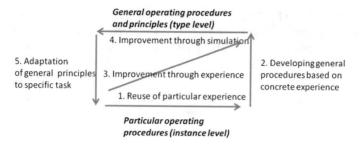

Fig. 5.3 Modes of knowledge reuse

achieved and the ambitions to increase the level of maturity. Aiming too high will result in waste due to extra processing, and aiming too low might result in waste through undercommunication, with possible results being waste due to unnecessary searching, interpretation work, and misunderstandings.

Figure 5.3 illustrates modes of process improvement within an organization.

How process improvement is performed varies depending on the knowledge maturity of the processes in an organization. When the knowledge is only at the individual level, reuse is between personal experiences at the instance level to a new situation at the same level (mode 1 above). This can also occur within the community. When formalizing knowledge, one typically enters mode 2 in Fig. 5.3 and develops general procedures, products, or rules typically based on the experiences from a number of instances. Traditionally, this mode is achieved by humans through workshops, focus groups, or other methods of gathering experiences from many instances. In addition, external reference processes might be consulted in this mode. In some settings, one could also imagine using more automated techniques (such as process mining (van der Aalst et al. 2011)). We will return briefly to this area in the next chapter. Process improvement in the traditional sense that was described in Chap. 1 is mode 3, therein creating a new type-level process based on an existing type-level process and existing instances resulting from applying the type-level process, potentially on a higher maturity level. One might also apply the improvement purely based on the type-level model, e.g., through process simulation, indicated as mode 4. The final mode (mode 5) is relevant when the new (individual and project) task is to use the type-level process model in new concrete instances, e.g., as guidance, but typically while adapting the generic process description to the specific task. In, e.g., a workflow system, this activation would be automatic. In between the automatic workflow activation and a purely manual activation, one finds the approach of interactive activation, a mode often used in connection with emergent and interactive workflows (Krogstie and Jørgensen 2004).

Process improvement is typically the result of a reflective process (reflection on action). Reflection might also be relevant within the task (reflection in action) for rapid adaptations; however, our prime focus in this section is reflection on action for learning and knowledge maturing over time. Reflection entails adding an additional dimension to existing knowledge representations.

To further discuss potential tool support for reflection, we use a model of computer-supported reflective learning from the MIRROR project (Krogstie et al. 2012), as depicted in Fig. 5.4. Although this is meant to address both individual and collaborative reflection, our main focus here is collaborative reflection.

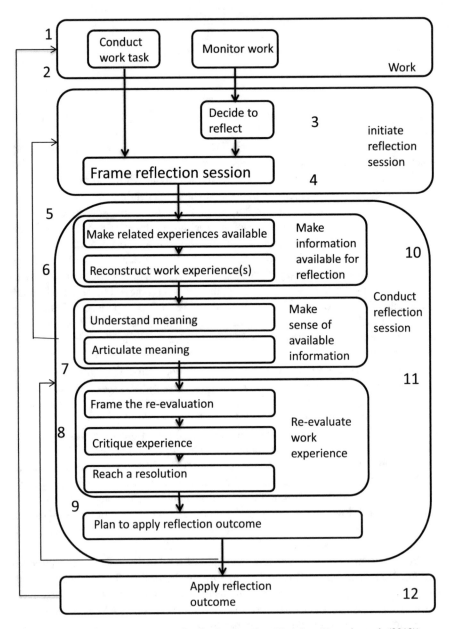

Fig. 5.4 Model of computer supported reflective learning (Based on Krogstie et al. (2012))

Overall, when performing process improvement, it is important to ensure that the relevant data for improvement are captured as part of work, frame the improvement sessions, have the necessary information available in the session, and ensure the availability of the improved knowledge after the sessions. Note that even if the reflection sessions are singled out above, they might often be conducted in practice closely integrated with normal work activities. What to have available when performing reflection is obviously very dependent on the mode of knowledge reuse (see Fig. 5.3). For example, in mode 1, only instance-level information is available (typically only from the current project). In mode 3, both the information on the type-level process and the information on one or more instantiations of the type-level process are useful to have available (in addition to knowledge about how the knowledge was adapted to the specific project). More precisely, looking back at Fig. 5.4, we find the following:

1. One needs to support data relevant to reconstructing and reflecting on experiences from work.
2. Data on, e.g., behavior might also be useful (e.g., tracking what part of the process is used as described in the case in Sect. 4.2).
3. Tools can contain reminders about suitable times for reflection (e.g., after a project release) or provide information relevant to the decision to reflect on action (e.g., when situations of waste are discovered during work).
4. In addition to the trigger for reflection, it can be important to have sufficient information relative to the context of the work that triggered the reflection.
5. When people involved in reflection are not present at the same place, methods of sharing the experience and other experiences relevant to the reflection can be important.
6. Relevant data from different sources might be important to introduce into the reflection process both at the instance level and at the type level, as indicated above.
7. To make sense of the experiences, one might need information about the surrounding context.
8. How to conclude based on a reflection might be structured in a certain form or according to concepts found, e.g., in a common ontology or terminology; this information would be used to structure the newly developed knowledge.
9. The results from the reflection should be captured, e.g., in a process repository or linked to the original knowledge sources.
10. The entire process should be shared via methods for using the working environment.
11. In addition, how the reflection session is performed can be improved using experiences about how it has been conducted.
12. The results from the reflection must be made available via the normal work tools or influence the normal work practice in the organization.

As we understand, models that are developed have different characteristics and needs. One dimension is the relevance over time and space.

- Relevance in time: This describes how long the models are relevant. In one extreme, models may only be relevant in a meeting; in contrast, the other extreme is whereby they are relevant for the lifetime of the organization. As an example of an intermediate case, a requirements model for a new IT system is typically only relevant in practice in the project developing the system, although ideally it should be relevant over the entire life cycle of the application system because the system is bound to be maintained over a number of years (Krogstie and Sølvberg 1994; Krogstie 1995, 2012).
- Relevance for whom: Is the model only relevant for a small group, for a department in the organization, for the entire organization, or even beyond the organizational boundaries? Observing the knowledge maturity model, relevance for whom can often change over time.

Another differentiation is relative to the formality of the modeling language and modeling approach. The choice of the formality of the modeling practice should be based on where these fit on the knowledge maturity spectrum. Sense-making initiatives generally require a low level of formality of practice, whereas when developing a quality system such as in Sect. 4.2 or an enterprise architecture acting as a corporate memory, a more formal approach is needed. The choice of methods, tools, and languages, as well as the choice of managing practice, should reflect the level of need for formality. Formality can be relative to a number of areas:

- Formality of modeling language: The utilized modeling language may have a formally defined syntax and semantics. In particular, a requirement for computer-assisted analysis and automatic activation mandates the use of a well-defined formal semantics of the language. Most other usage areas are also made easier with languages that have a formal syntax, although sense-making with a limited relevance in time for a limited number of actors can often best be supported by languages with a less formal syntax.
- Formality of tool support: The approach is supported more or less well by available modeling tools. Whereas sense-making and modeling as context for development can be supported by ad hoc tools (unless there is a need for traceability back to these models), the other goals warrant more formal tool support, especially where the time and actor scope are not a small, short-term group. In particular, this applies to computer-assisted analysis and automatic or interactive activation; moreover, manual enterprise models supporting quality assurance, as reported in the case reported in Sect. 4.2, also mandate advanced tool support to be able to retrieve the correct version of the relevant model.
- Formality of modeling process: The modeling can be conducted rather ad hoc or according to a well-defined plan. Note that modeling for sense-making and communication can be part of the early stages of a formal modeling process. Thus, approaches to participatory modeling using for instance 4EM (Sandkuhl et al. 2014) provide a rigorous modeling methodology, wherein the participatory component is only a part of the overall process.
- Formality of management. This includes the following:

- Management of the modeling language (in case there are language developments and adjustments using meta-modeling facilities, particularly a focus in the case reported in Sect. 4.1 but also exemplified in Sect. 4.2).
- Management of the usage of the modeling language (with more or less formal guidelines for the application of the modeling language, e.g., as reported in the case in Sect. 4.2).
- Management of the modeling tools: Ensure that the right versions of the tools are available for everyone involved when needed.
- Management of the models: Ensuring, e.g., versioning, and status tracking of models. Ensure that process owners are designated and have the necessary authority to manage the evolution of the models including having mechanisms to capture feedback and improvement suggestions on the current models.

It is important to recognize the differences between the three areas, namely modeling, models, and work processes, and to assign these areas to three different roles. The practice of managing the modeling process, the models, and the work processes being modeled must be based on the identified contexts and potential values and on the chosen modeling practice. If the context is pure sense-making and if the models are to be discarded after they are modeled, the establishment of a practice for the managing of the model and work process is not necessary. The closer the context of use is to develop an enterprise architecture or quality system to be used and evolved over a long time period, the more important it is to have a formal managing practice. Depending on the contexts of use and the modeling practice, it must be decided whether the models and the work processes should be managed after the modeling activity. It is important to differentiate between the management of the work processes itself and the models.

To increase the likelihood of dissemination, we have developed a model of the framework and related areas in the Troux Architect modeling tool. Figure 5.5 is a screenshot of the top level of this model, indicating the areas of information provided (but not showing the internal links between different areas). The different parts are briefly described below:

- The value framework process is the process described above in this chapter.
- The development processes include tasks related to modeling according to the defined goals of modeling in addition to more general process patterns.
- Management processes apply to processes across individual projects, including the following:

  - Manage modeling tools (as part of a development architecture).
  - Manage models (including model versions).
  - Manage the use of reference models (and follow-up on their evolution independent of the use in the company).
  - Align modeling initiatives.
  - Perform training (on modeling languages, approaches, and tools).
  - Evolve modeling languages (in case a meta-modeling approach is used).
  - Manage value framework (evolving this model).

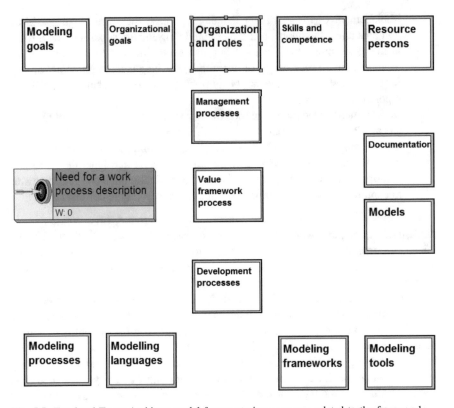

Fig. 5.5 Top-level Troux Architect model for structuring resources related to the framework

- Modeling goals include the goals of modeling with relationships to other parts of the framework where they apply.
- Organizational goals are goals that can be achieved within the company with the help of modeling and thus influence what are the relevant goals of modeling.
- Modeling processes that can be performed.
- Modeling languages list both standard modeling languages and modeling languages that have been developed for the organization in particular often on the basis of existing standardized languages, including specific guidelines for modeling as we saw examples of in both Sects. 4.1 and 4.2.
- Modeling frameworks bundle the modeling value framework into relevant other frameworks with larger scopes (such as the Zachman framework and TOGAF for enterprise architecture).
- Modeling tools list those tools that are relevant to the organization (both formal and more informal and manual tools).
- Documentation includes additional documentation on methods, languages, models, and modeling tools.

- Resource persons include persons competent in modeling in the organization and also potentially resource persons available externally.
- Skills and competence lists relevant to competencies, both related to the domain of the organization and related to IS development and modeling in particular.
- Organization and roles indicate the particular organization and roles defined for IS development and modeling.

Aspects within the different areas are interrelated as appropriate (not shown here).

5.2 Applying the Value Framework

Through several case studies, we have identified the expected and experienced value of modeling work and models, as well as experienced challenges. In this section, we present some of the reported (potential) value. We will later analyze how the framework addresses the reported challenges.

5.2.1 Identifying Potential Value

The stakeholders in our case studies presented many valuable outcomes in addition to those initially intended for the modeling project. Some of these are as follows:
Communication:

- The high-level process models encouraged an agreement among the management participants that was vital for the remainder of the project, therein creating important common references, identification, and enthusiasm.
- The process models triggered communication, being something to which everyone could relate. A quote from one of the participants underlying this was as follows: "Three boxes and some arrows: This is a fantastic communication tool."
- Communication was initiated and facilitated by and through the models.
- Modeling is seen as a mechanism for extracting knowledge from people's heads and representing this knowledge externally.

Learning:

- The modeling process itself turned out to be a learning experience for the participating domain experts, therein increasing their knowledge about the processes linking their own area with other areas of the organization.

- Through the workshop sessions, the participants obtained a substantial amount of knowledge from interacting with each other, "new" information was uncovered, and understandings were improved.
- People better understand their own views after a modeling session.
- The participation of the domain experts in the modeling process of a domain is important. The result would not have been the same if modelers from outside created the models based on interviews only.
- The models helped address and store the competence of people in the organization.
- Training was quicker when process models were used.

Long-term benefits:

- The process model gives the organization one language and one tool for everyone in the organization, namely a common frame of reference.
- Simple and effective diagrams indicate what is important to the organization.
- Through modeling as-is (the current situation), and not simply to-be (the requested future situation), current best practice is secured and remembered.
- The models are used in marketing toward potential customers. There is marketing value in telling the world that the organization has documented the processes.

5.2.2   Addressing Challenges to Modeling

To extract the additional value from the modeling initiatives and the models, in the following, we will address some of the major identified challenges in our case studies and examine how the framework could indicate a solution to these challenges. For each paragraph, we state the challenge and then how it is addressed using the framework.

Challenge 1: During organizational changes, models may have to be merged as processes from different parts of the organization (or across organizations) and are to be unified. The use of different modeling tools and languages for different models increases this challenge.

Example: Several as-is processes were to be harmonized and their documenting models merged into a common process model. The models were created for different user groups and therein originated from different organizational units and also from different countries. The modeling processes were also different and involved different types of people.

Framework application: Such models are most likely based on different methods, languages, and tools and created for different objectives, uses, and stakeholders. The historic context and the organizational installed base of the modeling and managing practice of each of the models should be investigated to establish a reuse strategy and to choose the correct current modeling and managing practice.

Challenge 2: To address situations in which the modeling begins as an informal activity but where the resulting models develop into a process defining tool to be implemented/activated in the workflow sense. The original language and tools often do not meet new expectations for the model to be kept updated, operationalized, scalable, and extendable with new functionality. The experience shows that the chosen tool and language often do not apply to this new situation.

Framework application: Awareness of where on the scale of knowledge maturity the models were initially created and where on the scale the models have ended up (and where they can be expected to end up). Sense-making models do not require a very high level of formality, whereas enterprise architecture models often do require such formality. Being conscious about this makes it easier to identify what has to be changed in the modeling and managing practice to fit the new situation.

Challenge 3: To keep the models and other descriptions updated and consistent.

Example: It becomes difficult to keep the models updated as the complexity increases and the number of non-integrated tools increases.

Framework application: The framework suggests careful analysis of the expected modeling context before choosing the modeling practice. Considering the future complexity when choosing methods, language and tools will simplify model management. The framework also states the importance of viewing the management of the models as a specific activity, therein stressing the importance of appointing someone responsible for the model. This is a different role than the modeling responsibility or the work process responsibility (process owner), but the person in this role must work closely with people in these roles.

Challenge 4: To implement the use of models as standard practice in the organization, particularly outside the modeling team.

Example: It is often challenging to make the models an integrated part of the organization and to involve the different stakeholders to the extent that they feel a sense of ownership and responsibility for the models. When the individuals performing the modeling leave the project and the modeling is left to the domain experts to complete, implement, and evolve, experience shows that the focus on the models often fades. If the modelers leave too early, the models may not be implemented in the organization at all.

Framework application: Identify all the expected users and other stakeholders during the initial phase of the modeling activity, examine their expected areas of use, and identify potential value on short and long time frames. By choosing a modeling practice to increase the value across all identified stakeholders, ownership and usefulness are improved even for stakeholders not participating in the modeling. If many stakeholders should be involved in the modeling, one can use techniques such as "Modeling Conference" and other types of participatory modeling activities described later in this chapter (Gjersvik et al. 2004).

Challenge 5: To produce views of the model according to different needs.

Example: Specific users and specific objectives of use require adapted views of the model. The development of these views is often time-consuming and challenging both technically and in terms of what to include.

Framework application: Identify the users and other stakeholders as parts of the context, analyze their background knowledge and needs, and determine for what purpose each stakeholder is going to use the models. In the extreme, one might end up with separate views for each stakeholder, which would be very time-consuming to keep up to date and might hinder the model's ability to act as a common picture of the organization for all stakeholders. Methods, language, and tools should then be chosen based on this. The production of model-generated workplaces in AKM (Lillehagen and Krogstie 2008) is an example of an attempt to make view generation efficient. In addition to personal views, one might want to have ad hoc collaborative views in the so-called virtual obeyas (Rossi et al. 2016).

Challenge 6: In some cases, the models might restrict and limit communication.

Example: High-level models are easy to agree upon; however, real gaps between the model and the current situation remain uncovered. A model is only one view of the world. When a model is the main artifact used for communication, the discussions often exclude those issues not included in the model.

Framework application: Carefully identify the context and the potential value of the modeling and models before creating the models. Consciousness about how to increase the potential value of communication will potentially help creating a more fitting model. Awareness of the limitations of a model and its restrictions is the key.

Challenge 7: The models are used in situations for which they were not intended.

Example: Models are often initially created primarily having one clear objective. This is challenging when others want to use them as a basis for other work, especially if the original assumptions on the use and purpose of the models are not documented.

Framework application: Through an analysis in the early phase of the modeling activity, identify the primary use as well as potential future uses and additional potential value. Looking upon this in relation to process knowledge maturity might help to predict possible directions of model use. The accommodation of indications of future uses of the models should be considered when choosing the modeling and the managing practice. When in a reuse situation, where a modeling initiative is going to reuse previously developed models, it is important to investigate the context in which the models were created and what modeling and managing practice have been used. The decision on a reuse strategy should be based on this investigation.

Challenge 8: To be conscientious about correctly distributing the responsibility of the modeling, models, and processes.

Example: One person was responsible for everything related to the processes and the models.

Framework application: The framework makes distinctions between the activities of managing the modeling, the models, and the work processes. One role is related to the management of the modeling, another to the management of the models, and a third to the management of the work processes. Process owners in large organizations are seldom those most familiar with process modeling.

5.3 Evaluation of Process Modeling Languages

As we have observed, using the appropriate modeling language is a very important aspect of developing models of high quality. The SEQUAL framework also includes this part, and a longer description of aspects relative to quality of modeling languages is found in Krogstie (2012). In recent years, BPMN has become the de facto standard, and at least parts of BPMN are used in many organizational settings. On the other hand, it is clear that there are process modeling situations in which BPMN is not the best fit, and as we have seen in Chap. 4, adaptations of standard modeling languages are quite common among those using modeling on a larger scale. Thus, here, we will examine investigations related to the quality of BPMN extending the treatments of Aagesen and Krogstie (2010, 2015).

5.3.1 Quality of BPMN

The importance of evaluating available methods for modeling increases as the number of available methods grows because the results will guide the users in selecting the best-fit method for the task at hand. In addition, when taking a standard modeling language such as BPMN as a basis, we have observed in the previous chapter how one in a large organization specializes the language to the particular organizational setting and goals of modeling, therein highlighting the importance of also examining the quality of the modeling language. We exemplify this here by more closely examining the quality of BPMN.

By evaluating existing methods, one will not only be able to compare their suitability for solving the problem at hand but also help determine the skills required of the user and model audience before performing the modeling task. By using formalized frameworks in the assessment of newly developed methods and comparing the evaluation with results from earlier studies, it would be possible to determine whether the overall appropriateness of the new method is better than that of its predecessors. All modeling languages will have deficiencies; thus, even when having decided upon a modeling language, it is important to know how one can avoid some of the problems with these by using appropriate use of tools and methods.

Different approaches to evaluating modeling languages include analytical and empirical methods, and both single-language and comparative evaluations have been developed. Empirical methods should investigate the possibility for modelers to use the language, comprehension of models developed in the language, and the ability to learn from and act according to the knowledge provided in the models (Gemino and Wand 2003; Krogstie et al. 2006). While analytical evaluations can be conducted as soon as the specification of the language is made available, empirical evaluations would in most cases require the users of the new method to have some experience with its use; for that, the method would need some time with the user community before evaluations can take place. Empirical studies might involve the investigation of whether the results from the analytical studies are supported and to what extent they have an impact in practice. Such studies would also involve performing case studies and surveys to discover whether the method is as appropriate as expected and whether it is used according to expectations.

BPMN has been around for many years and has been used extensively. It has been evaluated both analytically and empirically by a number of researchers. Even if BPMN 2.0 is relatively new, as discussed in Chap. 1, the core notation used for communication and analysis is similar to BPMN 1.X; thus, it is reasonable to build on evaluations of previous versions of the language when they focus on modeling at the descriptive level. The following section briefly introduces the evaluation approaches, followed by their outcomes. The evaluation results will be summarized below. For details about the evaluations, please refer to their original reporting in the referenced papers.

5.3.2 Ontological Analysis Using the Bunge–Wand–Weber Framework

The Bunge–Wand–Weber (BWW) framework defines a representation model based on an ontology defined by Bunge in 1977 (Wand and Weber 1993; Recker et al. 2006) and is an example of a reference ontology/model extensively used in the conceptual and process modeling fields. Two main evaluation criteria are ontological completeness and ontological clarity. Ontological completeness is decided by the degree of construct deficit, indicating to what extent the modeling language maps to the constructs of the BWW representation model. Ontological clarity is determined by construct overload, where the modeling language constructs represent several BWW constructs, namely construct redundancy, where one BWW construct can be expressed by several language constructs and a construct excess, having language constructs not represented in the BWW model.

BWW-based evaluations are presented in Recker et al. (2005 and 2007) and Rosemann et al. (2006), and their findings include the following:

- Representation of state. The BPMN specification provides a relatively high degree of ontological completeness (Rosemann et al. 2006) although with some limitations. For example, states of things cannot be modeled with the BPMN notation. You can associate state names with data objects, though. This situation can result in a lack of focus in terms of state and transformation laws not being able to capture all relevant business rules.
- System structure. Systems structured around things are underrepresented, and as a result, problems will arise when information must be obtained about the dependencies within a modeled system.
- Representational capabilities compared with other approaches. A representational analysis was conducted in Rosemann et al. (2006) on different approaches that show that BPMN appears to be quite mature in terms of

representation capabilities. This can perhaps be partly explained by the fact that the previous approaches such as EPC and Petri nets influenced the development of BPMN. It is interesting that among all the process modeling notations only BPMN of the is able to address all aspects of things, including properties and types of things. From this, it is possible to conclude that BPMN appears to represent a considerable improvement compared with other techniques for this type of modeling. The combination of ebXML and BPMN would provide maximum ontological completeness (MOC) with minimum ontological overlap (MOO) according to Recker et al. (2005).

5.3.3 The Workflow Pattern Framework

Whereas the BWW ontology looks at individual concepts, the Workflow Pattern Framework (van der Aalst et al. 2003; Russell et al. 2006) provides a taxonomy of generic, recurring concepts and constructs relevant in the context of process-aware information systems (Wohed et al. 2005) (see also Ouyang et al. (2010)). The patterns have been used to examine the capabilities of business process modeling languages, such as BPMN, UML activity diagrams, and EPCs; Web service composition languages, such as WCSI; and business process execution languages, such as BPML, XPDL, and BPEL (Russell et al. 2006).

The patterns are divided into control-flow patterns, data patterns, resource patterns, and exception patterns. Workflow pattern-based evaluations are presented in Recker et al. (2007) and Wohed et al. (2005, 2006). The outcomes of the evaluations include the following:

- Representation of state. The limited representation of state in BPMN presents difficulties in representing certain control-flow patterns (Wohed et al. 2006). There are further inherent difficulties in applying the Workflow Pattern Framework for assessing a language that does not have a commonly agreed-upon formal semantic or an execution environment. There are several ambiguities that can be found in the BPMN specification due to the lack of formalization (Wohed et al. 2006). This has been improved in BPMN 2.0.
- Multiple representations of the same pattern. The simple workflow patterns have multiple BPMN representations, and capturing the most advanced patterns requires deep knowledge of the attributes associated with BPMN modeling constructs that do not have a graphical representation.
- Support for instances. Workflow and environment data patterns are not supported due to the lack of support for instance-specific data for a task or sub-process with a "multiple instance" marker.
- Resource modeling. Support for representation of resources in BPMN is minimal, but the modeling of organizational structures and resources is regarded to be beyond the scope of BPMN. The authors state that the lane and pool constructs contradict this.

5.3.4 Evaluating BPMN Using SEQUAL

SEQUAL is described in Chap. 2 and extended in Chap. 3. For language evaluation, it is the language quality as a means to achieve model quality that is particularly relevant, and this is briefly described in Chap 2. A longer description is found
in Krogstie (2012). Evaluations of BPMN using SEQUAL are performed by
Nysetvold and Krogstie (2006) and Wahl and Sindre (2005) and are also discussed
in Recker et al. (2007). In relation to BPMN, the following findings were mentioned
by Wahl and Sindre (2005):

- Missing support for business-specific terms. Wahl and Sindre (2005) confirmed
  that the language does not contain business-specific terms even though the
  purpose of the language is the modeling of business processes.
- Understanding and use of constructs. The language notation is similar to that of
  other available languages with the same purpose (such as UML activity diagrams) and would be helpful for users familiar with different approaches of this
  type. The goal of BPMN is, however, to be understandable to more than simply
  users with previous process modeling experience, and grasping the complexity
  of the most advanced aspects of BPMN is, according to the authors, unrealistic
  without extensive training. This is somewhat confirmed by the case study
  reported by zur Mühlen and Ho (2008) (see below); however, this is partly
  considered in the leveling of BPMN 2.0 described in Sect. 1.5.
- Diagram layout. The authors also argue that it would be difficult to externalize
  relevant knowledge using only BPMN if the knowledge in question extends
  beyond the domain of business processes. There are few strict guidelines in the
  BPMN specification itself on how to lay out diagram constructs in relation to
  each other, which produces the potential to create BPMNs with poor layouts.
  Therefore, a number of style guides have been proposed by, e.g., Silver (2012),
  which are included as part of the guidelines described in Chap. 2 which is
  included in the extended SEQUAL framework for business process models in
  Chap. 3.

Nysetvold and Krogstie (2006) conducted an empirical evaluation of BPMN,
therein comparing it to EEML (Krogstie 2008) and UML activity diagrams (Booch
et al. 2005) using a specialization of the SEQUAL framework tailored to the
specific goals of modeling and the organizational setting. The usage area to be
supported was process modeling in relation to the implementation of a
service-oriented architecture (SOA) in an insurance company. The evaluation
ranked BPMN highest in all categories except domain appropriateness, in which
EEML had the best performance. However, EEML lost to BPMN on both tool and
modeler appropriateness. The evaluation on domain appropriateness partly over-
lapped the evaluations above, e.g., by including an evaluation relative to the support
for modeling control patterns. Other parts of this evaluation were particularly
adapted to the expressed needs of the case organization based on existing experience with process modeling and SOA development.

- Comprehensibility appropriateness is the category that was appointed the second highest importance because the organization regarded the ability to use the language across the different areas of the organization and to improve communication between the IT department and the business departments to be very important. In this category, BPMN and UML activity diagrams ranked equally high, which is not surprising given that they use the same swimlane/pool metaphor as a basic structuring mechanism.
- Participant appropriateness and tool appropriateness were given equal importance, and BPMN ranked somewhat surprisingly high in both areas. When observing the evaluation not taking tool appropriateness into account, the three languages ranked almost equal. Thus, it was in this case the focus on the chosen implementation platforms (BPEL and Web services) that resulted in BPMN being ranked highest. On the other hand, the focus on tool appropriateness did not appear to hamper the use of the language as a communication tool between people, at least not in this case. However, the example models used for the evaluation were quite simple. Tool appropriateness is further improved in BPMN 2.0, as described in Chap. 1, with explicit support for interchanging models between tools and supporting model execution.
- In the organizational appropriateness category, BPMN and activity diagrams ranked almost equal. The organization had used UML and activity diagrams for some time; however, tools supporting BPMN were also available to the relevant parts of the organization.

5.3.5   Evaluation of the BPMN Notation

A more detailed overview of notational quality aspects was provided in Moody 2009, where the following 9 principles for diagram notations are proposed:

(1) Semiotic clarity: There should be a 1:1 mapping between graphical symbols and concepts (using the error categories of BWW).
(2) Perceptual discriminability: How easily and accurately can symbols be differentiated from each other?
(3) Semantic transparency: How well does a symbol intuitively reflect its meaning?
(4) Complexity management: What constructs do the diagram notation have for supporting different levels of abstraction, information filtering, etc.?
(5) Cognitive integration: Does the notation provide explicit mechanisms to support navigation between different diagrams?
(6) Visual expressiveness: To what extent does the notation utilize the full range of available visual variables?
(7) Dual coding: Using text in an appropriate manner to complement graphics.
(8) Graphic economy: Avoiding an excessive number of different symbols.

(9) Cognitive fit: Trying to adapt the notation to the audience, i.e., possibly using different dialects with different stakeholder groups.

These factors have been integrated with the treatment on comprehensibility and participant appropriateness in SEQUAL (Krogstie 2012). An evaluation of BPMN 2.0 according to these criteria can be found in Genon et al. (2011). Not surprisingly for complex languages such as BPMN, they identify a number of deficiencies with the notation:

(1) Semiotic clarity: BPMN 2.0 has 242 concepts in the meta-model and 171 graphical structures, thus indicating to a mismatch. They found a 23.6 % symbol deficit, 5.4 % symbol overload, 0.5 % symbol excess, and 0.5 % symbol redundancy.

(2) Perceptual discriminability: In BPMN, four shapes are used to generate the majority of symbols. Variations are introduced by changing border style and thickness and by incorporating additional markers. Grain (texture) is used to discriminate between different types of events and activities. All five visual variable values used are distinct, which is good; however, they quickly become hard to distinguish when zooming out of the diagram. The use of color should be decided by the tool developers.

(3) Semantic transparency: In BPMN 2.0 process diagrams, symbols are conventional shapes on which iconic markers are added. Symbol shapes do not seem to convey any particular semantics, but partly build upon symbols used in similar languages: One negative exception is data object; its symbol suggests a "sticky note" (a rectangle with a folded corner). This icon is typically used for comments and textual annotations (e.g., in UML), not for core constructs. The visual notation of "data object" can thus be argued to be a case of semantic perversity. The differentiation between event and activity subtypes is also purely conventional; it depends on styles of borders that are not immediately perceived. There are also other examples of semantically opaque and in some cases perverse icons in BPMN 2.0. The pentagon is used in relation to event triggers and has multiple meanings. An error is signified by a lightning symbol. The icon for condition looks like a list. A Web service is depicted as 2 gears.

(4) Complexity management: BPMN includes four types of diagrams. In a diagram, only the relevant information for this viewpoint is represented. BPMN process models achieve modularity through two constructs, namely (1) link "events" used within and between diagrams and (2) support of subprocesses, a traditional mechanism for the hierarchical structuring of process models. To be effective, different levels of information should be displayed in independent diagrams instead of expanding into their parent diagram, as suggested in the style guide of Silver (2012).

(5) Cognitive integration: Although we, under complexity integration, point to certain mechanisms for dividing up the overall model, no techniques (e.g., as a navigation map) are available to reinforce perceptual integration across diagrams.

(6) Visual expressiveness: The BPMN process diagram notation uses half of the visual variables: Location (x, y), shape, grain, and color carry semantic information, whereas size, orientation, and brightness are not used. Visual variables in BPMN were appropriately chosen according to the nature of information, which here is purely nominal (i.e., there is no ordering between values). Location can also be used to encode intervals; however, it is used in BPMN only for enclosure (a symbol is contained in another symbol), which is only a small portion of its capacity. Visual variable capacities are rather well exploited, and grain is even completely saturated. However, as we discussed above, this causes discriminability problems. The perceptible steps between shape values are a major problem of the current notation. Current shapes belong to only two categories (circles and quadrilaterals), whereas there is no semantic relationship between the referent concepts within a shape category. Color is one of the most cognitively effective visual variables. BPMN uses only two colors—black and white—to allow "throwing" (filled) and "catching" (hollow) events to be distinguished. Hence, the color capacity is underused.

(7) Dual coding: BPMN uses dual coding for conditional and complex gateways only.

(8) Graphic economy: BPMN 2.0 process models have a graphic complexity of 171. This is at least an order of magnitude beyond novice capabilities. Zur Mühlen and Recker observed that, in practice, because only a limited amount of the language is used, the experienced graphic complexity of BPMN is significantly lower than its nominal complexity (zur Muhlen and Recker 2008). Their study (discussed further in Sect. 5.3.9) showed that most process diagrams designed for novices use only the basic symbols, namely event, activity, gateway, sequence flow, data object, and association, in addition to a few refinements (cf. the limited part of BPMN used in the case presented in Sect. 4.2). The practical complexity is thus approximately 10. This is certainly substantially more manageable than the full language; however, it remains high compared to popular languages (Davies et al. 2006) such as ER diagrams (complexity of 5) and DFDs (complexity of 4). YAWL van der Aalst and Hofstede (2005), which is a newer process modeling language more closely related to BPMN, has a complexity of 14.

(9) Cognitive fit: The objective of BPMN is to "provide a notation that is readily understandable by all business users, from the business analysts that create the initial drafts of the processes, to the technical developers responsible for implementing the technology that will perform those processes, and finally, to the business people who will manage and monitor those processes" (OMG 2011). It is questionable that one can address all differences, e.g., in expert-novice capacity, and the use of different representational media (tool and blackboard) with the same language, which is also partly considered in the proposed leveling of the language (descriptive, analytical, executable).

5.3.6   Combined Semiotic, Ontological, and Workflow Pattern Evaluation

Recker et al. (2007) propose a generic framework for language evaluation based on the combination of ontological, semiotic, and pattern-based evaluation presented above. They reported on the first attempt to classify existing theoretical frameworks for process modeling language evaluation using this framework. Their work provides an evaluation of existing frameworks as well as an evaluation of BPMN. For more information on the framework, refer Recker et al. 2007. Some general statements on BPMN can be summarized from the analysis based on the study by Recker et al. (2007), which partly confirms the findings of the studies performed by the stand-alone approaches:

- Representation of state. BPMN lacks the capabilities to model state-related aspects of business processes and is limited, if not incapable of, modeling states assumed by things and state-based patterns.
- Specialization of constructs. BPMN lacks attributes in the specification of the language constructs.
- Weak support for resource modeling. There is a lack of support for representing resource patterns, and the evaluation provides the same comment as Wohed et al. (2006) regarding the lane and pool constructs, which are additionally criticized for being overloaded.
- Redundant constructs. There is a relatively high degree of construct redundancy, which might explain why there are as many as three different BPMN representations for the same basic workflow patterns (Wohed et al. 2006).

5.3.7   Semistructured Interviews of BPMN Users

One effort to seek empirical evidence of theoretical propositions is facilitated by following up on a BWW representational analysis with semistructured interviews with BPMN users. The research questions for this study were initially to discover the representational shortcomings of BPMN in light of the BWW framework and to discover which of these were perceived as actual shortcomings by the BPMN users. This study involved 19 participants from six organizations distributed over four Australian states. The results are reported in Recker et al. (2005, 2006). A follow-up of this study was achieved as a Web-based survey performed between May and August 2007 and included 590 BPMN users from different parts of the world. A presentation of the results is available in Recker (2008). Interviews based on weaknesses discovered by representational analysis uncover how this affects the users (Recker et al. 2006).

- Work-arounds to fit local needs. The general impression regarding construct deficits is that even though the participants claim that they do not need to model state changes, business rules, or system structures, they find work-arounds and represent this information outside the BPMN model itself. In modeling events, as many as 74 % did not experience any limitation in using BPMN to this end, and the severity of the problem declined for users using the expanded set compared with interviewees using the core set of elements. This is in contradiction to the theoretical proposition claiming that there would be confusion connected to using the expanded set.
- Construct overload. The analytical evaluation proposed that there would be ambiguities regarding the lane and pool constructs. This was supported by the interviews and is mainly based on the fact that these constructs are used to represent a range of different real-world constructs, as also discussed in Recker et al. (2007).

In reporting the Web-based quantitative survey (Recker 2008), the following issues were identified:

- Support for business rule specification. Rule specification is an essential task in understanding business processes, and it would be beneficial to find that process modeling solutions acknowledge this better and provide support. This is suggested by one of the participants to be as simple as an additional graphical symbol, implying that there is a business rule at work. Note that one of the activity types of BPMN 2.0 supports this on a simple level.
- Weak support for resource modeling. The ambiguity that comes with the flexible semantics of lanes and pools is contradictory to their ease of use in modeling. One word of advice here is to provide better support for differentiating the multiple purposes for which lanes and pools can be used.
- Understanding and use of constructs. The survey shows that there is some doubt related to the use of gateways, off-page connectors (link events), and groups. Basically, there is confusion as to when to use these concepts and why. This might stem from the fact that they are constructs of the model and not the process modeled. In regard to events, there is some frustration related to selecting the right type of event.

5.3.8 Case Study of BPMN in Practice

Zur Mühlen and Ho (2008) followed the redesign of a service management process at a truck dealership in the USA using action research. The study included reports on experiences from using BPMN with participatory modeling of the as-is and to-be process and the activation of the models for simulation purposes, therein providing the following results:

- Understanding and use of constructs. Experience from the case study shows that the core set is used and understood. In cases where the entire set of BPMN constructs is used, the audience tends to disregard the richer meaning provided by the extended set (zur Mühlen and Ho 2008). The applied notation is primarily limited to the core constructs.
- Work-arounds to fit local needs. The use of constructs different from what are suggested in the specification has been observed. Modelers purposely create syntactically incorrect models to improve readability and to simplify the modeling task. One example of this is placing activity constructs across lanes to indicate that there are several organizational units participating in completing a task. This is not uncommon. When using BPMN in the case in Sect. 4.2, understanding (pragmatic quality) was also regarded as more important than using the language correctly (syntactic quality), although as observed having too low syntactic quality might hurt comprehension.
- Tool dialects. The tool used had its own BPMN dialect that was not fully compliant with the official BPMN specification. We will further examine different implementations of the BPMN in different tools below.

5.3.9   Statistical Analysis of BPMN Models

Similar to the work by Dijkman et al. (2007) of mapping models to Petri nets for analysis, zur Mühlen and Recker (2008) translated BPMN models into Excel spreadsheets and used the representation with different mathematical tools for statistical analysis and comparison. The investigated models were collected from three different groups: models used in consulting project, models created as part of BPMN education seminars, and models found online. Investigated phenomena include the general use of constructs, their frequency of use, and the correlation of use of different constructs.

- Modeling constructs used similar to those of natural language. By arranging constructs by frequency, the study revealed a distribution similar to the distribution previously observed for natural languages. This suggests that the use of BPMN constructs for expressing business processes mirrors the use of natural language. This would further suggest that expressiveness is based on the modelers existing vocabulary and that one will use whatever constructs one knowingly has available. The study found further support for this through observing that precise semantics are used by the consultant group and for models created in seminars, thus suggesting that this is based on formal training increasing the modeling vocabulary. Similar to many natural languages, BPMN has a few essential constructs, a wide range of commonly used constructs, and an abundance of virtually unused constructs (zur Mühlen and Recker 2008).
- Precise constructs replace the need for text annotations. Another issue discovered by mapping the correlation of constructs is based on the negative

correlation between the extended set gateways and text annotations. Text annotations seem to act as a substitute for formal events and gateway types by informally describing behavior.

- Practical language complexity does not equal theoretical complexity. Based on the result, the study also made an attempt to measure the practical complexity of BPMN based on the number of semantically different constructs used in each model. On average, this resulted in the number of different constructs used as 9 (consulting), 8.87 (Web), and 8.7 (seminars). There is, however, variation in what constructs are used, but nevertheless this has provided an image of a far less complex language in practice compared with its theoretical complexity. Altogether, six pairs of models were found out of 120 models examined that shared the same constructs, but there were several models sharing the same construct combinations or subsets.

- Models focus on choreography or orchestration, not both. By organizing the model subsets using Venn diagrams showing what subsets were used in combination, the study revealed that either modelers focus on process orchestration by refining models by extended gateways or they focus on process choreography by adding organizational constructs such as pools and lanes (zur Mühlen and Recker 2008).

5.3.10 Business Processes Are More Than What Is Possible to Represent in BPMN

Silver (2012) emphasized, as we have also noted above, that there are a large number of concepts relevant to process modeling that are not possible to represent in BPMN at a sufficiently detailed level. These include the following:

- At the enterprise or line of business level:

  - High-level business context, describing the company's relationship to competitors, regulators, suppliers, business partners, customers, community, etc.;
  - Strategic objectives and performance metrics;
  - Controls and constraints;
  - Markets and customers;
  - Products and services;
  - Locations.

- At the operational and cross-process level:

  - Value chains and process portfolios;
  - Operational goals and objectives;
  - Policies;
  - Performance metrics and KPIs;

- Organizational structures and roles.
- At the process-specific level:
  - Activity resource requirements;
  - Revenue and costs;
  - Job aids (instructions for human performers).
- Technical aspects:
  - IT systems;
  - IT services;
  - Detailed data structures.

5.3.11 Evaluation of BPMN Modeling Tools

Even if much can be said about the modeling language as such, the practical usage of the language in particular for large-scale use is dependent on the tool support of the language. Evéquoz and Sterren (2011) provided an evaluation of the following BPMN tools:

- Activiti BPM Platform 5.7,
- Bonita Open Solution 5.5.2,
- IBM Blueworks Live,
- Imeikas BPMN2 Visual Editor for Eclipse,
- Intalio BPMS Designer 6.0.3 Community Edition,
- ITP-Commerce Process Modeler 5 SR6 (Professional),
- JBoss jBPM5 5.1,
- Joinwork Process Studio 3.1,
- MID Innovator for Business Analysts—Enterprise Edition 11 R4,
- Oracle BPM Suite 11 gR1,
- Signavio-Oryx BPM Academic Initiative,
- Visual Paradigm Business Process Visual ARCHITECT 4.2 SP2.

The languages were evaluated according to the three levels of BPMN described in Sect. 1.5 in addition to a simple level (to be used manually on a whiteboard by process stakeholders). An example model for each of the four levels was developed for use in the evaluation. Modeling 4 reference processes for each of 12 tools should have resulted in 48 models. However, 9 diagrams (8 "complete" and 1 "analytic") could not be modeled due to insufficient palette support in the tools. Of the 39 resulting processes, only 7 were found to benefit from full support of the tools, whereas for the other 32, work-arounds had to be found. Signavio-Oryx was the only tool that offers full support of the BPMN 2.0 to model all 4 reference processes. The limitations that appeared the most often were related to the following:

- Unavailable events—16 occurrences;
- Annotations (unavailable shapes, no directional annotation flows)—14;
- Subprocesses (unavailable subprocess types, wrong depiction)—10;
- Pools (no pools, no black box pools, only one pool)—9;
- Some activity types not available—7.

To evaluate how the selected BPMS supports BPMN 2.0 export, the 39 processes was exported. Of the 39 processes exported, only 8 processes, produced by only three tools, were found fully valid (i.e., including proper schema declaration). When not considering missing XML schema declaration, 21 processes were exported in a valid manner. The following validation errors were encountered the most often:

- Missing required attribute—10 occurrences;
- Incomplete element content—10 occurrences;
- Invalid child element—10 occurrences;
- Invalid attribute or element—9 occurrences;
- Duplicate identifier—8 occurrences;
- Reference to undeclared identifier—5 occurrences;
- Invalid data type—4 occurrences.

Note that this evaluation was conducted less than a year after the official release of the BPMN 2.0 standard; thus, many minor errors are expected to have been solved since then.

An evaluation of the extent the modeling guidelines outlined in Sect. 2.3.4 (and included in the process modeling specific version of SEQUAL in Chap. 3) is supported in modeling tools which is presented in Snoeck et al. (2015). The following tools were evaluated:

- Camunda Modeler,
- ARIS Express,
- Bonita,
- Visual Paradigm 12.0,
- Bizagi Modeler, and
- Signavio Process Editor.

Overall, the large majority of guidelines (85.71 %) seem to be known by tool builders. Nevertheless, there are major differences between tools. Signavio was found to have the highest degree of overall support (57.14 %), followed by Bizagi (50 %), ARIS Express (30.36 %), Visual Paradigm (28.57 %), Camunda (25 %), and Bonita (19.64 %). In general, the group of presentation guidelines is the best supported category of guidelines. However, there are large differences in how this support occurs concretely. Visual Paradigm and ARIS Express have the highest degree of support for the guidelines regarding the layout of the model. Furthermore, Bizagi scored highest regarding label-style guidelines, despite having lower degrees of support for the other domains. Additionally, Camunda Modeler provides strong support for the label-style guidelines. Finally, Bonita appears to have the weakest average support, although certain individual categories score fairly highly. The different scores per category and subcategory indicate that tool vendors each have different preferences about which categories to support (see the paper for more details on this).

5.4   Achieving Quality in Business Process Models Through Modeling Methodology

Whereas SEQUAL over the years has evolved into a very comprehensive framework, it has been found to be difficult to understand and use in practice by many (Reijers et al. 2015). A number of guidelines for modeling based on this framework have been developed (Krogstie 2012), although having these guidelines put into use through methodologies and modeling tools requires further research and development. Here, we will provide an overview of an approach for using SEQUAL to guide the modeling process. The modeling task follows the SPEC cycle (see Fig. 5.6, which is extended based on ideas in a framework originally described in Sindre and Krogstie (1995)).

- **P—Preparation**: In this state, the organization is performing actions in preparation for creating the model. Here, one can use the framework presented in Sect. 5.1 as checklist for matters to take into account, including:
  - Deciding on the scope and goals of the project and identifying stakeholders. Defining both primary and secondary values to be achieved.
  - Deciding on the reuse of existing internal or external reference models.
  - Selecting participation strategies and participants from the identified stakeholder groups (Gjersvik et al. 2004; Persson and Stirna 2010).
  - Deciding on the format of the model and modeling languages to be used. When using a domain-specific modeling approach, modeling tasks are first initiated with a process defining the modeling language to be used (Kelly and

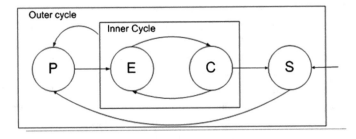

Fig. 5.6 The SPEC cycle of modeling (Krogstie 2012)

Tolvanen 2008; Krogstie et al. 2005). A process for this is described in Sect. 4.1.

- Preparing for the use of different supporting tools and techniques.
- Training participants in the use of the selected modeling languages, tools, and techniques as necessary.
- Eliciting knowledge (for the modeler to obtain more knowledge on the domain).
- Planning the subsequent modeling tasks (based on the goals of modeling).

- **E—Expansion**: Growing the model. During expansion, modeling statements may be made more or less uncritically, i.e., thorough validation is not undertaken, and errors might be introduced. Regardless, as long as some valid statements are made, the model's degree of completeness will increase.
- **C—Consolidation**: The model statements (especially those captured in the previous expansion phase) are consolidated with respect to perceived validity, comprehension, and agreement.
- **S—Suspension**: The modeling activity is suspended; for instance, because expansion does not produce further statements, the model has been agreed upon and baselined, or the project may have been aborted.

In practice, many modeling processes are time-boxed, with organizational goals limiting the process linked to calendar time and cost. The process (especially when performed as part of the development of a new system) usually has a relatively large P-phase and 3–4 inner cycles of expansion, followed by a change in layout and comprehension and consolidation, as indicated in Fig. 5.7, before a model is baselined. In the projects we have studied so far, the first expansion phase is the one that introduces the most statements, and the number of new statements decreases in later phases. It might also be necessary to return to the preparation phase, as discussed in more detail below. A similar pattern within requirements specification work was reported in Nguyen and Swatman (2001). Pinggera et al. (2012) reported similar patterns in business process modeling, although there are large differences between different modeling tasks in terms of the length of the different phases based on the modeling strategy. We note that a lot of the data for this has come from following novice modelers doing modeling alone. Thus, it is not always representative of industrial modeling practices.

An important aspect of modeling is to be able to represent the knowledge as held by people as directly as possible. An earlier practical limitation was that the techniques and tools used were difficult to use, thus often necessitating by design or by chance the involvement of an intermediary analyst. Newer approaches have demonstrated the possibility of involving stakeholders more directly, often with the guidance of modeling facilitators. This is found in particular in enterprise modeling with, for instance, the 4EM approach (Sandkuhl et al. 2014) and in the Socio-Technical WalkThrough (STWT Böhmann et al. (2011)). In addition, techniques supporting interactive workflows (Lillehagen and Krogstie 2008) can be said

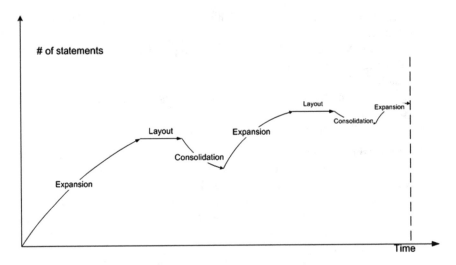

Fig. 5.7 Example of growth of model over time

to support this even more directly than traditional participatory model development techniques.

We will briefly describe two techniques: STWT (Böhmann et al. 2011) and Modeling Conference (Gjersvik et al. 2004).

5.4.1 Socio-Technical WalkThrough (STWT)

The goal of STWT is to provide a systematic communication process through a series of workshops that will result in knowledge integration among different parts of an organization. It should be systematic and structured to solve difficulties concerning their relationship and improve interrelationships. This technique is also seen as a systematical intervention because it should be able to integrate knowledge of several stakeholders that is capable of being different and fully conflicting.

STWT is somehow similar to Cognitive WalkThrough or Groupware WalkThrough; however, in contrast, STWT considers all the perspectives of stakeholders and designs a solution. This technique is meant to simplify the communication process among different stakeholders and technical parts of the organization. This task is performed around the development of a graphical process model. This graphical model shows the work process involving different individuals of an organization and their interaction with information systems that are used or are going to be used.

The Socio-Technical WalkThrough is planned to be performed in different workshops; therefore, this model is a type of primary step and serves as a basis for all these workshops. This walk-through is making progress by producing a diversity of questions and attempting to encourage all stakeholders to participate.

Because the most important goal of STWT is to support communicating among different individuals and tasks in an organization, it is highly important that all the participants recognize their different viewpoints and proposals in different workshops in the modeling of work processes. Therefore, the modeling language must be able to provide all these different techniques to participate in achieving the goal of modeling. As a result, this incompleteness feature of tools is the necessary specification of tools for expressing all the available paths to the destination.

To present these different approaches through graphical documentation, different languages for modeling can be used; however, one that best suits STWT is SeeMe (Herrmann 2006), but a subset of BPMN has also been used in certain projects. SeeMe is a semiformal language, which is useful when representing both social and technical aspects of an organization. Although it contains an explicit indicator for incompleteness and uncertainty, it provides complete specification of relationships and also has the ability to decompose elements

To implement STWT, two key roles are needed in addition to the different stakeholders. These key roles are facilitator and modeler. On the one hand, the facilitator is the individual who encourages participants to present their approaches to the model by asking several open questions, therein not being affected by their personal ideas and views. On the other hand, the facilitator should be able to translate these different perspectives into the process model; therefore, they are also helping the modeler to create suitable models. The modeler should also work with modeling tools and create a model in a consistent and correct manner that is understandable by all participants. As a prerequisite, they should be an expert in modeling with the applied tool.

5.4.2 The Modeling Conference Technique

The Modeling Conference is a method for participatory construction and development of enterprise models. This technique takes as a starting point business process modeling to understanding how organizations work. Similar to STWT, the Modeling Conference technique focuses on participation by all stakeholder groups and the link between organizational learning and process institutionalization through the use of technology.

The core of the Modeling Conference method has been adopted from the Search Conference method (Emery and Purser 1996). The Search Conference is a method for participatory, strategic planning in turbulent and uncertain environments. The method is based on a few basic ideas:

- Open-system thinking,
- Active adaptation,

- Genuine participation,
- Participant learning.

The concrete result of a Search Conference is a set of action plans, addressing various challenges that the conference has prioritized and that people at the conference have committed themselves to implementing. The plans may not always be congruent or coordinated, but there is a shared understanding among the participants on why each of the plans is important for parts of the system. This may be summarized in two core points:

- Action plans: "(…) multiple action plans focused on different parallel initiatives stand a better chance of diffusion than those that concentrate all their resources on one big hit" (ibid., p. 63).
- Shared frame of reference: "(…) the Search Conference does not just result in more information and data about the environment. Rather, the Search Conference process also yields a shared view of the environment as conflicts or perceptual disagreements are made rational, data and information are integrated, and common ground is discovered" (ibid., p. 67).

The Modeling Conference combines process modeling and search conferences by performing process modeling in a structured conference setting, thereby promoting broad participation. This is performed according to the following guidelines:

- The entire process is performed in one room (or a set closely located rooms when parallel group work is performed). All relevant actors in the process should be present or represented during the modeling tasks. In many cases, this also includes outside actors such as users, owners, customers, and public authorities.
- The tasks alternate between group work and plenary work.
- The participants primarily represent themselves but are jointly responsible for the content and results of the conference.
- The model experts facilitate the work and are responsible for the method used during the conference (but not the result).
- The modeling language, tools, and overall method must be simple so that the participants can focus on the content.
- The main outcome of the conference is a process model, which names the key processes, products, and roles. Additional results are related to this process model.

The modeling language used includes the following concepts and notation:

- Process: A series of tasks that produce a specific product. One example is "write paper."
- Product: The result of a process and an item in demand by a customer. One example is the product "scientific paper," which is a product of the

above-mentioned process. A process may have several products. We distinguish between end products and intermediate products.

- Customer: Someone who demands and uses the product of a process. Often, the customer is another process. For instance, the process "review paper" is a customer of the process "write paper" and demands the product "scientific paper."

The modeling conference preferably lasts at least one and a half days. Every group has a large sheet of paper on the wall on which they work. All symbols are precut and can be attached to the sheet of paper. Through these simple symbols and physical methods of working together, one obtains substantial flexibility and intensive learning; however, these aspects also limit the form of the work. The results of the group work are presented in plenary sessions for discussion and joint construction of consolidated models.

The documentation obtained by a Modeling Conference is a report and a process model. The most important outcome of the conference is the ownership that the participants develop through the construction process, which makes the model an important common reference for further more detailed development.

The conference agenda is designed so that the actors of the conference should develop models based on their own local reality before they enter a discussion with actors having (presumably) different local realities. One always starts with homogenous groups, where people with the same background develop their process models. Following this, the participants are more comfortable with the modeling language and tools and have greater self-confidence about their own point of view. This is especially important in organizations where there is a high risk of some groups of actors (i.e., management or experts) having model power over other participants as a result of having a previously developed model available (Bråten 1973). One subsequently mixes the participants in heterogeneous groups, where the entire modeling task is performed again.

The difficult point in the agenda is after the second modeling task, where the models of several groups are to be merged into one. This is conducted in a plenary session. The conference leader needs to be very attentive to the reasoning of the different groups so that he or she is able to combine the elements from different models into one coherent whole without steering the process too much. It is important that this plenary session is allowed to take the time it needs to obtain a consensus about the model.

A case study of the use of this technique was reported in Gjersvik et al. (2004). In that study, one could identify differences in acceptance and ownership scores between participants and non-participants; i.e., participation in the development of process models, through the use of model conferences, generates higher acceptance and ownership of the models. It may also be concluded that it seems that a process model refined by a process modeling group is accepted as better than the different models generated as a result of each independent Modeling Conference.

5.5 Summary

In Chapter 1, we outlined the different possible usage areas or goals of modeling. With this and the specialized SEQUAL framework for business process model quality presented in Chap. 3, we have described a framework for how to obtain value on the longer term from business process models. The main empirical background for this framework is described in the cases presented in Chap 4. We have also discussed aspects related to the quality of business process modeling languages and business process modeling methods as the means to achieving high-quality process models. In particular, on the areas of modeling methods and modeling tools, the treatment in this book is on a very high level, and we suggest you to look at the referenced material to investigate these areas in more detail.

References

Aagesen, G., Krogstie, J.: Analysis and design of business processes using BPMN. In: vom Brocke, J., Rosemann, M. (eds.) Handbook on Business Process Management. Springer, Berlin (2010)

Aagesen, G., Krogstie, J.: BPMN 2.0 for modeling business processes. In: vom Brocke, J., Rosemann, M. (eds.),Handbook on Business Process Management. Springer, Berlin (2015)

Böhmann, T., Burr, W., Herrmann, T., Krcmar, H.: Implementing International Services a Tailorable Method for Market Assessment, Modularization, and Process Transfer. GABL, Wiesbaden (2011)

Booch, G., Rumbaugh, J., Jacobson, I.: The Unified Modeling Language: User Guide, 2nd ed. Addison-Wesley, Reading, Boston (2005)

Bråten, S.: Model monopoly and communications: systems theoretical notes on democratization. Acta Sociol. J. Scand. Soc. Assoc. 16(2), 98–107 (1973)

Davies, I., Green, P., Rosemann, M., Indulska, M., Gallo, S.: How do practitioners use conceptual modelling in practice? Data. Knowl. Eng. 58, 358–380 (2006)

Dijkman, R.M., Dumas, M., Ouyang, C.: Formal semantics and analysis of BPMN process models. Queensland University of Technology, Brisbane (2007)

Emery, M., Purser, R.E.: The Search Conference. A Powerful Method for Planning Organizational Change and Community Action. Jossey-Bass Publishers, San Francisco (1996)

Evéquoz, F., Sterren, C.: Waiting for the Miracle: Comparative Analysis of Twelve Business Process Management Systems Regarding the Support of BPMN 2.00 Palette and Export. Technical Report IIG-TR 2011.03 (2011)

Gemino, A., Wand, Y.: Evaluating modeling techniques based on models of learning. Commun. ACM 46, 79–84 (2003)

Genon, N., Heymans, P., Amyot, D.: Analysing the cognitive effectiveness of the BPMN 2.0 visual notation. In: Malloy, B., Staab, S., van den Brand, M. (eds.) SLE 2010, LNCS 6563, pp. 377–396. Springer, Berlin (2011)

Gjersvik, R., Krogstie, J., Følstad, A.: Participatory development of enterprise process models. In: Krogstie, J., Siau, K., Halpin, T. (eds.) Information Modelling Methods and Methodologies. Idea Group Publishers, Hershey (2004)

Herrmann, T.: SeeMe in a Nutshell. The Semi-Structured Socio-Technical Modeling Method (2006)

Kelly, S., Tolvanen, J.-P.: Domain-Specific Modelling: Enabling Full Code Generation. Wiley, Hoboken (2008)

Krogstie, J.: On the distinction between functional development and functional maintenance. J. Soft. Maintenance **7**, 383–403 (1995)

Krogstie, J.: Integrated goal, data and process modeling: from TEMPORA to model-generated work-places. In: Johannesson, P., Søderstrøm, E. (eds.) Information Systems Engineering From Data Analysis to Process Networks, pp. 43–65. IGI, Hershey (2008)

Krogstie, J.: Model-based Development and Evolution of Information Systems: A Quality Approach. Springer, Berlin (2012)

Krogstie, J., Sølvberg, A.: Software maintenance in Norway: a survey investigation. In: Muller, H., Georges, M. (eds.) Proceedings of the International Conference on Software Maintenance (ICSM'94), pp. 304–313. IEEE Computer Society Press, Victoria (1994)

Krogstie, J., Jørgensen, H.: Interactive models for supporting networked organisations. Paper presented at the 16th conference on advanced information systems engineering (CAiSE 2004), Riga, Latvia, 9–11 June (2004)

Krogstie, J., Dalberg, V., Jensen, S.: Using a model quality framework for requirements specification of an enterprise modeling languages. In: Siau, K. (ed.) Advanced Topics in Database Research, vol. 4. Idea Group Publishing, Hershey (2005)

Krogstie, J., Sindre, G., Jørgensen, H.D.: Process models representing knowledge for action: a revised quality framework. Eur. J. Inform Syst. **15**(1), 91–102 (2006a)

Krogstie, J., Dalberg, V., Jensen, S.M.: Process modeling value framework. In: Manolopoulos, Y., Filipe, J., Constantopoulos, P., Cordeiro, J. (eds.) Selected papers from 8th International Conference, ICEIS 2006, vol. LNBIP 3, pp. 309–321. Springer, Paphos (2008)

Krogstie, B., et al.: Computer support for reflective learning in the workplace: a model. In: International Conference on Advanced Learning Technologies (ICALT) 2012, ACM: Rome (2012)

Krogstie, B.R., Schmidt, A.P., Kunzmann, C., Krogstie, J., Mora, S.: Linking Reflective Learning and Knowledge Maturing in Organizations Proceedings ARTEL 2013 (2013)

Kump, B., et al.: The Role of Reflection in Maturing Organizational Know-How. In: 1st European Workshop ARNets11, in Conjunction with EC-TEL 2011. Palermo, Italy (2011)

Lillehagen, F., Krogstie, J.: Active Knowledge Modeling of Enterprises. Springer, Berlin (2008)

Lin, Y., Strasunskas, D., Hakkarainen, S., Krogstie, J., Sølvberg, A.: Semantic annotation framework to manage semantic heterogeneity of process models. Paper presented at the CAiSE'2006, Luxembourg (2006)

Moody, D.L.: The "Physics" of notations: toward a scientific basis for constructing visual notations in software engineering. IEEE Trans. Softw. Eng. **35**, 756–779 (2009)

Nguyen, L., Swatman, P.A.: Managing the Requirements Engineering Process Proceedings REFSQ 2001. Interlaken, Switzerland (2001)

Nysetvold, A.G., Krogstie, J.: Assessing business process modeling languages using a generic quality framework. In: Siau, K. (ed.) Advanced Topics in Database Research Series, vol. 5, pp. 79–93. Idea Group, Hershey (2006)

OMG: BPMN v2 Specification. Technical report, OMG. (http://www.omg.org/), http://www.omg.org/spec/BPMN/2.0/, Jan (2011)

Ouyang, C., et al.: Workflow management. In: vom Brocke, J., Rosemann, M. (eds.) Handbook on Business Process Management, vol. 1. Springer, Heidelberg (2010)

Persson, A., Stirna, J.: Towards defining a competence profile for the enterprise modelling practitioner the practice of enterprise modelling. In: PoEM 2010, Delft, 2010. Springer, Berlin (2010)

Pinggera, J., Zugal, S., Weidlich, M., Fahland, D., Weber, B., Mendling, J., Reijers, H.: Tracing the process of process modeling with modeling phase diagrams. In Proceedings ER-BPM'11, pp. 370–382 (2012)

Recker, J.: BPMN Modeling—Who, Where, How and Why. BPTrends (2008)

Recker, J., Indulska, M., Rosemann, M., Green, P.: Do process modelling techniques get better? A comparative ontological analysis of BPMN. In: 16th Australasian Conference on Information Systems, Sydney, Australia (2005)

Recker. J., Indulska, M., Rosemann, M., Green, P.: How good is BPMN really? Insights from theory and practice. In: 14th European Conference on Information System (ECIS 2006), pp. 1–12, Gothenburg, Sweden (2006)

Recker, J., Rosemann, M., Krogstie, J.: Ontology—versus pattern-based evaluation of process modeling language: a comparison. Commun. Assoc. Inf. Syst. **20**, 774–799 (2007)

Reijers, H., Mendling, J., Recker, J.: Business process quality management. In: vom Brocke, J., Rosemann, M. (eds.) Handbook on Business Process Management, 2nd ed. Springer, Berlin (2015)

Rosemann, M., Recker, J., Indulska, M., Green, P.: A study of the evolution of the representational capabilities of process modeling grammars. Adv. Inf. Syst. Eng.-CAiSE **4001**:447–461 (2006)

Rossi, M., Cocco, M., Kristensen, K., Parrotta, S., Terzi, S., Krogstie, J., Ahlers, D.: LEAN Virtual Obeya in Book from the LinkedDesign Project. Elsevier, Amsterdam (2016)

Russell, N., ter Hofstede, A.H.M., van der Aalst, W.M.P., Mulyar, N.: Workflow control-flow patterns: a revised view. BPM Center Report BPM-06-22, BPMcenter. org, pp. 6–22 (2006)

Sandkuhl, K., Stirna, J., Persson, A., Wißotzki, M.: Enterprise Modelling—Tackling Business Challenges with the 4EM Method. Springer, Berlin (2014)

Silver, B.: BPMN Method and Style. Cody-Cassidy Press (2012)

Sindre, G., Krogstie, J.: Process heuristics to achieve requirements specification of feasible quality. In: Pohl, K., Peters, P. (eds.) Second International Workshop on Requirements Engineering: Foundations for Software Quality (REFSQ'95), pp. 92–103. Jyvälskylä, Finland (1995)

Snoeck, M., Moreno-Montes de Oca, I., Haegemans, T., Schedeman, B., Hoste, T.: Testing a selection of BPMN tools for their support of modelling guidelines. In: Proceedings PoEM (2015)

van der Aalst, W.M.P., ter Hofstede, A.H.M.: YAWL: yet another workflow language. Inf. Syst. **30**(4), 245–275 (2005)

van der Aalst, W.M.P., ter Hofstede, A.H.M., Kiepuszewski, B, Barros, A.P.: Workflow patterns. Distrib. Parallel Databases **14**, 5–5 (2003)

van der Aalst, W., et al.: Process Mining Manifesto, Business Process Management Workshops 2011, Lecture Notes in Business Information Processing, vol. 99, Springer, Berlin (2011)

Wahl, T., Sindre, G.: An analytical evaluation of BPMN using a semiotic quality framework. In: Proceedings of EMMSAD'2005, pp. 533–544 (2005)

Wand, Y., Weber, R.: On the ontological expressiveness of information systems analysis and design grammars. J. Inform. Syst. **3**(4), 217–237 (1993)

Wesenberg, H.: Enterprise modeling in an agile world. In: Proceedings of the 4th Conference on Practice of Enterprise Modeling, Oslo, Norway (2011)

Wohed, P., van der Aalst, W.M.P., Dumas, M., ter Hofstede, A.H.M.: Pattern-based analysis of BPMN—an extensive evaluation of the control-flow, the data and the resource perspectives (revised version). BPM Center Report BPM-06-17, BPMcenter.org (2005)

Wohed, P., van der Aalst, W.M.P., Dumas, M., ter Hofstede, A.H.M.: On the suitability of BPMN for business process modelling. In: Business Process Management—BPM 2006, Vienna, Austria. Lecture notes in computer science, vol. 4102, pp. 161–176 (2006)

zur Mühlen, M., Ho, D.T.: Service process innovation: a case study of BPMN in practice. In: Hawaii International Conference on System Sciences, Proceedings of the 41st Annual (2008)

zur Mühlen, M., Recker, J.C.: How much language is enough? Theoretical and practical use of the business process modeling notation. In: Proceedings CAiSE'08. Springer-Verlag, Montpellier, France (2008)

Chapter 6
Some Future Directions for Business Process Modeling

As observed earlier in this book, both the depth and breadth of interest in business process modeling has increased over the last decades. This increased interest has moved the bar concerning the reasons why people want to use business process modeling approaches, and it has also resulted in increasingly expressive and applicable—and thus complex—modeling languages. We also observe that it is possible to aim for a large number of potential modeling goals. One interesting aspect is that when using models in an industrial setting to obtain long term benefits, the models do not have only one goal. Rather, they aim to be *multivalent*: to provide value toward achieving a number of different potentially conflicting goals, often pushing for even greater expressiveness of the modeling languages to use. On the other hand, practical large scale applications of business process modeling typically use only a pragmatic and often small subset of the standard languages.

In the next section, we will investigate how process modeling in particular has developed given these conflicting requirements and discuss how it might continue to develop in the future as computer systems themselves evolve to support modeling to a greater extent.

6.1 Business Process Modeling Integrated with other Types of Modeling

Modeling languages through the 1980s were primarily mono-perspective (e.g., ER-diagrams for structural modeling and DFD for process modeling); however, methods to more closely integrate the various modeling languages appeared during the 1990s. An early example of such an approach was Tempora (Loucopoulos et al.

© Springer International Publishing Switzerland 2016
J. Krogstie, *Quality in Business Process Modeling*,
DOI 10.1007/978-3-319-42512-2_6

1991), which aimed to create an environment for the development of complex application systems. The underlying idea was that development of a CIS should be viewed as developing the rule base of an organization, which would then be used throughout the development and evolution of the system. However, rules are difficult to visualize; thus, Tempora had three closely interrelated languages for conceptual modeling: ERT, an extension of the ER language; PID, an extension of the DFD; and ERL, a formal language for expressing organizational rules that was also extended to include deontic notions (Krogstie and Sindre 1996). The basic modeling constructs of ERT were entity classes, relationship classes, and value classes. The language also contained most of the usual constructs from semantic data modeling such as generalization and aggregation, derived entities and relationships, and some extensions for temporal aspects that were specific to ERT. The PID language was used to specify processes and their interactions in a formal way. Its basic modeling constructs were processes, ERT views (which were links to a structural ERT model), external agents, flows (both control and data), ports to depict logical groupings of flows as they enter or leave processes, and timers, which could act as either clocks or delays.

A way to combine the models in these languages was developed as a basis for generating prototypes directly from the models (Krogstie et al. 1991; Lindland and Krogstie 1993). In addition to linking PID to ERT models and ERL rules to ERT models and PIDs, there was the possibility of relating rules in rule hierarchies.

As observed in the BPMN evaluation in Sect. 5.3, we find a similar picture here. The process models act as the central artifacts, but often it is desirable to extend the models to cover concepts normally captured through other modeling perspectives. Note that the same pattern occurs in the certification example in Sect. 4.1, where the new language had the processes at its center, but one also wanted to be able to represent relevant rules, data, and organizational entities in an integrated manner. The petroleum industry case in Sect. 4.2 actively pursues a more full-fledged enterprise modeling approach that was not focused solely on the core process models. EEML (Krogstie 2008), which furthered the work from Tempora, also sported a central process modeling language, but with data, actor, and rule modeling as full-fledged perspectives integrated into the process modeling. Enterprise modeling languages such as ArchiMate and 4EM (Sandkuhl et al. 2014) also cover many perspectives in an integrated manner but still preserve the possibility for focusing specifically on business processes. At the same time as these (process) modeling languages were being extended with concepts from other perspectives, we observed in both cases from Chap. 4 that a very limited set of language constructs was chosen for the core models to keep them manageable. This subset has actually been further reduced through use (e.g., removing the possibility of intermediate events in the case presented in Sect. 4.2).

Multiperspective modeling (such as GEMAL (Andersson and Krogstie 2015)) flattens this hierarchy further, treating processes as just one of many perspectives that are all on equal levels, leaving the modeler free to use any modeling perspective as the main one. This type of modeling is believed to be primarily applicable for expert modelers for early sense-making. In contrast, a perspective that leans toward process modeling, where additional aspects are particularly related to the process model, is believed to still be useful (although potentially limiting if used in the wrong way) for extensive use of modeling.

6.2 Beyond the Activity—Business Process Modeling across Organizational Levels

Another primary observation is that the type of process modeling language used varies across organizational levels. The way to model the top-level processes (the process maps) in the oil and gas case in Sect 4.2 is different than the way to represent the intermediate level models, which are different from the workflow models in the BPMN variant. Malinova and Mendling (2015) comes to a similar result. They found that BPMN is neither complete nor clear for modeling process maps. Thus, if organizations use BPMN to design their process maps, they will encounter multiple BPMN elements that embody the same semantics as one process map concept and vice versa: One BPMN element may be used to represent multiple process map concepts. These findings illustrate that many concepts are specializations of others. An underlying reason is that BPMN models and process maps have differing purposes; that is, while the purpose of a BPMN model is to show the details of a process, the purpose of a process map is to depict an abstract overview of all the processes for an entire company; hence, process maps show how BPMN models fit together while excluding their details.

Going back to the differentiation of the "as-is," "to-be," and "ought-to-be" models from Chap. 1, this concept can also be used to illustrate how it can be beneficial to use different modeling approaches at different levels of abstraction.

Process modeling at a company level often starts with the company vision and business value. It is also important to develop both corporate future goals and target architecture in the form of a "Future Operating Model" (an ought-to-be model), as well as detailed workflows that include both as-is and to-be activities.

To achieve this, one needs a combined top-down and bottom-up approach. The Future Operating Model is a top-down model that describes best practices for the way the organization wants to operate in the future (ought-to-be). In contrast, the workflow model is a bottom-up model that shows how the enterprise operates with today's (as-is) systems and organization and how it will operate with tomorrow's (to-be) systems and organization.

The Future Operating Model describes best practices derived from previous experience, technological development, regulatory requirements, and so on and shows ambitions and plans on a general level: It models how the enterprise should operate in the future. This model is used for both understanding and planning programs and projects.

The model is used to perform basic analyses and to help answer questions such as:

- "What is our enterprise doing?"
- "Are we doing the right things?"
- "How are our main processes and value chain operations being performed?"
- "Could we redesign our basic processes?"

The preceding questions lead to analysis that should be conducted before going into the details such as:

- "Who/what does which tasks?" (Humans/machines).
- "Which IT systems are used for what tasks?"

Only after these basic analyses have been conducted and decisions made can one move forward to create detailed workflow models. A unifying overall process model such as this makes it possible for people with varied backgrounds—who come from different organizational units and disciplines and have worked in different ways in the past—to agree on common work processes and value chains. A unifying model contributes to common terminology for processes, concepts, information objects, and so on. A generic overall model also contributes to process modeling standardization so that work processes can be described the same way across different departments and disciplines, which is important for communication and reuse. The process hierarchy provides a total overview of the enterprise and agreements about best practices. Experience shows that it is the transitions in the value chain that often slips, and this becomes explicitly evident in this type of overall end-to-end model. In this model, it is also important to keep customer/client relationships in focus and to ensure that customer interactions with the company are explicitly modeled.

As illustrated in Fig. 6.1, the Future Operating Model is a top-down planning model that shows value chains, but also value shop and value networks if relevant, whereas the workflow model is a bottom-up implementation model that shows the detailed workflow for defined parts of the value chain. The left side of Fig. 6.1 shows a top-down process breakdown structure, from an "overall view" that proceeds over several levels down to "processes/activities." The right side shows a bottom-up workflow model built up in levels from Applications and Roles to IT Services and Procedures for Implementation (Orchestration).

Modeling a top-down generic model can be accomplished using different notations. A case from the hospital sector presented in Fossland and Krogstie

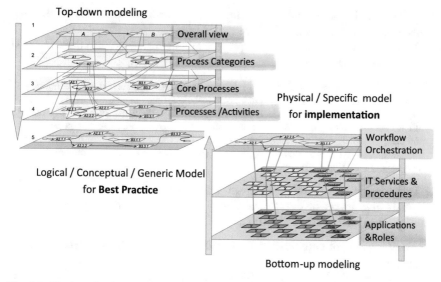

Fig. 6.1   The interplay between top-down and bottom-up modeling (Fossland and Krogstie 2015)

(2015) used IDEF0, which is regarded as a best practice for building logical/generic/conceptual process models with a "process breakdown structure."

The ought-to-be model should be made independent of specific applications or organization structure, making it viable for use even when technological innovations and organizational changes such as mergers or divisions occur. The workflow model is a bottom-up implementation model (e.g., in BPMN as in the case presented in Fossland and Krogstie (2015)) that shows detailed workflows for defined parts of the value chain. Based on the level of dynamicity of the process (cf. Fig. 1. 10), other less rigid modeling languages than BPMN (e.g., languages supporting interactive process modeling (Krogstie and Jørgensen 2004; Lillehagen and Krogstie 2008)) can be more beneficial. Additionally, work on combining imperative process modeling such as BPMN and declarative process modeling is being pursued in so-called hybrid models (Maggi et al. 2014).

6.3   Welcome to the Machine—Tools from Interpreters to Modelers as Part of Big Data Ecosystems

Whereas modeling has traditionally been conducted by humans, with the availability of large amounts of data, machine learning algorithms, and tool support, tools are now being given more active modeling roles. For process modeling, this increase is most obvious based on the collection of event data in the field of process mining, but in connection with big data developments, there is a need to model on the type level based on models on the instance level (data) (Conti et al. 2012; Lukyanenko and Parsons 2013).

Process mining is described in the process mining manifesto (van der Aalst et al. 2011) in the following way:

> Process mining techniques are able to extract knowledge from event logs commonly available in today's information systems. These techniques provide new means to discover, monitor, and improve processes in a variety of application domains. There are two main drivers for the growing interest in process mining. On the one hand, more and more events are being recorded, thus, providing detailed information about the history of processes. On the other hand, there is a need to improve and support business processes in competitive and rapidly changing environments.

Thus, in process mining, data—in particular event data—are regarded as essential. Five levels of event data quality are described in the process mining manifesto (van der Aalst et al. 2011):

1. Event logs are of poor quality. Recorded events may not correspond to reality, and events may be missing.
2. Events are recorded automatically, often as a by-product of some information system. Coverage varies. No systematic approach is followed to decide which events are recorded. Moreover, it is possible to bypass the information system. Hence, events may be missing or not recorded properly.
3. Events are recorded automatically, but no systematic approach is followed to record events. However, unlike the logs at level 2, there is some level of guarantee that the events recorded are trustworthy (but not necessarily complete). Consider, for example, the events recorded by an ERP system. Although events need to be extracted from a variety of tables, the information can be assumed to be correct (e.g., it is safe to assume that a payment recorded by the ERP actually exists).
4. Events are recorded automatically and in a systematic and reliable manner; logs are trustworthy and complete. Unlike the systems operating at level 3, notions such as process instance and activity are supported in an explicit manner.
5. The event log is of excellent quality, both trustworthy and complete according to the needs, and events are well defined. Events are recorded in an automatic, systematic, reliable manner. Privacy and security considerations are addressed adequately. Moreover, the events recorded (and all their attributes) have clear semantics. This implies the existence of one or more ontologies. Events and their attributes point to this ontology.

Event data are as other data clearly models and can be viewed from the perspective of model quality. The above description of quality levels of event data primarily relates to physical, syntactic, and semantic quality (in an objectivistic sense). Process mining can be looked upon relative to the so-called BPM life cycle (van der Aalst 2016). The life cycle describes the different phases of managing a particular business process.

- In the design phase, business processes are modeled.

- In the configuration/implementation phase, the model is activated by being transformed into an executable system. If the model is already in executable form, this phase may be very short (automatic activation). However, if the model is informal, it only acts as the context of change for a traditional development project.
- After the system supports the modeled processes, the enactment/monitoring phase starts. In this phase, the process is instantiated, and the process instances are running while being monitored.
- The diagnosis/requirements phase evaluates the process instances and monitors emerging requirements due to changes in the environment of the process (e.g., changing laws, policies, or environmental factors).

Poor performance or new demands from the environment may trigger a new iteration of the BPM life cycle starting with the redesign phase. According to van der Aalst (2016) until recently, there were few connections between the data produced while executing the process instances and the business process modeling. Process mining offers the possibility to close the BPM life cycle. Data, in particular event data recorded by the system, can be used to provide a better view of the actual processes, i.e., deviations can be analyzed and the quality of models to be closer to the actual situation can be improved although one should be aware of the risk of premature closure (Krogstie 2012).

The focus on event data in process mining points to that this area is part of the larger area of data science (van der Aalst 2016). As discussed also in Chap. 2, data in general can also be looked upon as models (Krogstie 2013). There is no "true," objective data, and data are always captured under some presumption of what is relevant. We will look at the area of quality of big data relative to the possibility of automatic development of (process) models, extending the presentation given in Krogstie and Gao (2015), also taking into account that event data from future process mining will not come from individual systems in one company, but from a multitude of systems in a number of different more or less uncoordinated organizations as discussed in Sect. 1.3.

Big data have been "conceptualized" by using a number of "V" words similar to the 6-V framework described below. Big data aspects are found in a number of domains (Chen et al. 2012):

- *Volume* refers to the large amounts of data that can be exploited. The database field has always had to cope with increasing volumes—as exemplified by the fact that one of the main conferences in the field already established in the 1970s is called VLDB, which stands for very large databases. Still, the exponentially increasing volumes provide new challenges when datasets are too large to be stored and analyzed using traditional database technologies. Modern big data tools use distributed systems to store and analyze data across databases that are potentially spread around the world using different cloud computing solutions. On the other hand, more data as such do not necessarily mean better results (Boyd and Crawford 2012).

- *Velocity* refers to the speed at which new, relevant data are generated and distributed, which can potentially occur at any time. Technology now allows us to analyze data while it is being generated, without ever storing it in traditional databases.
- *Veracity* refers to the messiness or trustworthiness of the data. With many forms of big data, data quality and accuracy are less controllable than it was discussed in Chap. 2 (consider Twitter posts with hash tags, abbreviations, typos, and colloquial speech as well as the questionable reliability and accuracy of the content).
- *Variety* refers to the different types of data that one might want to look at in concert. In the past, efforts focused mainly on structured data that fit into tables or relational databases. However, a large percentage of the world's data are unstructured (text, images, video, voice, etc.). Other relevant data might come from human interaction with systems. With big data technology, one can now analyze and bring together data of different types such as messages, social media conversations, photographs, clickstreams, sensor data, video, and voice recordings. Note that the variety aspect is not specific to big data; the same issues are found within large organizations as they attempt to address data integration (Krogstie 2013; Martin et al. 2012) internally or in collaboration with business partners, where the data stem from data warehouses or from less structured, ad hoc sources. On the other hand, in big data ecosystems, data by definition reside in and are controlled and evolved by many different organizations. This limits the possibilities for standardizing on one representational format for the typically secondary use of data found in big data ecosystems used by many different consumers.
- *Visualization.* To be able to obtain value from the data, it must be abstracted and visualized in a manner that makes the data useful for the end user, applying and extending techniques in the area of information visualization (Ware 2000). In our context, visualization relative to process models is of particular interest (van der Aalst 2016).
- *Value.* Having access to big data provides no advantage unless it can be turned into some value. Another term used in this regard is *viability*.

We can position the big data characteristics (considering data sources as part of the digital ecosystems described in Chap. 1) in relation to the quality levels of SEQUAL in the following way:

Deontic quality: It is closely related to the description of the point *value* in the list above: Are we able to utilize the data for our particular purpose? *Viability* is a subarea of this that can be related to the discussion of feasible quality in SEQUAL. Although one might achieve value through additional processing, the cost of such processing might be regarded as higher than the benefit. Based on the goal of the data use, and also partly dependent on the data sources to be matched and aggregated, different weights might be assigned to the different quality levels described below. From the point of view of data-enabled digital ecosystems, the use of data from many sources is secondary: The data were not originally created to fit the purpose of use in the ecosystem setting. Additionally, there might be many secondary users who would like to use the data in different ways to achieve different goals. A framework for personalization of big data quality deliberations is found in Embury et al.'s study (2009) which investigates some of these issues. Note that traditional models within an organization might also need to fulfill many different goals, as discussed earlier in this book based on Heggset et al. (2014) and Krogstie et al. (2008), but because those situations are within a well-defined organizational setting, they might be easier to tackle.

Social quality: Provenance issues relating to the trustworthiness of the data source as part of *veracity* are central at this level. In combination with *variety* (which includes data from a number of different sources evolving in an uncoordinated fashion by autonomous actors constituting parts of a digital ecosystem), new issues potentially arise compared to traditional data and model quality discussions because some sources might be more trustworthy than others. Variety might also be an issue internally in organizations, for example, matching personal data held in local spreadsheets with data from enterprise systems such as ERP or PLM system (Krogstie 2013). However, because these sources lie within the same organization, the possibility for enforcing compliance is larger than in a big data ecosystem setting. Due to *velocity* aspects, one might need to quickly and automatically deduce a source trust level using a trust model (Artz and Gil 2007) based on existing metadata for the data source, which thus would also need to be available.

Pragmatic quality: This type of quality is related both to machine understanding of data sources and to human understanding of the results. From a machine-understanding standpoint, the issues here are very different for different types of data (e.g., between structured and unstructured data). In particular, *velocity* drives the increased need to devise tool understanding techniques. When using automated means to structure data, one must use some preconceived model for interpreting the different data sources; this model should also be made available as metadata for human consumers of the end result. Conversely, from the standpoint of a human understanding the results (e.g., visualized as process models), this must also be supported by taking empirical quality into account when devising the *visualizations*. Another approach that can be used is to provide personalized output —a personalized view of data—in which case it might be important to make the user model used in the personalization controllable and scrutable by the user (Asif and Krogstie 2014). Given the expanding types of stakeholders typically involved, personalization is of increasing importance. Different techniques can be used for different types of stakeholders, supporting multiple views for different stakeholder types using the same model to enhance individual comprehension. On the other hand, as discussed earlier, personalization can be at odds with the goal of using the generated model as a framework for building common understanding.

Semantic quality: Whereas traditional quality aspects such as completeness, accuracy, and consistency are not discussed specifically in the big data literature, the area *veracity* points more generally toward a focus on data and model quality. One reason for the *variety* of sources used in many big data scenarios and applications is to achieve improved completeness: Not all relevant data can be found in one data source. On the other hand, *variety* is accompanied by the traditional challenges in data integration quality (Martin et al. 2012), requiring data matching on different levels of abstraction and precision. When data are produced by sensor networks, there may be redundancy issues (e.g., reporting location every second even from an object that is not moving). Such redundancies should be filtered out, as should erroneous readings due to noise, for example, an indication that an object suddenly moved a large distance in a short time. Moreover, this filtering must be performed in the correct sequence. To avoid issues of poor physical quality (see below), it is often possible to abstract the data, in which case it is important that the abstracted dataset maintains the important characteristics of the original dataset (Wad 2008). This illustrates an interesting side of big data not typically experienced in traditional modeling and data representations, namely that the modeling (i.e., abstraction) is partly performed by algorithms rather than solely by humans. From the digital ecosystem point of view, the federated approach will bring new challenges concerning how we regard the semantic quality of the overall model. Whereas semantic quality in smaller domains can be followed up much as is typically proposed in traditional data quality literature (i.e., looking at the feasible (perceived) completeness and validity), one would to a larger degree need to be able to live with inconsistencies across federations (Krogstie 2012). Consequently, it would be important to be able to identify those aspects of the models across domains that need to be consistent for integration purposes and equally important to identify the inconsistencies we can live with given the current need to utilize the different data sources.

Syntactic quality: *Variety* comes into play here because not all data sources have a strictly defined meta-model with a predefined syntax. Therefore, to match the different data sources, certain presumptions must be made about the structure and contents of data, meaning one needs to instill structure if it is not there and in some cases assign meaning (as discussed under semantic quality) to data based on statistics and qualified guesses. As data usage and terminology evolves, the underlying data model may evolve as well. Thus, even if a match between the languages used for federated sources was established at a certain point in time, it might cease to be valid at a future point in time.

Empirical quality: Support for empirical quality will be increasingly incorporated into tools that build up models from raw data using techniques such as process mining (van der Aalst et al. 2011) to integrate information visualization tools and modeling tools. Note that guidelines for aesthetics are partly incompatible; therefore, one must make choices based on usage and interpretations of the representation. In connection with maps for example, (Shekhar and Xiong 2008) states that "different combinations, amounts of application, and different orderings of these techniques can produce different yet aesthetically acceptable solutions." Because data visualizations must often be auto generated (to address issues of *velocity*), aspects described under this level are even more important for pragmatic quality than for traditional models developed mostly manually by human modelers, where a model that is not empirically ideal might work just fine because the original modelers are familiar with the overall model structure.

Physical quality: *Volume* is particularly relevant on this level because it can be difficult to have access to all the relevant data at the same time. Rather than being based on central repositories, available data storage must be distributed and federated, utilizing standard interchange formats and supporting mash-ups using data from different sources stored at different places. This brings up a new issue: Determining what part of the total model must be available for each data reuse. This is complicated because the accessibility of the right (most current) data is influenced by the *velocity* of data changes. To support provenance, it might also be necessary to store the full chain of the data revisions (the data movement effect plan (D'Andria et al. 2015)), not only the last version. In general, provenance metadata should be represented independently of the technologies used for data storage. One area that is underdiscussed in current big data literature is the security aspects, even though the use of big data-oriented techniques on personal data is rife with privacy challenges. People's growing awareness of such issues may potentially make it more difficult for those working with big data techniques to access all the data that is of interest; for example, users may adopt anonymous surfing methods. This notes a need to be open about how big data (e.g., location data) will be used (Biczok et al. 2014), both for its primary usage area and for secondary usage areas.

6.4   Summary

Although modeling is only one of many aspects of BPM, it is an important area both directly and indirectly. For instance, van der Aalst 2013 lists the following as key concerns in BPM.

- Process modeling languages,
- Process enactment infrastructure,
- Process model analysis,
- Process mining,
- Process flexibility,
- Process reuse.

All of these areas to some extent involve the manual or automatic development or use of business process models.

As we have attempted to illustrate in this book, quality in business process modeling can be achieved by appropriately balancing the purposes of modeling, the people involved, the tools, modeling languages, and techniques used.

In this book, we have looked at different aspects of this problem area, both theoretically and through in-depth investigations of cases where process models are used on a large scale in business organizations. In the main cases of this book, we have focused on process models being mainly manually activated, noting that there are other works that go in more detail on interactive activation (e.g., Lillehagen and Krogstie 2008) and automatic activation (e.g., ter Hofstede et al. 2010).

In this final chapter, we have indicated some of the directions in which process modeling approaches are headed. Even though we ended by describing visions of more automatic modeling, parts of the use of business process modeling will continue to be an activity intended to support human thinking, communication, and knowledge development.

References

Andersson, A., Krogstie, J.: Implementation and first evaluation of a molecular modeling language. In: Proceedings EMMSAD 2015 LNBIP 214. Springer, Berlin (2015)

Artz, D., Gil, Y.: A survey of trust in computer science and the semantic web. Web semantics: science. Serv. Agents World Wide Web 5(2), 58–71 (2007)

Asif, M., Krogstie, J.: Externalization of user model in mobile services. Int. J. Interact. Mobile Technol. (iJIM) 8(1), 4–9 (2014)

Biczok, G., Martinez, S.D., Jelle, T., Krogstie, J.: Navigating Mazemap: indoor human mobility, spatio-logicalties and future potential. PERMODY IEEE (2014)

Boyd, D., Crawford, K.: Critical questions for big data. Inf. Comm. Soc. 15(5), 662–679 (2012)

Chen, M., Mao, S., Liu, Y.: Big data: a survey. Mobile Netw. Appl. 2014(19), 171–209 (2012)

Conti, M., et al.: Looking ahead in pervasive computing: challenges and opportunities in the era of cyber–physical convergence. In: Pervasive and Mobile Computing, vol. 8, no. 1, pp. 2–21, Feb 2012

D'Andria, F., Field, D., Kopaneli, A., Kousiouris, G., Garcia-Perez, D., Pernici, B., Plebani, P.: Data Movement in the Internet of Things Domain Service Oriented and Cloud Computing, vol. 9306, pp. 243–252. Lecture Notes in Computer Science (2015)

Embury, S.M., Missier, P., Sampaio, S., Greenwood, R.M., Preece, A.D.: Incorporating domain-specific information quality constraints into database queries. J. Data Inf. Qual. (JDIQ) 1(2), 11 (2009)

Fossland, S., Krogstie, J.: Modeling as-is, ought-to-be and to-be—experiences from a case study in the health sector. In: Proceedings PoEM 2015, Valencia, Spain (2015)

Heggset, M., Krogstie, J., Wesenberg, H.: Ensuring quality of large scale industrial process collections: experiences from a case study. In: The Practice of Enterprise Modeling, pp. 11–25. Springer, Berlin (2014)

Krogstie, J.: Integrated goal, data and process modeling: from TEMPORA to model-generated work-places. In: Johannesson, P., Söderström, E. (eds.) Information Systems Engineering from Data Analysis to Process Networks, pp. 43–65. IGI, Hershey (2008)

Krogstie, J.: Modeling of digital ecosystems: challenges and opportunities. In: Proceeding PRO-VE 2012. Springer, Berlin (2012)

Krogstie, J.: Evaluating data quality for integration of data sources. In: Proceedings PoEM 2013, pp. 39–53, Riga, Latvia (2013)

Krogstie, J., Sindre, G.: Utilizing deontic operators in information systems specifications. Requir. Eng. J. 1, 210–237 (1996)

Krogstie, J., Jørgensen, H.: Interactive models for supporting networked organisations. Paper presented at the 16th conference on advanced information systems engineering (CAiSE 2004), Riga, Latvia, 9–11 June 2004

Krogstie, J., Gao, S.: A semiotic approach to investigate quality issues of open big data ecosystems. In: Proceedings ICISO (2015)

Krogstie, J., McBrien, P., Owens, R., Seltveit, A.H.: Information systems development using a combination of process and rule based approaches. Paper presented at the third international conference on advanced information systems engineering (CAiSE'91), Trondheim, Norway (1991)

Krogstie, J., Dalberg, V., Jensen, S.M.: Process modeling value framework. In: Manolopoulos, Y., Filipe, J., Constantopoulos, P., Cordeiro, J. (eds.) Selected Papers from 8th International Conference, ICEIS 2006. LNBIP, vol. 3, pp. 309–321. Springer, Heidelberg (2008)

Lillehagen, F., Krogstie, J.: Active Knowledge Modeling of Enterprises. Springer, Berlin (2008)

Lindland, O.I., Krogstie, J.: Validating conceptual models by transformational prototyping. In: 5th International Conference on Advanced Information Systems Engineering (CAiSE'93). Springer, Paris (1993)

Loucopoulos, P., McBrien, P., Schumacker, F., Theodoulidis, B., Kopanas, V., Wangler, B.: Integrating database technology, rule-based systems and temporal reasoning for effective information systems: the TEMPORA paradigm. J. Inf. Syst. 1, 129–152 (1991)

Lukyanenko, R., Parsons, J.: Is Traditional Conceptual Modeling Becoming Obsolete? Conceptual Modeling, vol. 8217, pp. 61–73. Lecture Notes in Computer Science (2013)

Maggi, F.M., Slaats, T., Reijers, H.A.: The Automated Discovery of Hybrid Processes Business Process Management. Springer, Berlin (2014)

Malinova, M., Mendling, J.: Why is BPMN not appropriate for process maps? In: Proceedings ICIS 2015 Forth Worth (2015)

Martin, N., Poulovassillis, A., Wang, J.: A methodology and architecture embedding quality assessment in data integration. ACM J. Data Inf. Qual. 4(4), 17 (2012)

Sandkuhl, K., Stirna, J., Persson, A., Wiβotzki, M.: Enterprise Modelling—Tackling Business Challenges with the 4EM Method. Springer, Berlin (2014)

Shekhar, S., Xiong, H.: Encyclopedia of GIS. Springer, Berlin (2008)

ter Hofstede, A.H.M., van der Aalst, W.M.P, Adams, M., Russel, N.: Modern Business Process Automation: YAWL and its Support Environment. Springer, Berlin (2010)

van der Aalst, W.M.P.: Business process management: a comprehensive survey. ISRN Soft. Eng. 37 (2013)

van der Aalst, W.M.P.: Process Mining: Data Science in Action, 2nd edn. Springer (2016)

van der Aalst, W.M.P., et al.: Process mining manifesto. In: Business Process Management Workshops 2011, vol. 99. Lecture Notes in Business Information Processing. Springer, Berlin (2011)

Wad, C.: QoS: Quality Driven Data Abstraction for Large Databases. Worcester Polytechnic Institute (2008)

Ware, C.: Information Visualization. Morgan Kaufmann (2000)

Appendix
Special BPMN Notation in the Petroleum Industry Case

In the case described in Sect. 3.2, a specialized BPMN notation was used. The main part of this language is described in Figs. A.1, A.2, and A.3.

In Figs. A.4, A.5, A.6 and A.7, we see the original and improved process models from the experiment reported in Sect. 3.2.

© Springer International Publishing Switzerland 2016
J. Krogstie, *Quality in Business Process Modeling*,
DOI 10.1007/978-3-319-42512-2

Symbol name	Symbol	Description and naming convention
Activity related symbols		
Task	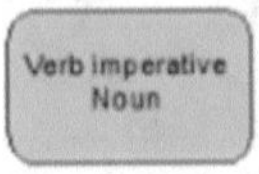 Verb imperative Noun	This symbol represents an activity. You shall define the title of this symbol as a verb imperative that reflects the activity performed in order to add value to the asset. The noun shall reflect the asset.
Optional Task	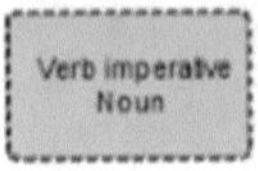 Verb imperative Noun	This symbol describes an optional activity. You shall define the title of this symbol as a verb imperative that reflects the activity performed in order to add value to the asset. The noun shall reflect the asset.
Collapsed sub-process	 Verb imperative Noun	This symbol represents a part of the workflow diagram that is collapsed to increase the visual quality of the workflow. The symbol is drawn using a standard-size activity shape with a [+] symbol attached. You shall define the title of this symbol as a verb imperative that reflects the activity performed in order to add value to the asset. The noun shall reflect the asset. The symbol shall be linked to the corresponding workflow diagram with an identical title.
Call task	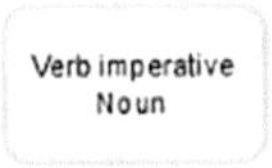 Verb imperative Noun	This symbol is used to address a workflow diagram in a different work process model. The external workflow diagram is addressed with a reference or a link in the task. The title of the call task shall be identical to the workflow diagram name that it calls.

Fig. A.1 Modeling of tasks

Collaboration activity	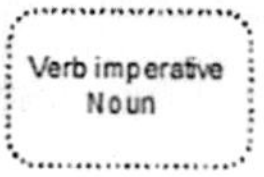 Verb imperative Noun	This symbol is used to group activities when they are executed in cross lanes collaboration. The activities grouped by this symbol shall not be sequenced in time or contain dependencies. The verb imperative shall reflect the activity performed in order to add value to the asset. The noun shall reflect the asset.
Event related symbols		
Start event	 Noun Verb past participle	A start event describes the state of the asset that triggers initiating work according to the workflow diagram. You shall define the title of this symbol as a noun reflecting the asset. The verb past participle shall reflect the activity performed in order to add value to that asset.
End event	 Noun Verb past participle	An end event describes the state that terminates conducting work according to the workflow diagram. You shall define the title of this symbol as a noun reflecting the asset. The verb past participle shall reflect the activity performed in order to add value to that asset.
Gateway related symbols		
Parallel gateway		When you have a parallel sequence in your workflow diagram you shall use a parallel gateway to visualise the parallel divergence and convergence. You shall not name parallel gateways.
Diverging exclusive gateway	 Control Noun	An exclusive gateway visualises a control of exclusive divergence and/or convergence. The title of this symbol shall consist of 2 pieces of information: • Term: Control • noun that reflects the object submitted to control Example: Control water-pressure level
Converging exclusive gateway		The converging exclusive gateway is used if the design require a need to merge the flows from the exclusive gateway prior to a common end event. You shall not merge the flow from exclusive gateways if requirements unique to one flow apply to any of the preceeding activities after the merge. You shall not name converging exclusive gateways.

Fig. A.2 Modeling of events and gateways

Other symbols		
Sequence flow	*Free text* →	This symbol is used to show the sequence in which activities and conditions are performed. A sequence flow can be given a title that describes the flow. It is mandatory to add a title when exclusive split applies to the flow. Then the title shall be the adjective reflecting the result of the control. If possible, the text shall be placed on top of the symbol close to the arrow exit.
Data symbol	Noun or Adjective	This symbol is used to describe a physical collection of information. The symbol can be used in workflows when it is necessary to indicate the creation or use of information in an activity. The title of this symbol shall be a noun in singular or an expression in singular starting with a noun or an adjective.
Data association	·········>	This symbol is used to link data symbols together with other symbols of this diagram.
Association	·············	This symbol is used to link text annotation symbols together with other symbols of this diagram.
Lane	Noun	A lane horizontally frames relevant activities and conditions. A lane inherits the name of the process role of which it represents.
Presence of requirements	 ⚠	This symbol is used to show the presence of one or more governing elements classified as requirement. Symbols that may have requirements linked to them are: • Any type activity symbol except the collapsed sub-process. • Any type gateway symbol In addition this symbol can be visualised on workflow diagrams.
Presence of information		Used to show the presence of one or more governing elements classified as information

Fig. A.3 Other modeling constructs

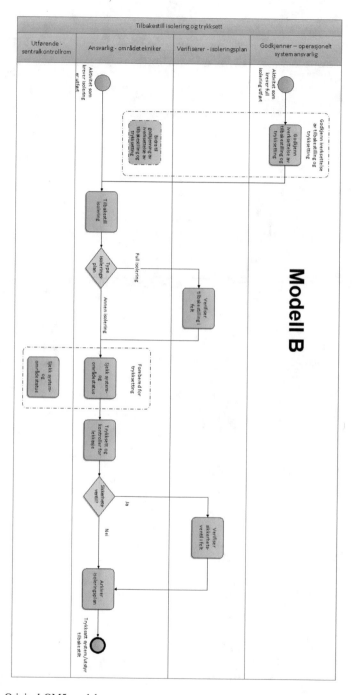

Fig. A.4 Original OM5 model

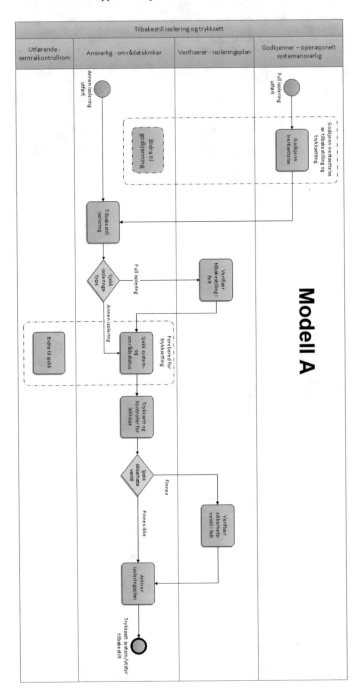

Fig. A.5 Improved OM5 model

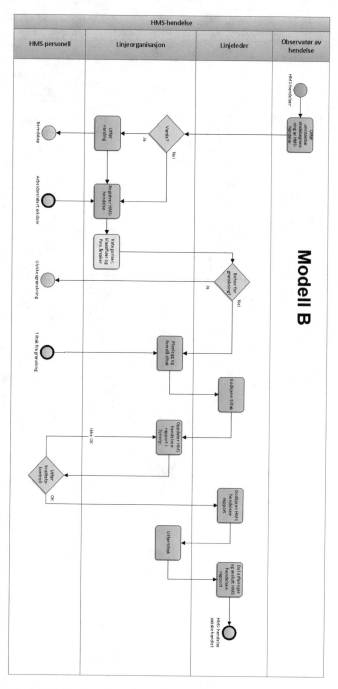

Fig. A.6 Original SF103 model

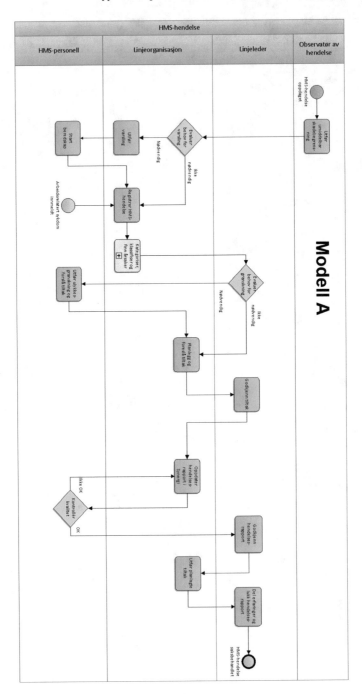

Fig. A.7 Improved SF103 model

Index

A
Agreement, 130
AKM, **31**
Animation, 129
ARIS, 158, 171, 217
As-is model, **28**
Audience, 105
Availability, 110

B
Big data, 231
BPM in the large, 157
BPMN, 19, *39*, 158, 163, 205, 229
    quality, 205
Business process, 1
    quality, 5
    value dimension, **6**
Business process modeling, **27**
    case, 139
BWW, 70, 206

C
CASE, 157
CDIF, 22
CIS, 106
CMM, **12**
Completeness, 121
Conceptual modeling, **18**
Conference, 221
Consistency checking, 123
Constructivity, 123
Currency, 110

D
Data models, 60
Data quality, 55
Deontic quality, 134

DFD, 27, **36**, 227
Digital ecosystems, **15**
Docmap, 159
Driving questions, 124

E
EEML, **34**, 228
4EM, 198, 228
Empirical quality, 111
Encoding, 111
Enterprise modeling, 157
Enterprise models, 63
ER, 60
ERP, 232
Error correction, 119
Error detection, 119
Error prevention, 118
Explanation generation, 129
Expressive economy, 117

F
Feasible agreement, 134
Feasible completeness, 134
Feasible comprehension, 134
Feasible validity, 134
FRISCO, 20

G
GEMAL, 229
Goals of modeling, 104, 143
    case, 170
GoM, 85
Graph aesthetics, 113
Green BPM, *6*

H
Hierarchical abstraction, **20**

© Springer International Publishing Switzerland 2016
J. Krogstie, *Quality in Business Process Modeling*,
DOI 10.1007/978-3-319-42512-2

I
IDEF0, *37*, 140, 231
Information quality, 56
ISO/IEC 9126, 55
ISO-9000, 54

K
Kano-model, 55
KPI, **9**

L
Labelling, 120
Language development
    case, 148
Lean manufacturing, **11**
Learning, 135

M
MDA, 21
Meta-modelling, 22
METIS, 149
Model execution, 129
Model filtering, 127
Modeling, 27
    participatory, 219
Modeling perspective, **23**
Model inspection, 127
Model integration, 131
Model monopoly, **30**
Model refactoring, 117
Model rephrasing, 127
Model reuse, 123
Model translation, 129
MOF, 22

O
OMG, 22
Ontology, 107
Ought-to-be model, **28**, 106, 229

P
Paraphrasing, 129
Participant training, 126
PEP, *7*
Perceived completeness, 122
Perceived validity, 122
Persistence, 110
Physical quality, 109
7PMG, 86
Pragmatic quality, 125
Process harmonization, 139
Process impact, 145

Process improvement, 195
Process map, 160, 229
Process maturity, **12**
Process mining, 195, 231

Q
Quality
    business process, 75
Quality of modeling language
    case, 151
Quality of process model
    case, 146

R
Reference model, 91

S
SAP ERP, 92
SeeMe, 221
Semantic quality, 120
Semiotics, 19, 56
Sense-making, **30**, 143
SEQUAL, 65, 103, 208, 234
Sharing economy, *6*
SIF-index, 4, 158
Signavio, 109, 216
Simulation, 130
Social quality, 130
Socio-Technical WalkThrough, 220
SRS, 58
Structural perspective, 60
Syntactic incompleteness, 117
Syntactic invalidity, 117
Syntactic quality, 117

T
Tempora, 227
To-be model, **28**
TOGAF, 200
Troux Architect, 149

U
UML, **34**

V
Validity, 120
Visualisation, 129

W
Workflow, 31
Workflow patterns, 207

Printed in the United States
By Bookmasters